The Three
Edwards

The Three Edwards

War and State in England
1272–1377

Michael Prestwich
Reader in Medieval History
University of Durham

METHUEN

First published in Great Britain in 1980 by
George Weidenfeld & Nicolson Ltd
91 Clapham High Street, London SW4

First published as a University Paperback in 1981 by
Methuen & Co. Ltd
11 New Fetter Lane, London EC4P 4EE

Printed in Great Britain by
Fletchers Limited, Norwich

British Library Cataloguing in Publication Data
Prestwich, Michael
The three Edwards: war and state in
England, 1272–1377. – (University paperbacks; 755)
1. Great Britain – Politics and government –
1154–1399
I. Title
942.03   DA225

ISBN 0–416–30450–8

For Maggie

Contents

Illustrations

Between pages 176 and 177

The effigy of Edward Despenser (d. 1375) (*Walter Scott*)

Berkeley Castle (*National Monuments Record*)

The coronation of Edward III (*Bibliothèque Nationale, Paris*)

Sir Geoffrey Luttrell with his wife and daughter-in-law (*by courtesy of the Trustees of the British Museum*)

Hawking (*by courtesy of the Trustees of the British Museum*)

A fourteenth-century naval battle (*by courtesy of the Trustees of the British Museum*)

A gold noble minted in celebration of the victory of Sluys (*by courtesy of the Trustees of the British Museum*)

A guiennois showing the Black Prince (*by courtesy of the Trustees of the British Museum*)

Edward III and David II of Scotland (*by courtesy of the Trustees of the British Museum*)

The capture of David II at Neville's Cross (*Bibliothèque Nationale, Paris*)

Death reaching out for his victim (*Bodleian Library, Oxford*)

Edward III, Tewkesbury Abbey (*National Monuments Record*)

Edward III outside the walls of Rheims (*Bibliothèque Nationale, Paris*)

Windsor Castle (*Crown Copyright – reproduced with permission of the Controller of H.M. Stationery Office*)

St George's Chapel, Windsor (*by permission of the Dean and Canons of Windsor*)

Jousting (*National Monuments Record*)

Edward III from the Great East Window in York Minster (*National Monuments Record*)

The funeral effigy of Edward III (*by permission of the Dean and Chapter of Westminster*)

Maps

Preface

The idea for this book was not mine; I owe a considerable debt of gratitude to John Roberts for suggesting to my publishers that I should write it. The opportunity was one which I welcomed, for the period it covers is one on which I had been lecturing at St Andrews for ten years, and which, more seriously, presents intriguing questions as to how the medieval English state in its most developed form responded to the varied problems presented by war. There is a far greater unity to the period when England was ruled by the first three Edwards than might appear from the very different fates and reputations of the kings. This book is intended more as a work of synthesis than as the presentation of original research on a massive scale, though I must acknowledge the generosity of the Research and Travel Funds of the University of St Andrews which enabled me to consult manuscripts and obtain microfilms. Many of my fellow academics may be infuriated by the absence of footnotes: I can only plead the instructions of my publishers, which I welcomed, as had full references been given, the book would have appeared much later in print, at a much higher price. I must apologize, however, to the many scholars on whose work I have relied heavily and whose achievements I have often not been able to acknowledge properly.

I have benefited greatly from reading the unpublished doctoral theses of E. B. Fryde, 'Edward III's War Finance, 1337–1341' (Oxford, 1947), and C. J. Given-Wilson, 'The

Court and Household of Edward III, 1360–77' (St Andrews, 1977). I have learnt much from my research students while I supervised them; I would like to thank Sharron Uhler and Nancy Messimer. Many St Andrews undergraduates will find parts of this book familiar; I have gained much from teaching them. Ann Kettle and Chris Given-Wilson both deserve my grateful thanks for reading through most of the manuscript in draft, and correcting many errors of style and content. I would also like to thank Paula M. Iley and Jane R. Thompson of Weidenfeld and Nicolson. My greatest debt is of course to my wife, who has read through all the drafts, and has helped in many other ways. Her criticisms have been invaluable, as has her work on the maps and genealogical tables. Without her, this book would never have been written.

Durham   Michael Prestwich
July 1979

Chronological Table

Edward I

1272 Accession of Edward I
1274 Return of Edward to England; investigation of local administration
1275 Statute of Westminster I
1277 First Welsh War
1278 Statute of Gloucester; *quo warranto* inquiries set up
1282–3 Second Welsh War
1285 Statute of Westminster II
1286–9 Edward in Gascony
1290 Death of Eleanor of Castile
1291–2 The hearing of the Great Cause
1294–5 Madog's rebellion in Wales
1294–8 War with Philip IV of France
1296 Edward's first campaign in Scotland; deposition of John Balliol
1297 Constitutional crisis; issue of the Confirmation of the Charters
1298 Battle of Falkirk
1304 Siege of Stirling Castle
1306 Rebellion and enthronement of Robert Bruce in Scotland
1307 Death of Edward I

Edward II

1307 Accession of Edward II
1308 Marriage to Isabella of France; coronation; first exile of Piers Gaveston

1309 Statute of Stamford; return of Gaveston
1310 Appointment of the Ordainers; campaign in Scotland
1311 Publication of the Ordinances
1312 Death of Piers Gaveston
1314 Battle of Bannockburn
1315–16 Famine
1316 Lincoln Parliament
1318 Treaty of Leake
1319 Siege of Berwick
1321 Exile of the Despensers
1322 Defeat of Thomas of Lancaster at Boroughbridge
1322–6 Ascendancy of the Despensers
1326 Invasion of Isabella and Mortimer
1327 Deposition of Edward II

Edward III

1327 Accession of Edward III; his first campaign against the Scots
1327–30 Rule of Isabella and Mortimer
1329 Death of Robert Bruce
1330 Edward's personal rule established
1332 Edward Bruce's invasion of Scotland; battle of Dupplin Moor
1333 Battle of Halidon Hill
1337 Hundred Years War begins
1339 Confrontation with the French at Buirontosse
1340 Battle of Sluys
1340–1 Political crisis in England
1346 Battles of Crécy and Neville's Cross
1347 Capture of Calais
1348 Onset of the Black Death
1351 Statute of Provisors; Statute of Labourers
1352 Statute of Treason
1353 Statute of *Praemunire*
1355 Black Prince's raid to Narbonne
1356 Battle of Poitiers
1359–60 Edward III's last campaign in France
1360 Treaty of Brétigny

CHRONOLOGICAL TABLE

1363 Establishment of the Calais staple
1367 Battle of Nájera
1369 Renewal of war with the French
1371 Dismissal of the clerical ministers
1375 Treaty of Bruges
1376 Good Parliament; death of the Black Prince
1377 Death of Edward III

Introduction

The century during which England was ruled by the first three Edwards was one of striking contrasts. A confident and masterful Edward I conquered Wales and built Caernarfon in consciously imperial style; his son Edward II was defeated by the Scots in battle, and suffered the abject humiliation of deposition. Edward III won great triumphs against the French, but his reign also saw the population, which had reached its medieval peak, cut down by the ravages of plague.

The three kings were men of very different qualities, with little more in common than a strong and healthy physique. The workings of heredity are mysterious, and it may be that all three inherited more characteristics from their mothers, none of whom was English, than from their fathers. Edward I's reign was marked by military conquest and legislative progress; the king was always reluctant to compromise with his opponents, but the reign was one of positive political achievement. The community of the realm found a new focus in the developing institution of parliament, and the country gained a much-needed unity after the troubles of Henry III's reign. The apparently secure edifice collapsed under the incompetent Edward II. He did not understand the important art of patronage, and he lost the trust of the nobility as he turned to unsuitable favourites such as Piers Gaveston and the Despensers. After the defeat of his main baronial opponent Thomas of Lancaster, Edward II's reign took on an increasingly tyrannical aspect until it was ended by a revolution headed by his own queen, Isabella. The reputation of English arms had plummeted as Edward II had failed to maintain the impetus of the war against the Scots which his father had begun; under Edward III the wheel of fortune turned again. News of the great victories of Sluys, Crécy and Poitiers reverberated through Europe. Two kings, David of Scotland and John of France, were held captive in England and forced to pay huge ransoms. Edward III's new Order of the Garter became a renowned symbol of chivalry. Edward III learnt the political lessons of his father's reign, restored the prestige of the monarchy and established a remarkable rapport with the nobility. Only in the last years of his life, with the onset of senility, did the underlying strains of many years of warfare begin to threaten his achievement.

Despite the obvious contrasts between the three reigns, there is more to connect them than the coincidence of the kings' names. The period is given a coherence by war, for all its vicissitudes. The need to organize and finance campaigns on a far greater scale than hitherto posed major problems for the government, and placed great burdens on the people. Success in war brought political peace and unity at home, but failure was divisive. Even Edward I and Edward III faced considerable difficulties when their overambitious military schemes in the Low Countries proved to be beyond their resources, while failure against the dogged resistance of the Scots was a recurrent background to the turbulent politics of Edward II's reign. The importance of war in this period stretched far beyond the traditional bounds of military history. The central constitutional development was the evolution of parliament, and it was the pressures of war which gave the institution much of its unique character. The need to obtain national consent for war taxation was of prime importance in the development of a system of representation, while the development of the parliamentary peerage was closely connected with the system used to summon magnates to fight. In economic terms, the burdens of recurrent taxation and the seizures of food supplied for the armies affected the prosperity of the countryside and were a matter for frequent complaint.

INTRODUCTION

Even the question of law and order was bound up with war. Criminals were given encouragement by the lavish grant of pardons in return for service on campaign, while the crown was on occasion compelled to reduce the severity of its policies as a concession in return for grants of taxation.

This book is not intended to be a comprehensive history of England in a full and complex period, nor does it aim to provide a mere narrative of events. Such questions as the development of parliament, the character of the aristocracy, and the impact of war and natural disasters on the economy are considered in analytical chapters, while the Scottish wars are dealt with as an integral whole, rather than being incorporated into a more general account of the three reigns. Consequently, some apparent omissions in the narrative chapters are remedied in other sections of the book. Inevitably, there are some aspects of life which are not covered. The Church and intellectual activity lie largely beyond the scope of the volume, as do some aspects of the economy. Nevertheless, it is hoped that a coherent story emerges from these pages, a story of how the country responded to the pressures of war, and of the part played in the process by the three kings.

I have attempted to avoid becoming too enmeshed in the inevitable technicalities of the medieval historian's trade. Some explanation is perhaps required of the currency in this period. The main coins in circulation in England were silver pennies; gold was first minted in 1344. For accounting purposes, the system of £ s d, which survived until very recently, was used, as well as the mark. This latter unit was worth 13s 4d, or two-thirds of a pound. There is no way in which medieval monetary values can be translated into the constantly changing values of modern money. It may help to note that the total currency in circulation during the period varied from about £500,000 to over £1,000,000, that only the elite of the nobility enjoyed incomes over £5,000 a year, and that the wage of an ordinary soldier was 2d a day.

1

The Leopard
or the Lion

Edward I

Edward was an unusual name in thirteenth-century England. In a country where the aristocracy was largely French-speaking, English names were not fashionable. Henry III, however, was devoted to the cult of Edward the Confessor, a king who had displayed some of his own qualities of piety and incompetence. This explains his choice of name for his eldest son, and the accession of Edward I to the throne in 1272 marked the beginning of just over a hundred years of rule by kings called Edward. The name was not Edward I's immediate choice for his heir: the future Edward II had elder brothers, John, Henry and Alphonso, but all three died young. Edward II came under pressure from the French to call his eldest son Philip after his father-in-law Philip IV, but the memory of his own masterful father was too strong and the boy was duly christened Edward. The line of Edwards looked as if it might continue indefinitely; Edward III's eldest son, the Black Prince, and his eldest grandson bore the name in turn. This was an age of high mortality, however, and Edward III outlived them both. In 1377 it was the Black Prince's surviving son, Richard of Bordeaux, who inherited the throne.

Edward I's reign falls into well-defined phases. The first stretches from his return to England from crusade in 1274 until his departure for his duchy of Gascony in south-west France in 1286. These were the years of the conquest of Wales, and of the king's major legislative measures. On his return from Gascony in 1289 his attention was soon drawn to Scotland, with his adjudication in the lengthy proceedings to determine who had the right to the Scottish throne. The king's prestige was arguably never higher than in the early 1290s, but he soon faced increasing problems at home and abroad. Rebellion in Wales and hostility from the Scots, combined with war with France, posed a severe test. The scale of the demands imposed on the country led to political and constitutional crisis in 1297. In the last decade of the reign it was the problem of Scotland which dominated all else, and which defied resolution.

Edward I was in Sicily late in 1272 when he learnt that he had become king. That exotic country, still bearing the strong imprint of Arab influence and notorious for the treacherous nature of its people, was used by Edward as a staging post for his voyage to and from the Holy Land on crusade. At the age of thirty-three, the eldest son of Henry III and Eleanor of Provence was a man of considerable, if chequered, experience. The years after 1258, when a baronial opposition under Simon de Montfort attempted to fetter King Henry and to establish a new system of government, were difficult ones for the young Edward. The baronial leader was his uncle by marriage, and for a time he fell under his spell. Eventually he emerged as one of de Montfort's most determined opponents, and with his allies, mainly drawn from the Welsh marches, he roundly defeated the baronial army at Evesham in 1265. A poem written during these years compared the future king to a leopard, considered in the Middle Ages to be a devious beast. 'He is a lion by his pride and ferocity; by his inconstancy and changeableness he is a pard, changing his word and his promises, excusing himself with fair speech.'[1] This was the man on whose tomb a much later generation was to inscribe the words *pactum serva*', 'keep faith'. Edward was determinedly ambitious for himself and for his family, and for him self-interest outweighed consistency. He was always prepared to manipulate the law to his own advantage, rather than abide by its spirit.

In the aftermath of the defeat of Simon de Montfort, Edward's was not a voice of moderation, even though he

was well aware of the value of many of the reforms that had
been proposed by his father's opponents. He did not welcome the policy of peace with the Welsh Prince Llywelyn,
for this thwarted his own ambitions in a country where he
had been granted extensive lands in 1254. His dispute with
the Earl of Gloucester, who had done much to ensure the
royalist triumph at Evesham, threatened to plunge the
country into renewed civil war. The great adventure of
the crusade must have been a welcome diversion from a
difficult situation; in his determination to fulfil his crusading vow, Edward displayed a single-mindedness which
contrasted with his earlier changes of side in the political
conflicts in England.

Edward's intention in 1270 was to join the crusading
expedition led by St Louis which landed in North Africa.
He and his followers, however, only arrived after the
French king's death: instead of abandoning the project, like
most of the crusaders, he sailed for Sicily and then to the
East. His force was too small to do much in military terms,
but Edward's crusade has become famous for the romantic
story of the attack on the future king by a Moslem assassin.
His wife, Eleanor of Castile, is said to have sucked the
poison from the wound. Regrettably, the story is highly
suspect: an earlier version has Edward's great friend the
Savoyard noble Otto de Grandson perform this task, but
the most reliable account tells of an operation by surgeons,
with the wailing Eleanor ordered firmly from the room –
she was told that it was better that she should be in tears
than the whole land of England weep. Eleanor fully
supported her husband's military ambitions; it was
during the crusade that she had a translation made for
him of the Roman manual on the art of war written by
Vegetius.

Perhaps the most important result of the crusade was
that Edward established firm and lasting friendships with a
select group of companions. From the Welsh Marches there
were Roger Clifford, Payn de Chaworth, and the Earl of
Pembroke, William de Valence. Robert Tibetot was to serve
Edward loyally in the future wars in Wales. Otto de Grandson was the first of a distinguished group of Savoyards who

7

aided him in many ways. John de Vescy was a former
Montfortian who gave his loyalty to Edward on the
crusade, and so demonstrated that the bitterness of the past
could be forgotten. Such men were to give Edward their
wholehearted support, and provide him with a solid
foundation for his enterprises.

The new king's return to England was leisurely. His
recovery from the assassin's wound was slow, and he was
diverted by the need to attend to affairs in his duchy of
Gascony. Edward held the duchy from the King of France,
a situation always liable to cause problems. The powerful
Gaston de Béarn was in revolt against Edward, and
appealed to the jurisdiction of Philip iii as the ultimate
feudal overlord of Gascony. Agreement was eventually
reached in this case, but conflict between the kings of
England and France over Gascony was to recur in a far more
serious form in the future.

It was not until August 1274 that Edward finally reached
England. There had been surprisingly little trouble since
the death of Henry iii. Rumours that the new king would
never return had caused a minor rising in the north. The
king's brother Edmund of Cornwall had threatened to use
force to pursue his vendetta against Robert de Ferrers,
whose earldom of Derby he had acquired by questionable
means in the aftermath of the civil war. The Earl of Gloucester had intervened and written to the king's ministers: 'It
does not seem that there can be peace in the land, nor can
the king's lordship be respected, if the people of the land
can raise forces in time of peace to attack others without consideration and without judgement.'[2] Gloucester
demonstrated his sense of responsibility again after the
king landed, when he entertained Edward at Tonbridge
and ended, at least for a time, his feud with him.

The coronation was a magnificent affair. The two halls at
Westminster were re-decorated 'so that on entering and
gazing at such beauty, the eye was replete with delights
and pleasure'.[3] A mass of temporary accommodation was
put up for the crowd of guests, and a large number of
kitchens were built. Delicacies such as swans and peacocks
were provided as well as vast quantities of beef, mutton,

pork and poultry. One story has it that at the banquet which followed the ceremony in Westminster Abbey five hundred horses were turned loose, to be kept by anyone who managed to catch them. This was a celebration by young men – by a new generation filled with a new confidence – and the story may well be true. The festivities were not limited to the nobles at the feast; the citizens of London were able to drink red and white wine flowing from the public drinking fountain in Cheapside.

What sort of king would Edward be? Would he fulfil the gloomy prophecies of the gifted chronicler Matthew Paris, who told a macabre story of the young Edward gratuitously ordering the mutilation of a young man he met going peaceably along the road, or would the leopard change his ways? In legal doctrine it was argued that Edward the king was a different person from the Lord Edward, heir to the throne, but reality might not match the fictions of the law.

The signs in 1274 were certainly promising. In October a massive inquiry was set up to investigate local administration. Part of its purpose was to fulfil the promise made by Edward at his coronation, when by one account he lifted the crown from his head and stated that he would never wear it until he had recovered all the crown lands granted out by his father. The scope of the inquiry was much wider than the investigation of encroachments on royal rights, however, and was extended to cover the activities of all local officials, from sheriffs to castle constables. The technique was not wholly new. Henry III had ordered investigations into usurpations of royal rights, and in 1258 the baronial justiciar Hugh Bigod had begun a major inquiry into the activities of both royal and seigneurial officials. The scale of Edward I's inquest, however, if not its nature, was novel, and it was significant that the king was prepared to use and adapt some of the methods of those who had opposed his father. The results of the massive inquiries, produced by interrogating local juries, were recorded on what are now known as the Hundred Rolls. So extensive is the evidence that they provide that no succinct summary is possible. No government since the making of

Domesday Book had been provided with so massive a dossier. The evidence that it gave of individual corruption and general misgovernment was alarming. When the returns had come in, the first statute of Westminster was drafted in 1275. With fifty-one clauses, many of them highly technical, this statute attempted to correct most of the abuses which had been revealed. Legal proceedings were subsequently begun so that action could be taken against corrupt officials. In 1278 justices were ordered to inquire into the question of the alleged usurpation of royal rights by magnates, by means of legal actions known as *quo warranto*. Edward intended to rule firmly.

The crusade had been an extremely expensive venture. By the thirteenth century the days when men would sell all they possessed to travel to the Holy Land to fight the infidel were long gone, and Edward had to pay heavily for the contingents that accompanied him. The total cost of the expedition was probably in the region of £100,000, and Edward had been forced to borrow over £23,000 from the Italian banking company of the Ricciardi of Lucca to finance his return to England. The same firm also paid £7,600 in England to Edward's loyal servant Robert Burnell. These heavy debts had to be paid off. In parliament in 1275 the king negotiated a customs duty on wool and leather exports, at the rate of 6s 8d on each sack of wool. At a second parliament in the same year he obtained the grant of a tax: everyone was to pay a fifteenth of a valuation of their movable property. With a yield approaching £80,000, this tax did much to remedy the king's financial problems. In 1275 Edward laid the foundations of the financial system that was to serve him for the rest of the reign: loans from Italians and tax receipts were used to meet the needs of extraordinary expenditure, and the customs revenues provided a regular income out of which the lenders could be repaid.

Edward was not a man to be satisfied with policies of legal reform and financial stability, which were in any case matters better dealt with by ministers, rather than by a king who always had a healthy impatience with technicalities.

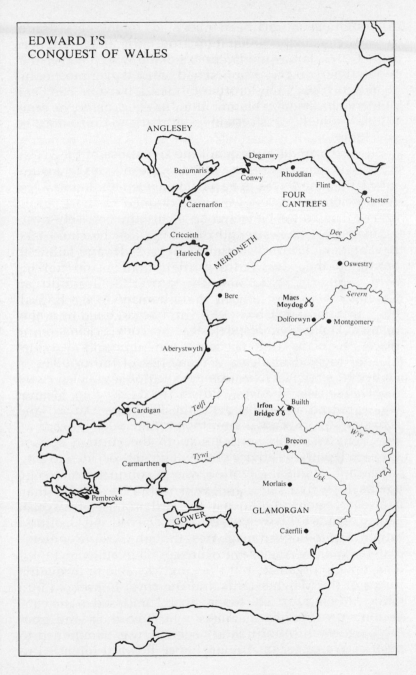

EDWARD I'S
CONQUEST OF WALES

ANGLESEY

Beaumaris

Deganwy

Conwy

Rhuddlan

Flint

Chester

FOUR
CANTREFS

Caernarfon

Criccieth

MERIONETH

Dee

Harlech

Oswestry

Bere

Maes
Moydog

Severn

Dolforwyn

Montgomery

Aberystwyth

Builth

Irfon
Bridge

Cardigan

Teifi

Brecon

Wye

Carmarthen

Tywi

Morlais

Usk

Pembroke

GOWER

GLAMORGAN

Caerfili

Although his ultimate ambitions lay with the crusade, Edward's main preoccupation from 1276 until 1284 was with Wales. Following the peace made with the Welsh at Montgomery in 1267 Edward had handed over most of his estates in Wales to his brother Edmund, but if he had been prepared to abandon his ambitions in Wales before he came to the throne he was certainly not ready to do so once he was king.

Edward's ambition was not the sole cause of the Welsh wars. The magnates of the March were anxious to acquire new lands; there was to be a colonial element to the wars. Aggression, however, was not confined to the English. The Welsh prince Llywelyn ap Gruffudd unwisely over-estimated his own strength, thinking that he could take advantage of Edward's absence on crusade, and failing to appreciate the extent of the hostility to his plans from his own brother Dafydd and the powerful Gruffudd ap Gwenwynwyn. He refused to do homage to the English king, invaded English territory, and began building a new castle at Dolforwyn despite Ralph de Tony's claims to the place. His plans to marry Simon de Montfort's daughter Eleanor revived unpleasant memories of the troubles of Henry III's reign. There was no court of law which could resolve the issues between Edward and Llywelyn; Eleanor was captured at sea by the English; Prince Dafydd and Gruffudd ap Gwenwynwyn took refuge with Edward I – the scene was fully set for war. In the autumn of 1276 Edward I, with the advice of his magnates, decided to act.

Edward I's initial intention was to conduct a campaign against Llywelyn's strongholds in north Wales, rather than to attempt a general conquest. Edward promised the Welsh prince's lands to Llywelyn's brothers Dafydd and Gruffudd rather than to English magnates, though the king contemplated acquiring Anglesey for himself. The campaign took a long time to organize, but the king was able to throw the forces of the Marcher lords and the royal household into battle early in 1277. The feudal host, composed of the contingents provided by magnates who held their land from the king in return for military service, was summoned to meet at Worcester in August. Since Edward intended to advance along the coast of north Wales the venue had to be changed to Chester. Large numbers of workmen were employed to prepare a road for the army and by the end of August the king had over fifteen thousand men in arms, many of them recruited in south Wales. The campaign route led from Chester to Flint, on to Rhuddlan and then to the old English stronghold at Deganwy. From there troops were sent by sea to Anglesey, where they reaped the grain harvest. No major battle was fought, but Edward had done enough to display his strength to Llywelyn, and negotiations began. It is likely that the English lacked the resources, particularly food supplies, for a protracted conflict, and that they welcomed the chance to end the war.

The peace terms were tough. Llywelyn had to surrender the land between Chester and the Conwy known as the Four Cantrefs, which had been granted to Edward in 1254, but which the Welsh subsequently regained. His political authority was severely curtailed; although still prince, he was to receive homage only from the five lords of Snowdonia. A massive war indemnity of £50,000 was imposed. When Llywelyn appeared before Edward, however, he was released from this crippling burden, and with rare magnanimity the English king allowed the marriage to Eleanor de Montfort to go ahead; he even paid for the ceremony.

There were still considerable problems to be resolved. One of the most important ways in which lordship was expressed in the Middle Ages was through the exercise of justice, and Edward's intention of extending his rights of jurisdiction at Llywelyn's expense soon became plain. A particularly contentious clause in the peace treaty laid down that in lawsuits involving the prince, Welsh law should apply in Wales and Marcher law in the Marches, the lands held by English magistrates in Wales. The principle was reasonable, but its application was not. Edward's justices referred only one case to Llywelyn's court, and the prince found his claims consistently blocked through the interpretation of this clause. Archbishop Pecham expressed the English attitude well when he argued that the laws and customs referred to in this treaty could only mean those laws which the English had customarily used in Wales, since Welsh law itself was contrary to all reason and justice. Llywelyn found himself involved in a complex and humiliating dispute with his former enemy Gruffudd ap Gwenwynwyn. Interminable procrastination tested his patience to the limit, and must have convinced him of the English king's bad faith. In about 1322 the men of north Wales were to demand English common law in preference to their native law, but in the aftermath of Edward 1's initial campaign, the constant delays, chicanery and corruption inherent in the workings of the English legal system inevitably disenchanted them.

A further indication of Edward's intention of exercising effective lordship over Wales is provided by the castles he built to consolidate the campaign, at Flint and Rhuddlan along the line of his advance, and further south at Aberystwyth and Builth. On his return from crusade, Edward had been entertained by count Philip of Savoy at his newly built castle of St Georges d'Esperanche. He was impressed by the building, with its freshly plastered walls gleaming in the sun, and he recruited its architect, Master James of St George, into his service. Master James was the architect for the new castles in Wales, and he was helped by a select group of fellow Savoyards. The most up-to-date techniques of fortification were used to overawe a people whose leaders scarcely had the resources to mount a full-scale siege. Rhuddlan featured two great twin-towered gates and a double line of defences. The river was diverted and a dock built, to ensure that the castle could always be supplied from the sea. A domestic touch was provided by the little fishpond with a fenced garden which was created for the queen.

In 1282 the Welsh revolted. This was not a result of the harsh treatment of Llywelyn, but rather of the inadequate rewards provided by Edward for his former ally Prince Dafydd. Llywelyn could not stand by, and chose to give aid to his brother. Concerted attacks were made on English-held castles throughout Wales. The English were quick to respond: plans were made at a council at Devizes in April, and troops were assembling in May. Far more elaborate victualling arrangements were made than had been for the first campaign; Edward even called on his overseas dominions of Gascony, Ponthieu and Ireland for aid. The strategy was based on that which had served so well in 1277. The main host advanced in the north, near the coast so that supplies could be provided by the navy, while the Marcher lords were active to the south. The crossing to Anglesey was to be achieved this time by constructing an elaborate bridge of boats.

Despite this careful planning, matters did not go well initially. The Welsh had some success in the south, and the crossing to Anglesey was delayed. Truce negotiations began but Luke de Tany disobeyed orders and advanced towards the bridge. He was ambushed and his knights driven into the sea to drown under the weight of their armour. This setback hardened the king's determination. He sent for reinforcements and planned a winter campaign, but before he moved news came of a decisive English victory. A group of Marcher lords had lured Llywelyn into a trap at Irfon Bridge, probably by indicating that they intended to change sides. The Welsh prince had vainly shouted out his name in the battle to try to ensure that he would not be killed; an English squire ran him through in ignorance of his victim's identity. In·the new year Edward was able to conclude the war. Snowdonia was isolated, and Bere, the last Welsh stronghold, surrendered in April. In June the fugitive Dafydd was captured by his own men and handed over to the English – he was later tried and executed as a traitor.

The war of 1282–3 was one of conquest, in contrast to that of 1277. Edward intended to do far more than punish a rebellious vassal. In the statute of Wales in 1284 the English system of administration was extended, and the new counties of Flint, Anglesey, Merioneth and Caernarfon created. For the rest, Wales remained a country of Marcher lordships, controlled by families such as the Mortimers, Chaworths, Bohuns and Clares. The legal system of Wales was thoroughly overhauled, Edward declaring in majestic tones:

We have caused to be rehearsed before us and the nobles of our realm the laws and customs of those parts hitherto in use. Which being diligently heard and fully understood, we have, by the advice of the aforesaid nobles, abolished certain of them, some thereof we have allowed, and some we have corrected; and we have likewise commanded certain others to be ordained and added thereunto.[4]

The archaic system of criminal law was largely Anglicized, but Welsh law as a whole was not abolished. The principality, however, was. The tale of Edward presenting his baby son as a new prince to the Welsh people is wholly mythical.

As in 1277, the victory was consolidated by the building of castles. Snowdonia was ringed by Conwy, Caernarfon, Harlech and Criccieth. At Caernarfon Master James of St George abandoned his usual style and built a magnificent castle with polygonal towers and dark stripes of masonry enlivening the massive walls. This was a deliberate echo of the walls of Constantinople, for Edward I wished to express in stones and mortar a traditional Welsh legend that the father of the Emperor Constantine himself was buried at Caernarfon, where he had found a great castle with multi-coloured towers. Three eagles surmounting the turrets on the greatest tower of Edward's castle emphasized the king's imperial ambitions in Wales. The new castles were accompanied by town walls, and a deliberate attempt was made to encourage English settlers by giving them superior privileges to the local Welsh inhabitants.

The first Welsh war cost about £23,000, but the bill for the second probably reached £150,000, even though the leading magnates had rejected the king's plan that they should serve at his wages – they preferred to answer a traditional feudal summons, and fight out of their own resources. At a period when the income from royal lands stood at only £14,000 at most, the financial burden of the war was immense. Over £70,000 was advanced by the Ricciardi and John Kirkby was sent on a tour of England to raise loans as an advance against a tax which had not yet even been negotiated. A Lincolnshire chronicler sardonically remarked that although Kirkby asked how much religious houses and others were prepared to give, they did not profit from this as he simply taxed them as he wished. Kirkby raised over £16,500, but this was hardly enough. In the next year, in some desperation, the king arbitrarily seized the proceeds of a crusading tax which had been deposited in English churches. A subsidy of a thirtieth on movable goods was agreed in 1283, and assessed at over £42,000. The clergy also voted a tax, though with more reluctance than the laity. Thus the war was paid for, but the effort had been considerable, and the king was provided with a foretaste of the acute financial problems that a period of more continuous warfare would bring.

The victory achieved in 1283 did not end Edward's involvement in Wales. There was a revolt in 1287 while the king was away in Gascony, and in 1294 an extremely serious rising took place: this was not led by members of the old princely families, which had largely been destroyed, but had more of the qualities of a popular rebellion. The extension to Wales of the English system of taxation in the early 1290s was probably the main cause of the rising. The records reveal a very harsh assessment. In Merioneth the average was 4s 3d for each taxpayer, as against a mere 1s 9d in the Marcher lordship of Chirk. Edward's preparations for an expedition to Gascony provided an opportunity for revolt; it was even said that some Welsh troops recruited for this campaign turned the arms they had been given against the English.

Originality in strategy was not one of Edward's talents. Indeed, his initial invasion in 1277 had followed almost exactly the route pioneered by the Roman general Suetonius Paulinus in his attack on the Druids in Anglesey, and his techniques of warfare were foreshadowed by the twelfth-century writer Gerald of Wales. In 1294 the English king once again advanced from Chester and relied on his magnates to launch supporting attacks in the south. The Welsh had a striking success in capturing the royal baggage train, and Edward spent an uncomfortable time in his new castle at Conwy before fresh supplies could come by sea. Supplies of wine had run out, and the king insisted that the last gallon should not be reserved for himself, but should be shared out. As in 1282–3, it was not the king who won the decisive victory. This time it was the Earl of Warwick operating from Oswestry, who defeated the Welsh leader Madog at Maes Moydog in March 1295. A triumphant newsletter recorded the death of seven hundred Welshmen, 'and we only lost one squire, Sir Robert FitzWalter's tailor, and six footsoldiers, but at least ten horses were killed. For the Welsh waited for us so well, and attacked our people from the front, and they were the finest and bravest Welshmen that anyone has seen.'[5] The Welsh were no match for the experienced English cavalrymen and archers.

After the defeat resistance faded fast, and the king went on a triumphant circuit of a demoralized country. This time only one new castle was founded, at Beaumaris in Anglesey. There, Master James of St George laid out his most ambitious plan, for a fully concentric castle with two great twin-towered gatehouses, on a palatial scale. The towers still stand unfinished, a testimony to Edward's growing financial difficulties. A find of leather token coins in Anglesey, dating from this period, is striking evidence of the expedients to which the king's officials had to resort in order to satisfy the workmen. In a letter to the exchequer in 1296 they stated that they needed over 2,630 men at a cost of £250 a week, and ended plaintively, 'And, sirs, for God's sake be quick with the money for the works, as much as ever our lord the king wills; otherwise everything done up to now will have been of no avail.'[6]

By 1295 Edward I had succeeded in Wales, but it had taken him three major campaigns. Judgements on his enterprise have varied widely. For some historians, Edward's was a civilizing mission, bringing an advanced system of law to a backward people. For others, the English king was exercising an unwarranted degree of force in pursuit of personal ambition. For Englishmen in the late thirteenth century, there was every justification for Edward's actions. Wales was a disunited country, and Llywelyn had neither the kind of authority, nor the administration to exercise it, that Edward had in England. English propaganda had it that the Welsh were a people devoted to sexual licence, murder, robbery and every other sort of crime. To a clerk in the entourage of the Archbishop of Canterbury who wrote a brief history of the wars, Taffy was very definitely a thief. Edward had every right to intervene against Llywelyn in 1277, when the Welsh prince refused to perform homage to him, and the later campaigns all followed open acts of rebellion. However, there was less justification for the nature of the settlement imposed on Wales, with the abolition of the principality. The clear partiality with which the English justices administered the law was testified to by an official inquiry and does them little credit. Nor should Edward's achievement be overrated. English penetration of Wales had begun at the time of the Norman Conquest, and Edward's campaigns can be viewed as merely the last of a long series. His opponents were weak and divided, and it is hardly surprising that they were unable to withstand the great weight of resources brought to bear on them.

The years of success in Wales were also years of constructive reform at home. A series of wide-ranging statutes has given the reign a lasting and fundamental importance. The study of the legal reforms of Edward's reign is difficult and highly technical; the texts of the statutes are lengthy, and even contemporaries often found them obscure – modern scholars have shied away from editing them. This is not the place for a full examination of Edward's legislation, but in any assessment of the reign it is vital to try to outline some of the main principles that underlay it.

Edward I and his advisers were not attempting to codify English law; the sobriquet of the English Justinian given to him by nineteenth-century historians is deserved only in the loosest sense – nor was written legislation wholly new. In 1215 Magna Carta had altered many points of law, and the period of baronial opposition to Henry III after 1258 saw the production of many important texts promulgating changes in the law. There was no fixed concept under Edward I of what a statute was. Some were in French, others in Latin, and no authoritative record was produced of the statutes as they were made. It was possible for administrative orders later to acquire the status of a statute.

Nevertheless, there was no doubt that the statutes were a new form of law, which stood in contrast to customary law, dominated as it was by the precedents of the past. It is wrong to try to see any one general principle running through the whole range of statutes produced in the most fruitful years between 1275 and 1290, save for a very real desire to remedy grievances. The first statute of Westminster of 1275 was drafted 'because our lord the king had great zeal and desire to redress the state of the realm in such things as required amendment for the common profit of Holy Church and of the realm',[7] and it reflected the grievances revealed in the Hundred Rolls, even if it could not meet them in full. Petitions sometimes provoked legislation, and some cases that came before the courts raised general issues that were best resolved by statute. The repeated failure of a Flemish merchant to obtain his share of the profits of a partnership he had made with an English trader was the probable origin of the Statute of Acton Burnell of 1283, which set up a new procedure for the recovery of debts. A complex case which first came before the courts in 1281 concerning feudal overlordship was settled in 1285 by 'the special act of the king and his council', and a general principle was then set out in a clause of the second statute of Westminster, issued in the same year.

Edward i and his councillors had to deal with a wide range of problems. The famous first clause of Westminster ii, *de donis conditionalibus*, was designed to meet the obvious grievance of landowners who found that even if they laid down specific conditions on grants of lands such as those to a daughter on her marriage, the terms were often flouted. Unfortunately, poor drafting meant that the statute was not as effective as its authors intended. The interests of great landowners were protected in the statute of *Quia Emptores* of 1290, which ensured that if their feudal tenants disposed of some of their lands, the new holder would enter into the same feudal relationship with the lord as the former holder. In contrast, the legislation at Gloucester in 1278 had been directed against the magnates, for it had set up the *quo warranto* inquiries. In 1290 a new statute attempted to resolve some of the difficulties which these investigations had created, with a compromise which preserved the royal theory that all rights of jurisdiction derived from the crown, but permitted all those who could show that their ancestors had exercised such rights since 1189 to retain them.

Crime was a matter of much concern, and in Westminster II a system for keeping the peace was outlined, reviving provisions for all men to possess arms appropriate to their status so that law and order could be maintained. The crown extended its criminal jurisdiction in the statutes most strikingly over the question of rape. The case of one knight, Walter de Bek, who raped a ten-year-old girl, demonstrates the novel quality of statute law. As his offence was committed before 1285 he was allowed to go free, for it was only in the statute of that year that the crown gained jurisdiction in such a matter.

Some legislation was politically inspired. The statute of Mortmain of 1279, which forbade grants of land to the Church, was an act of retaliation against provocation by the new Archbishop of Canterbury, John Pecham. In fact, the statute was less drastic than it appeared, for the king was quite prepared to issue licences to those who wished to grant land to the Church, and techniques such as leasing provided other means of getting round its terms. In 1307 the king agreed to popular demands for another statute directed against the Church, this time concerned with the export of the proceeds of English livings held by foreign clergy. Edward was, however, far from consistently anti-clerical. In 1285 the writ *Circumspecte agatis* defined the extent of ecclesiastical jurisdiction, and permitted the church courts to hear a wide range of cases.

It is impossible that such a systematic and elaborate process as the production of the statutes could have taken place without the active approval and encouragement of the king. There is little evidence, however, to suggest that Edward was involved in the technical and detailed work of drafting in the way that Henry II had been. Chief justice Hengham made a categorical statement about the authorship of Westminster II: 'Do not gloss the statute; we know it better than you, for we made it.'[8] The king certainly presided over many cases, particularly in the first half of the reign, and it is possible to detect a certain royal impatience with the interminable arguments of the lawyers. One dispute over the validity of a writ was firmly terminated by Edward's ringing intervention: 'I have nothing to do with your disputations, but, by God's blood, you shall give me a good writ before you arise hence.'⁹ In 1297 a royal order forbade attorneys to plead in the exchequer, and stated that cases should be heard without pomposity, quibbling or trickery. Edward was fully prepared to bend the law to suit his own interests, but he felt strongly about corruption and miscarriages of justice. When he was in Gascony between 1286 and 1289 disquieting rumours reached him. He wrote a severe letter to the Earl of Cornwall, his lieutenant in England, on behalf of a laundress who had followed him abroad to complain that she had not received justice in a rape plea. On his return, Edward reacted to the complaints he had received by instituting an immediate inquiry into the misdeeds of his judges and ministers. As a result of the hearings, the judiciary was purged. The chief justice of common pleas, Thomas Weyland, fled into sanctuary, but was starved out and forced into exile. The Archbishop of Canterbury's curious argument in his favour – that he was not a bigamist as had been alleged but that he had merely kept two mistresses – failed to help him. Even the great Hengham was found guilty, but it was only on one of nine counts that a case was proven. He was fined no less than 8,000 marks, most of which he paid; clearly there were considerable profits to be made out of the law. One of the last men to be charged was the escheator Henry de Bray, a notorious figure, who attempted suicide first by jumping from the boat taking him to the Tower, and then by beating his head against a stone wall. There was great enthusiasm for the king's action against the judges, but the fact that all except Weyland were pardoned after payment of heavy fines led to accusations that the king allowed financial expediency to outweigh his concern for justice. Even those who had been found guilty did not mend their ways. In the 1290s Hengham was still drawing a pension from Christ Church, Canterbury. A letter from Margaret of Hardeshull to the chancellor begged him not to appoint Hengham to hear a dispute between her and Philip Marmion, because he was retained as one of the latter's clerks.

The decade of the 1280s was the period when Edward I's prestige on the continent was at its height, and one that witnessed his greatest achievements in England and Wales. With a Provençal mother and a Castilian queen, Edward was a cosmopolitan man. He had ambitions to act as the arbiter of Europe, and aimed to establish peace as a prerequisite for a crusade. In 1282 the Sicilians had risen against their lord, Charles of Anjou, and the ambitious Peter of Aragon was swift to take advantage of the situation. Edward refused to preside over Charles's and Peter's abortive attempt to resolve their dispute by single combat, and preferred a course of proper negotiations. When Charles of Anjou's son Charles of Salerno was taken prisoner in 1284, Edward worked hard to obtain his release, which he saw as essential if peace was to be obtained. The matter was one of his chief concerns during his stay in Gascony, and in 1287 agreement was reached with the new king of Aragon, Alfonso, for Charles to be set free. Matters did not go smoothly. Charles failed to provide the full sum of money agreed, and Edward not only had to provide funds, but also hand over a number of hostages as security for payment, including his two close friends John de Vescy and Otto de Grandson. A letter from an English diplomat in 1289 expressed pessimism about Charles's capacity as a ruler, and concluded, 'I fear that we have worked much in vain on his behalf'.[10] Edward took the cross in 1287, but with the disaster of the fall in 1291 of Acre, the last remaining crusader stronghold, and the king's growing preoccupations with affairs nearer home, he was never able to fulfil his ambition of travelling once again to the Holy Land. For a period, however, Edward had been able to play a central role in European politics; he had not only intervened with some success in the dispute between the Aragonese and the Angevins, but also sent an embassy to negotiate agreement between the quarrelling rulers of Brabant, Guelders and Holland. He had become the most respected prince in Europe. In the early 1290s he was even to send ambassadors to distant Trebizond and beyond, into the steppe lands of Central Asia, to negotiate with the Mongol Khan, whom he saw as a potential ally for a crusade. They returned with a leopard to add to the royal menagerie in the Tower and the first parasols to be seen in England.

The character of Edward 1's rule changed in the early 1290s. There were major changes in the king's immediate domestic circle and among his ministers. The air of confidence in military and legislative matters was lost, and financial pressures became more acute as the king was faced with wars which were not of his own choosing. Contemporaries noted other changes; one chronicler commented on the way in which years of plenty were succeeded by a period of dearth and high prices, which was to last for forty years.

The loss of some of those closest to the king must have affected him considerably. In 1290 the queen, Eleanor of Castile, died. Edward's great grief was immortalized in the magnificent series of crosses erected at the various stopping places of her funeral cortège between Harby, near Lincoln, where the queen died, and Westminster. Two elaborate tombs were constructed, one at Lincoln for her entrails and one at Westminster for her embalmed body. Eleanor's character does not emerge very clearly from the chronicles and records. Although she was described in conventional terms as 'a pious, modest and merciful lady, a lover of all English people and a support for the whole realm',[11] she was also an astute businesswoman, and like her husband acquisitive of land. The way in which she bought up debts owed to Jews was good business practice, but the technique was both unsavoury and unpopular. She had literary interests, for one romance was dedicated to her, and she even corresponded with an Oxford scholar about one of her books. Whereas none of Edward's own officials were men of intellectual distinction, she employed as keeper of her wardrobe Geoffrey of Aspall, the author of voluminous commentaries on Aristotle. Her main duty as queen she fulfilled admirably by bearing Edward possibly as many as sixteen children, although only six were living at the time of her death. Edward was to remarry in 1299 but his second queen, the King of France's sister Margaret, was never to occupy as strong a place in his affections as Eleanor had done.

In 1291 the king's mother, Eleanor of Provence, died. Although she had retired into religious life at Amesbury some years earlier, her influence on Edward had been considerable as her surviving letters show. Besides giving advice on foreign policy and asking favours for her friends, she could write in a more personal style:

Know dear sire that we are very badly served by you since we have heard no news of your estate, and of how things are with you, since you left us. We are letting you know that we are in good health, thanks be to God. We have left Gillingham sooner than we expected, because of the pollution of the air, which we found extremely smoky in the evenings, and have come to Marlborough, arriving on the Friday after Michaelmas. Thanks be to God, we are in good estate, as we greatly desire you to be.[12]

The quality of the air was a matter which greatly concerned Eleanor; on another occasion she warned Edward not to take his son north with him, because the bad air would make him ill. Alongside such perennial maternal desires to interfere in domestic matters, Eleanor probably influenced the king's policy towards the Jews. A pious lady, who insisted that one of her granddaughters became a nun, she had expelled all Jews from her estates in 1275. In 1290 the king followed her example, removing all Jews from England. A grateful people made a substantial grant of taxation, which considerably outweighed any financial loss incurred by the crown, which could no longer subject Jews to harsh and arbitrary taxation.

Another important influence on Edward in the first half of the reign was that of his chancellor, Robert Burnell. A man of considerable ability, he had served Edward before his accession. The king twice tried to have him elevated to the see of Canterbury, but he had to be content with the bishopric of Bath and Wells. With his wealth and illegitimate offspring, Burnell was not perhaps an outstanding ornament of the English Church from a spiritual point of view, but as a minister he was a man of greater probity than Walter Langton, who came to take his place as the king's most trusted official. Burnell's death in 1292 does much to explain the changing character of Edward's government in his later years, and the decline of his interest in legal reform.

The centre of the governmental machine was the royal household, and in particular the department of the wardrobe. The name is misleading; the wardrobe was responsible for almost all household expenditure, and it was through it that war was financed. It possessed a flexibility wholly lacking in the exchequer with its rigid accounting system. In 1290 important changes of personnel took place: Walter Langton became keeper, and another highly important minister of the later years of the reign, John Droxford, was appointed controller. At the same period Walter Beauchamp became steward of the household, a post he was to hold until 1303. The knights of the royal household were important both in war and in peace, when they performed many miscellaneous administrative tasks. In the early 1290s there were considerable changes in their ranks. The men of Edward's own generation who had served him so well in Wales were replaced by a group of younger men. Of the close friends who had been with him on crusade, only Otto de Grandson remained actively in his service through the decade. A man of astonishing longevity, he did not die until 1328 at the age of ninety.

Edward's position was transformed in 1294 by the outbreak of war with France. The confiscation of Gascony by Philip IV ushered in a period of almost continuous warfare. The conflict with France lasted until the autumn of 1297; there was also the Welsh revolt of 1294–5, and war with the Scots from 1296. The story of the French and Scottish wars will be covered in later chapters; for the present, what is important is that Edward faced the problems of recruiting troops, collecting food supplies and raising funds on an unprecedented scale. The total military expenditure from 1294–8 was probably at least £750,000, and in 1297 the strain on the country led to a major political and constitutional crisis. Concentration on war and its needs led to neglect of some of the king's earlier concerns. Only two general eyres, or major judicial inquiries, took place after 1294. No more major statutes were produced. Apart from Beaumaris, no large-scale castles were built.

At the outset, Edward obtained a remarkable degree of support from his people for the war with France. For three consecutive years he was voted taxes by the laity in parliament, and although the Dean of St Paul's died of apoplexy when he heard that the king intended to tax the clergy at an unprecedented rate of half their assessed income, the money was duly paid. The merchants willingly conceded a customs duty of forty shillings on each sack of wool exported, rather than see the crown carry through a scheme for the compulsory purchase of all the wool in the country. The one measure taken in 1294 which had an arbitrary and unreasonable air was the seizure by royal agents of all the money deposited in churches throughout the kingdom for safe-keeping. In the next year, however, the treasurer William March who had been responsible for the seizure was dismissed.

Finance was an acute problem. One major difficulty was that the crown no longer had the support of the Ricciardi bankers, for at the outset of the war Philip IV of France had driven them into bankruptcy by confiscating the assets the firm held in his country. Forced loans from the remaining Italian companies in England could be no substitute for the willing and substantial assistance that the Ricciardi had provided in the past. The financial system lost a great deal of its earlier flexibility, and although the crown amassed a considerable reserve of cash in 1294, it soon found that expenditure was fast exceeding income.

The clergy were the first to object to the king's financial demands. Pope Boniface VIII was anxious to end the war between France and England, and attempted to put pressure on the combatants by forbidding the clergy to pay taxes to the lay authorities. He did this in a celebrated bull *Clericis laicos* which was promulgated in 1296. The papal stand was supported by the Archbishop of Canterbury, Robert Winchelsey. Early in 1297 the king countered the refusal of the clergy to grant a tax by outlawing them. He made it known that if they paid a fine equivalent to the sum that they would have paid in taxation, they would re-enter his favour. Royal officials acted harshly. At Canterbury, the priory granary was sealed up, and the grain allowed to rot until fumes rose from the putrefying mass. The archbishop's horses were taken from him. Few churchmen continued their resistance for long, and as the receipts from fines mounted, the king relaxed his attitude. By July 1297 he reached agreement with the archbishop. In August, however, a convocation of the clergy agreed that no taxes could be paid without papal permission. The king's response was to order a new levy, justifying it in terms of the necessity of the times, which once again alienated the archbishop and the rest of the clergy.

Edward might have been able to deal easily enough with the opposition of the Church in 1297, had it not been for the increasing hostility of his lay subjects as the events of the year unfolded. At the Salisbury Parliament in February a dramatic scene took place when Edward asked the magnates to serve in Gascony. In 1295 he had been able to persuade the Earl of Arundel and some others to go only by means of blatant financial blackmail. Now the Earl of Norfolk Roger Bigod refused to comply with the king's plans. 'By God, O earl, either you go or hang', said Edward, to which the earl, quite correctly as events turned out, replied, 'By the same oath, O king, I shall neither go nor hang.'[13] The king's next move was to summon the magnates and all those who owned at least twenty-pounds-a-year-worth of land to muster at London. The summons took a new form. It did not appeal to the traditional obligations of fealty and homage, and did not specify where service was required. When the troops mustered, Bigod as Marshal of England with his colleague the constable, Humphrey de Bohun, Earl of Hereford, were asked to draw up lists of those present. They refused, on the grounds that this had not been a proper feudal summons, and were dismissed from their posts. Abortive negotiations took place between the king and his opponents at the end of July. A statement of the opposition case, known as the Remonstrances, set out the argument against the summons, and also stressed the impoverishment that was the result of heavy taxation and the seizure of victuals. The case thus made was not so much constitutional as practical, and it made excellent popular propaganda.

Edward was eventually forced to yield on the issue of military service. His plan was to send reinforcements to the English fighting in Gascony and to launch a new attack on the French from Flanders. He offered wages to all those who were prepared to sail with him for Flanders, but despite his blandishments, there was a poor response. Reports survive from three counties which show that only one man was prepared to go, and he was a household knight who was paid a regular fee by the crown. The cavalry which did go on the expedition was, indeed, largely composed of household forces. Not one single earl accompanied the king.

By the end of July the financial situation was desperate. Not only did wages have to be found for the expedition, but also the very substantial subsidies which had been promised to the English allies on the continent, notably the Duke of Brabant and the German king. There were both political and practical reasons why a full parliament could not be summoned, and Edward decided to raise a new tax, an eighth assessed on movable property, without obtaining full consent. He obtained the agreement of 'those standing about in his chamber',[14] as one hostile chronicler puts it. The king's arguments that he was putting himself in acute personal danger, and his reminders of the duty that men owed to their lord, carried little weight. Just as he was setting sail from Winchelsea the leading opposition earls, Bigod and Bohun, appeared at the exchequer with their retainers to forbid collection of the tax.

The two earls also took exception to the crown's dealings in wool. At Easter a seizure of wool had been ordered, and although it had brought in little, the measure was repeated at the end of July, when it was estimated that eight thousand sacks were needed. The government intended to export the wool and use the cash raised from the sales to finance the campaign. Again, no proper consent was obtained, and the earls had good grounds for requesting that the levy cease. The king's response was to ask whether he was not as free as any other man to buy wool in his kingdom, which wholly ignored the compulsory element in the operation. In fact, popular resistance to the measures was such that the two seizures probably yielded only about three thousand sacks between them. The arbitrary measures of taxation and wool seizure taken in late July provided the opposition with a strong constitutional argument to add to their earlier complaints about the burden imposed on the country.

As well as the general issues, individual grievances played an important part in the crisis of 1297. Archbishop Winchelsey was hard pressed by the king to pay debts that he owed to the crown; Roger Bigod was in a similar position. The Earl of Hereford had been harshly treated by the king in 1290, as a result of a private war with the Earl of Gloucester; Edward had also been aggressive towards the privileges of the Welsh Marcher lords, and it is significant that one of the meetings of the opposition was held at Montgomery on the Welsh border. John de Ferrers, a baronial leader, had a long-standing quarrel with Edward, because of the part the king had played in dispossessing his father of his lands and the title of Earl of Derby in the aftermath of the Montfortian civil war.

For much of the crisis the king and his opponents remained a discreet distance apart, but there were dramatic moments. On 14 July a carefully stage-managed ceremony took place at Westminster, when the king obtained from his subjects oaths of fealty to his young son Edward. Crying with emotion, the king begged forgiveness from his people, and promised to make full redress for his exactions. Bigod and Bohun stayed away, only taking the oath two days later. Another striking scene took place in September, when a royal clerk was deputed to make representations against Archbishop Winchelsey. He chose to do this in Canterbury Cathedral itself, at the very time that the archbishop was preaching, and the scene degenerated into a shouting match between the two men.

The opposition could not, however, divert Edward from his planned campaign, in which he considered that his honour was at stake. When he sailed in late August the country was on the verge of civil war; castles everywhere were put into a state of readiness. At Tickhill for instance, the moat was cleared, new ropes and locks bought for the drawbridge, iron bars fitted to the gate, and a palisade erected. A force of twenty crossbowmen and an equal number of archers was recruited. In the event these preparations were not put to the test. On 11 September the Scots routed an English army at Stirling Bridge, and the news at once created the sense of national unity which all Edward's histrionics and propaganda had failed to rouse. Agreement between the opposition and the regency government was reached by 10 October in a document known as the Confirmation of the Charters. The opposition had wanted to add new clauses to Magna Carta itself, but this was not acceptable, although the government were prepared to make significant concessions in a separate document. The Confirmation promised that no precedent would be made of the recent demands for taxes, impositions and prises – or seizures of goods – and it conceded that in future any similar measures would require the common consent of all the realm. The heavy customs duty of forty shillings, known as the *maltolt*, was abolished, and again it was stated that such a levy would not be taken in future without consent. The agreement was not entirely satisfactory. The new concessions did not have the authority that inclusion in Magna Carta would have given them, and the precise nature of the consenting body was not defined. For the time being however, it was sufficient, and the king, who perhaps fortunately had taken no part in the final negotiations because he was in Flanders gave his consent to the agreement on 5 November.

Edward I's own contribution to the settlement came after his return to England early in 1298. An elaborate judicial inquiry was set up to investigate all the administrative malpractices that had taken place during the period of wartime. The surviving records reveal a wide array of abuses. The recruitment of troops, the seizure of goods, the collection of taxes had all provided a host of minor officials such as sub-bailiffs and village constables with opportunities to enrich themselves at the expense of those least

31

able to protect themselves. The great prises of foodstuffs had been particularly liable to abuse: in 1296 the exchequer had ordered the levy of no less than 63,200 quarters of grain. The collectors accepted bribes to exempt men, they seized more than they were entitled to, and they kept some back for themselves: the records make the almost universal hostility to the government very easy to understand. The inquiry of 1298 showed that the king had not lost his concern for the justice and administrative order which had helped to inspire the Hundred Rolls, but there was no attempt this time to follow up the investigations with legislation.

The crisis of 1297 had been essentially the result of the abnormal demands that the king was compelled to make as a result of his over-extensive military commitments, rather than the product of a fundamental dissatisfaction with the government. The end of war with France did not, however, mean the end of domestic discord. There was amply justified suspicion that Edward did not intend to adhere to the terms of the Confirmation of the Charters, and with campaigns continuing in Scotland the pressures of war were still present. In 1300 a document known as the *Articuli super Cartas* dealt at length with a wide range of administrative abuses, notably with regard to purveyance, as the compulsory purchase of foodstuffs for the army was coming to be called. In order to obtain support for the war, the king was forced to concede the demands made of him, though in 1300 he did not collect the tax that was granted in parliament, since he objected to the conditions that were imposed. Argument increasingly centred on the issue of the royal forest, and the king's willingness to submit to a revision of the boundaries. The matter was regarded as a touchstone of the king's good faith, and concerned an important area of royal prerogative power. These years following the crisis of 1297 also saw the king abandon, under pressure, his attempts to reform the system of summoning men to fight in his wars, and develop a form of military obligation to replace the out-dated feudal service, which had provided an inadequate force for an insufficient period.

Although the king was in a weak position in his final

years as a result of his financial difficulties, his opponents did not gain in strength. Humphrey de Bohun died in 1298, and Roger Bigod was in severe financial straits. Archbishop Winchelsey's position was gravely weakened after 1305, for in that year a former royal clerk of Edward's, the Gascon Bertrand de Got, was elected Pope as Clement v. He was open to all Edward's insinuations and charges against the archbishop, and early in 1306 Winchelsey left England to defend himself at the papal court. Clement formally absolved the king from the concessions he had made, and in 1306 Edward cancelled the revisions of the forest boundaries. The king had learned some lessons from the events of 1297, and did not impose further arbitrary taxation. In 1303 he succeeded in negotiating a new customs duty of an extra 3s 4d on each sack of wool exported by foreign merchants, but he accepted the English merchants' refusal to pay such a subsidy themselves. Rather than engage in unpopular financial measures, the government ran up debts on an unprecedented scale by borrowing money from the Italian company of the Frescobaldi and by failing to pay all manner of creditors from great magnates to humble tradespeople. By the end of the reign, debts probably totalled some £200,000.

The man who came under fiercest attack from the opposition in Edward I's last years was the treasurer, Walter Langton. He had held the office since 1295, and his considerable wealth bore ample witness to his corrupt practices. Langton was accused of a remarkable range of crimes, from murdering his mistress's husband with her assistance, to performing homage to the devil. He undoubtedly abused his position, taking full advantage of every twist that the law presented. One of his techniques was to appoint men as sheriffs who held land he wanted. They would then be held to account for their term of office with the utmost stringency, and only when they handed lands over to Langton were they discharged by the exchequer. He was an efficient administrator, however, and even when he quarrelled with the heir to the throne, he received the king's full support. In 1307 he was pardoned all his offences, and it was not until Edward II's reign that action was taken against him. The king's support of an unpopular and corrupt minister is perhaps surprising in view of his action against the justices in 1289, and his dismissal of Langton's predecessor as treasurer, William March. Yet Langton was a very active and extremely loyal servant to Edward I and, though no great reformer, he deserves much of the credit for the reconstruction of royal authority after the crisis of 1297. He was later to display his devotion to Edward's memory by decorating his episcopal palace at Lichfield with scenes of the king's life and triumphs.

The final years of Edward I's reign were overshadowed by events in Scotland, but there were some achievements at home. A major campaign was begun in 1305 to deal with the growing problem of law and order. The records of the judicial commissions that were set up show that despite the work of legal reform the country Edward ruled was violent and unruly. The city of York, to which the royal administration had moved in 1298 to facilitate the organization of the war in Scotland, was shown to be under the control of an unscrupulous 'mafia' of local businessmen. Their power was broken by royal justices in 1306. The new measures, known as commissions of trailbaston after the staves carried by criminals, were not popular, as a contemporary poem shows: 'They take forty shillings for my ransom, and the sheriff comes for his fee, so that he will not put me in prison. Now consider, lords, is this right?' The author went on to explain that he had fought for Edward in Flanders, Scotland and Gascony, and was now forced into outlawry: 'I have spent all my time in vain to try to please such a man.'[15]

An occasion of great splendour took place in 1306 when the young prince Edward was knighted along with some three hundred others. They were all given splendid robes for the occasion, and Westminster Abbey rang with the clamour of trumpets and the shouts of joy; such was the crush that two unfortunate youths were suffocated in the crowd. A great feast took place at which two lavishly decorated roast swans were placed before the king; these were probably not real birds, but masterpieces of the confectioner's art. Edward then swore on the birds that he would set out for Scotland to avenge the death of John Comyn, recently murdered by Robert Bruce, and the others present swore to accompany him and to continue the fight under his son. The ceremony was modelled on Burgundian practice, and shows that the old king had not abandoned the enthusiasm he had shown in his youth for chivalry and its ceremonial pageantry.

Edward 1 died on 7 July 1307 on his way north to fight the Scots. He had been ill throughout the winter, and it was his strength that failed him, not his determination. One story has it that he asked that at his death his body should be boiled until the bones were clean of flesh: the rattling skeleton should then be carried north on every expedition against the Scots. Perhaps more credible is his wish that his heart should be taken to the Holy Land and that his executors should pay the wages of a hundred knights for a year on crusade. In the event neither wish was carried out and the body was simply taken for burial in Westminster Abbey, where it lies in an untypically plain undecorated tomb.

How can the character of Edward 1 be summed up? Had the changeable leopard of his youth been transformed, to continue with the contemporary metaphor, into the lion who terrified all the other beasts of the forest? There were contradictory elements about the king. A man of magnificent physical presence, who stood literally head and shoulders above other men, he had hesitant, possibly lisping, speech. Although he was a great military leader, he fought few battles as king. In 1294 he was even accused of cowardice, when an Irish knight alleged that William de Vescy had told him that Edward was the laziest knight in the realm, and that in 1265 he had refused to march against Simon de Montfort until shamed into action by Roger Clifford. The story was hotly denied, however, and there is no reason to doubt Edward's personal courage: in 1297 he faced a hostile mob in Flanders with bravery, and in the next year he showed considerable determination when he ignored an injury incurred on the previous day when his horse had trodden on him. At the siege of Stirling in 1304 he refused to retire to his tent to recover from the shock of having his mount felled under him by an enemy missile.

Such are the sources that survive from this period that they reveal little of the inner man: men who led lives of constant activity did not bare their souls in correspondence. The great mass of official records do, however, provide some revealing details. An entry for the repair of Edward's daughter Elizabeth's coronet after he had thrown it into the fire reveals his violent temper; in the course of the wedding of another daughter, Margaret, he hit a page on the head, wounding him so badly that he paid him twenty marks in compensation. A pleasanter note is struck by the record of a payment of £2 to the queen's laundress, after he had bet her that she could not follow the royal hunt. Payment of the exceptionally large sums of £40 each to the messengers who reported news of the births of a daughter and a grandson in 1306 gives some indication of the pleasure that Edward must have felt. A letter written to his second queen's physician shows a real concern for her well-being: she had been ill, and Edward gave orders that she was not to travel until she was fully recovered, 'and if you allow her to travel too soon, by God's thigh you will suffer for it'.[16] A letter to her confessor seems in contrast to be lacking in sympathy, at least by modern standards – Edward asked him to tell the queen that her sister had died, 'and truly we will bear this grief very lightly, since we have considered her dead and lost from the hour when she was first married'.[16]

Edward still possessed the leopard's deviousness in his later years. One story told of how he forged a letter and left it lying on his bed so that his queen, Margaret, would read it and report the contents to her brother Philip IV of France. A more authentic example of the king's capacity for guile is provided by a letter sent to the treasurer in 1306 ordering the imprisonment of Henry of Keighley, a knight of the shire who had been responsible in 1301 for a bill in parliament critical of the king. Edward asked that Keighley should be well treated, but that this should appear to result from the treasurer's kindness, rather than from royal orders. The king's motives on that occasion were commendable, but in another letter to the treasurer he behaved less honourably by approving an unpopular appointment, but asking that it should be made under Langton's authority rather than his own.

Edward shared fully in the chivalric culture of the age. In his youth he had been an ardent performer at the tournaments that were one of its chief characteristics. Although he prohibited tournaments after his accession to the throne because they diverted men's interests from his campaigns, his interests in other aspects of chivalry did not die. He was a devotee of Arthurian legend, and had the reputed grave of Arthur and Guinevere at Glastonbury excavated. He held round-tables for his knights, and at one of his feasts a squire appeared disguised as the Loathly Damzel, a figure in Arthurian legend. Yet some of the king's actions were hardly in accord with chivalrous concepts. It is not enough for Edward's apologists to excuse the imprisonment of the Countess of Buchan and Robert Bruce's sister Mary in cages in the castles at Berwick and Roxburgh by pointing out that latrines were provided for the ladies. Another incident which has aroused recent hostile comment took place at the siege of Stirling Castle in 1304, when the king refused to let the garrison come out until he had tried out his latest siege engine, even though they had offered to surrender. Contemporary chroniclers, however, did not comment adversely on this – one author remarked on the fact that when the garrison did leave, Edward was moved to mercy, sparing their lives rather than executing them as he was entitled to do.

In many ways Edward I was a conventional man. He possessed the normal pious instincts of the age; a fifteenth-century document even records a vision he is alleged to have seen of the Virgin Mary. He had a strong commitment to the crusading cause, and genuinely regretted that circumstances prevented him from setting out again to the East. The abbey at Vale Royal in Cheshire, which Edward founded in fulfilment of a vow made during a dangerous voyage enjoyed his generous patronage until in 1290 he inexplicably withdrew his support: 'the king has ceased to concern himself with the works of that church, and henceforth will have nothing more to do with them.'[17]

Perhaps he was disenchanted after Queen Eleanor's death, or possibly he found evidence of the misappropriation of the funds he had poured into the building scheme – Edward's piety was never such as to interfere with the political decisions he took towards the clergy, as the crisis of 1297 demonstrated.

Hunting was a favourite pastime for Edward. He had no taste for greyhounds, but was a keen and highly expert falconer. A typical letter to the official in charge of the birds reads:

We have fully understood from your letters, sent by the bearer of these, that the gerfalcon in your keeping has taken a crane, since you sent us the heads of the last two cranes he took. We are very pleased about this, and order you to take pains to exercise him, and look after him as well as you can.[18]

On one occasion the king ordered a wax image of an ailing falcon to be made and placed before the shrine of Thomas Becket to try to ensure its recovery. In 1300 Edward possessed two chess sets; he also played at dice, and the accounts record various payments to minstrels. When he was bled by his doctor in 1297 a harpist helped to keep the king's mind off the operation.

Generosity in a monarch can be more a fault than a virtue and it is hard to accuse Edward I of being lavish with his patronage. Those who served the king certainly might do well for themselves; Robert Burnell and Walter Langton used their positions to acquire great wealth and wide acres, but this was done by using – and abusing – their ministerial positions rather than by obtaining grants from the king. Edward was generous enough in parcelling-out estates in Wales to those who served him in his wars, notably in 1282 when the Earl of Lincoln, Earl Warenne, Reginald Grey and Roger Mortimer all received major lordships in the Welsh March. Later he attempted to reward his supporters by similar means in Scotland, but they were never able to gain effective control of their lands there. Within England itself Edward was far less munificent. He husbanded the stock of royal estates for the benefit of the crown and the royal family; he did not raise any of his close associates to the rank of earl. Otto de Grandson, one of his most loyal followers, obtained little land in England from Edward, although he received some estates in distant Ireland and was given custody of the Channel Isles. Edward naturally used the common currency of medieval patronage as one of the means by which he governed the country; he appointed men to the custody of castles, sold wardships, acceded to requests to permit the setting up of new markets and fairs, and distributed the ecclesiastical livings under his control. He was not, however, profligate in the rewards he gave his servants, and stands in striking contrast to his weak-willed son Edward II.

Edward could display striking loyalty to his servants, as in the cases of Burnell and Langton whose corrupt practices he overlooked. He might equally turn against men who appear to have served him competently – Jean de Grailly, seneschal of Gascony and one of the king's crusading companions, was disgraced and removed from office in 1287; William March, the treasurer, was dismissed in 1295; and John Langton, the chancellor, removed from his post in 1302. An official wrote to a colleague: 'Sire, know that at the time of writing there is no good news at court to tell you of, but there is some that is unpleasant, as follows. Sir John Langton the chancellor has been totally removed from the king's service, and the seal taken from him by the king's command, but for what reason I do not yet know.'[19] Anthony Bek, one of the king's most loyal and influential councillors was removed from favour in 1300, and his palatinate of Durham placed in the hands of royal officials. The purge of the judicial bench in 1289 was but the most striking of a number of incidents which must have made the king feared rather than loved as a master.

Edward had an undoubted reputation for justice. Even before his accession, the King of Cyprus asked him to arbitrate in a dispute between himself and his barons, and in the prime of his life his adjudication in the Great Cause (the succession dispute to the Scottish throne) testified to his renown. Equally telling is the faith placed in the king by a Florentine merchant who hopefully put before him a claim for the restitution of property destroyed by his rivals in Florence. The king was prepared to see his own personal animosities overridden in the cause of mercy and justice: in 1305 he declared that he would rather show mercy to a dog than to Nicholas Segrave, who was accused of treason, but he accepted the request of the magnates that Segrave should be released on the guarantee of thirty of their number. The Welsh and the Scots, of course, came to have a very different view of the king, but according to his own principles Edward treated them in a just and lawful fashion; by his lights such men as Prince Dafydd and William Wallace were traitors, not honourable enemies. Edward's exalted view of his own position could lead him to interpret the law in a way far too favourable to himself. As an examination of his dealings with the magnates, in chapter five, will show, he had little hesitation in sinking to very dubious means of manipulating the law, using such techniques as the support of false claimants in the courts. The great lawgiver was not impartial, but he did not operate beyond the bounds of the law as he interpreted it.

Edward was not a man to be diverted from his purpose – his succinct and sharp recorded utterances suggest a man of few doubts. Despite the evidence of his occasional trickery, he never employed the politician's gifts for compromise. In 1294 he committed himself to a campaign on the continent against Philip IV, and he carried out his aim with determination, despite the fact that when he left the country in August 1297 for Flanders, England was on the verge of civil war. The political compromise was worked out in his absence, and his opponents were right to suspect that once Edward returned he would do all he could to go back on the agreement that had been forced on him. Neither did he compromise in his struggle with the Welsh, and displayed a similar stubborn obstinacy against the Scots. His correspondence reveals a lack of concern with the details of administrative matters; he was capable of asking for the impossibly large quantity of a hundred thousand quarters of grain to be sent to Gascony in 1296, and of demanding the equally impossible number of sixty thousand soldiers for his Scottish campaign of the same year. There is no evidence that he was greatly worried by the growing insolvency of the crown in his later years, beyond a series of irritated letters to the exchequer asking them to send him more money. This was probably because the fundamental financial problems of the day were not tackled by the king. He should not be condemned for this – he was surely right to take the attitude that administration was a matter for officials, not for the king in person.

Edward I was not the kind of king who was greeted by cheering crowds as he travelled through the country; a letter from an official announcing that he intended to spend Easter at Nottingham asked that the local people should be comforted by being told that he would go as fast as he had come. The arrival of the court inevitably involved exactions such as the purveyance of food supplies, which explains this apparent unpopularity. In 1297, however, one Londoner went so far as to declare that the king's head should be impaled on a pike alongside that of Llywelyn of Wales. However few of Edward's subjects would have dared or wanted to go as far as that, even in the year of crisis. He was without doubt one of the greatest rulers of his time, and it was deservedly to Edward rather than to his own monarch that the Frenchman Pierre Dubois dedicated his treatise on the recovery of the Holy Land. Edward was a king to inspire fear and respect; contemporaries valued his many achievements and his death was not anticipated with any optimism. With news of his illness in 1307 preachers were prophesying evil days to come – when his death became known, the news was met with genuine and widespread grief.

2

The Proving Ground

The War against the Scots

On a stormy March night in 1286 Alexander III King of Scotland was killed when he fell from his horse and tumbled down a cliff in west Fife. The accident set off a course of events which led to war between England and Scotland – a war which continued, with some intermissions, into Edward III's reign. To examine this conflict it is necessary to move back from the point of time reached in the last chapter to the heyday of Edward I's reign, and to take the story on through the disasters of his son's reign to the resurgence of English arms under Edward III. Although there were some signal victories, this war was to be far less successful than Edward I's against the Welsh, or than the struggle against the French between 1337 and 1360: it was nevertheless of fundamental importance. The problem of Scotland dogged Edward I in his later years, and constantly overshadowed the troubled politics of his son's reign. The English learned much from the war, and it was as a result of experience in fighting in the north that their army was transformed by Edward III's reign into the most formidable fighting machine in Europe.

Whereas Edward I's conquest of Wales can be seen as the culmination of a long tradition of warfare, the situation in the north was very different. The origins of the Anglo-Scottish war did not lie in deep-seated antagonisms between the two countries, neither should the war be seen as a colonial venture by the English. The thirteenth century had been a period of peace with the Scots: Henry III's sister

Joan had married Alexander II of Scotland, and Edward I's sister Margaret, who died in 1275, was Alexander III's first queen. Many great families, like those of Balliol, Bruce and d'Umfraville held land on both sides of the border and, in contrast to the lords of the Welsh Marches, had no vested interest in war, and there is little to suggest that Edward I had ambitions to subjugate Scotland before the 1290s. Alexander III's second marriage to the French Yolande of Dreux in 1285 may have been seen as a threat to English influence, and Edward I's mother's report that Gilbert de Gresk, an Englishman who had served Queen Margaret, had had his lands confiscated because of his nationality, could well have angered the English king. The cause of Edward's war of conquest, however, lay in the disastrous circumstances of the northern kingdom in the aftermath of Alexander's death.

The stability of medieval kingdoms depended to a great extent on the ability of rulers to produce male heirs. By 1286 all Alexander's children by his first marriage had died, and his line was represented only by his granddaughter Margaret, the 'Maid of Norway'. His young queen Yolande was probably pregnant at the time of his death, but if so she miscarried. The magnates succeeded in maintaining the Maid's right to the throne, despite the ambitions of the Bruce family, and a marriage was negotiated with Edward I's heir Edward – a move which would ensure English support for the regime. The plan came to nothing, however, for the young girl died in 1290 on her way to Scotland. A grave crisis now threatened. There was no clearly-recognized heir to the throne; eventually, thirteen claimants were to appear.

To the credit of the Scots, the situation did not degenerate into civil war. The Bishop of St Andrews, however, was sufficiently alarmed to write to Edward I suggesting that he should come to the border to prevent bloodshed. The English king, however, needed no invitation to intervene – in his view, he was the superior lord of Scotland. In the twelfth century, William the Lion had done homage to Henry II for the kingdom of Scotland, and although later Scottish rulers had only acknowledged English suzerainty over the land they held in England, Edward had no doubt that he was the ultimate feudal superior of Scotland. This conclusion was reinforced by historical research undertaken at his request in the monastic chronicles.

Edward I summoned the Scots to meet him in a parliament at Norham in May 1291. His request that they should recognize his rights of overlordship caused some problems, but after an adjournment the contenders for the throne agreed to accept his judgement. They conceded that he should hold Scotland until the completion of the hearings, and in letters of safe-conduct, Edward conceded that no precedent would be made of the summons to Norham, and that the status of the realm of Scotland would not be prejudiced.

The majority of the contenders probably put in claims only in order to safeguard their rights should the throne once again fall vacant: the real issue lay between Robert Bruce, the Competitor and John Balliol. Both of these men appointed forty auditors, who formed the court along with twenty-four nominated by Edward I. As the genealogical table shows, both Bruce and Balliol were descended from David, Earl of Huntingdon, the former claiming because he was nearest in degree, the latter by virtue of the seniority of his line. The arguments were technical and complex: should feudal law, which favoured Balliol, be followed, or Roman law, which suited Bruce's case? Could the kingdom be divided like a barony between daughters and their descendants? An ingenious claim by the Count of Holland, one of the contenders, suggested that the Earl of Huntingdon had resigned his right to the throne, and this caused a lengthy adjournment. Eventually the verdict went in favour of Balliol, and he was duly enthroned in December 1292.

How impartial had Edward I been? He had placed the Scots under considerable pressure during the hearings: an English fleet off Holy Island prevented victuals reaching Scottish ports; troops were summoned from the north of England, mustering after the initial adjournment; and the treasurer ordered the collection of debts owed to the crown by John Balliol from his English estates. There is no reason,

THE SCOTTISH WARS
OF
INDEPENDENCE

Lochindorb

Spey

Stracathro

Tay

Methven
Perth
Dupplin
Stirling Moor
Bridge
Forth
Stirling Bannockburn
Falkirk
Dunbar
Edinburgh
Halidon Berwick
Hill
Bothwell Norham
Clyde
Tweed
Roxburgh
Loudoun
Hill

Annan

Dumfries
Caerlaverock
Carlisle

however, to suppose that the eventual verdict was the result of a cynical manipulation of the law – Edward went to great trouble to obtain advice, summoning university representatives to Norham and consulting lawyers overseas. Balliol's case was the strongest, even if it has to be admitted that it suited Edward to have as king of Scotland a man who was a substantial landowner in the north of England, and who seemed likely to prove more subservient than Bruce. The Great Cause, as the hearings were known, was a considerable triumph for Edward. Its importance was demonstrated by the magnificent record of the proceedings made by a public notary.

Once Balliol was king, Edward I sought to define his overlordship of Scotland. As in Wales, he pushed his claims far enough to provoke rebellion. The new king did homage to Edward, who almost immediately began to test his rights of jurisdiction. At Newcastle he heard the appeal of a Berwick man, Roger Bartholomew, who asked for reversal of judgements that had gone against him in Scottish courts. The English justice Roger Brabazon declared that Edward did not regard himself as bound by any promises that he had made during the interregnum in Scotland as far as the exercise of justice was concerned. Edward summoned Balliol to appear before him at Westminster to explain his failure to do justice – an unprecedented step. Nor did the English king confine his interference in Scotland to judicial matters. In 1294 he summoned Balliol and some leading Scottish magnates to perform military service in Gascony. Such service was normally implied in the act of homage, but the request was not one which the Scots had anticipated. It demonstrated the extent to which Edward attempted to take advantage of the unfortunate circumstances of the succession dispute in Scotland and its aftermath.

Balliol did not answer Edward's summons, but did little else to resist. A council of twelve seized power from him in 1295, and made a treaty with Edward's enemy Philip IV of France. War was bound to follow, and the rival hosts were summoned to muster in March 1296. An insertion was later made in the record of the Great Cause, noting an alleged warning given to Balliol, that if he did not govern satisfactorily, the King of England had a right to intervene. The clumsy manipulation of the evidence does Edward's officials little credit, and seems unnecessary – the Franco-Scottish alliance provided ample justification for war. At this time, Edward's intention was to attack Philip IV with the aid of a vast coalition of princes in the Low Countries, but the plan now had to be postponed until the situation in Scotland was resolved.

Edward's campaign was a determined one. Berwick was sacked with savage brutality: the inhabitants 'fell like autumn leaves',[1] to quote a contemporary simile. At Dunbar Earl Warenne routed the Scottish feudal host and all heart went out of Scottish resistance. At the powerful stronghold of Stirling the English found no garrison, merely a gatekeeper who promptly handed over the keys. In a tour of the country Edward received the homage of the defeated. Balliol himself was initially offered quite favourable terms by English negotiators, but, probably on Edward's orders, they insisted on his absolute and unconditional surrender. The royal arms were stripped from his surcoat in a humiliating ceremony and a system of direct English rule under Earl Warenne was set up. When Edward handed him the Scottish seal, he remarked with characteristic coarseness, 'A man who gets rid of a turd does a good job.'[2]

The campaign of 1296 was intended as a true conquest, as the removal of the Stone of Destiny from Scone to Westminster Abbey indicates. There was no question of reopening the Great Cause; Edward intended to rule as the 'true and immediate lord of the realm of Scotland'.[3] The government of the country was entrusted to Englishmen as far as possible, and it was even decreed that only Englishmen were eligible to be appointed to church livings in Scotland. The ease of the conquest was deceptive, however, and the campaign marked the beginning, not the end, of a long and exhausting struggle.

The Scots revolted in 1297. One of the leaders was Robert Bruce, grandson of the competitor to the throne, and himself a future king of Scotland. Up to this time the Bruces had been consistently loyal to Edward I: Robert's father and grandfather had pledged themselves to him before the opening of the 1296 campaign, but Edward had not rewarded them with the throne as they must have hoped, and Robert now tried to gain it forcibly. He and his allies were soon defeated, but better fortune awaited William Wallace and Andrew Moray. These men, the one of knightly rank and the other of baronial status, led a rising which had a truly popular character, in contrast to the baronial action in 1296. There was a widespread and not wholly unjustified fear that Edward I intended to exploit the resources of Scotland in support of his French war – rumour had it that he wished 'to seize all the middle folk of Scotland to send them overseas in his war, to their great damage and destruction.'[4] The report was very plausible, remembering Edward's attempt to obtain the service of the twenty-pound landholders in England; in 1294 the Welsh had been driven into revolt by English oppression; the threat of it now had a similar effect on the Scots. With all the government's resources devoted to the organization of the expedition to Flanders, little attention was paid to the problems of Scotland. In September 1297 an army under Earl Warenne was defeated by Wallace and his men at Stirling Bridge. The English treasurer of Scotland, the obese and unpopular Hugh Cressingham was killed and his skin cut up to make grisly mementoes for the victors. This battle demonstrated for the first time the vulnerability of the mounted knight in full armour to the common foot-soldier, but the lesson would have to be repeated many times before it was fully understood.

The English defeat at Stirling Bridge was a profound shock, but was not decisive. On the continent Edward I came to terms with Philip IV, each ruler abandoning his respective allies in Flanders and Scotland. In 1298 a major campaign in Scotland culminated in the English triumph at Falkirk. The Scots under Wallace did not swoop down on an unprepared enemy as they had at Stirling Bridge – instead, they were drawn up in strong defensive rings, known as schiltroms, and presented a thicket of spears to the English. Wallace addressed his men, saying 'I have brought you to the ring; now hop if you can.'[5] His tactics were intelligent, but the schiltroms could not resist successive assaults from the English infantry and cavalry. In the end they appear to have succumbed to an attack from the rear by a force which had outflanked them. Half of Edward's infantry force of some 25,700 were Welshmen, who refused to fight; nevertheless, the English were completely victorious.

Edward I, still troubled by the recalcitrance of the earls who had led the opposition to him in 1297, was unable to follow up his success at Falkirk properly – the English established control of only limited areas dominated by the castles they held in southern Scotland; no campaign took place in 1299, and the Scots recovered Stirling Castle after a lengthy blockade, during which the garrison were reduced to eating their own horses. In the next few years the war fell into a regular pattern: major summer offensives by large English armies failed to bring the Scots to battle; in 1300 a great host achieved little more than the capture of 'a poor little castle',[6] as one chronicler rather unfairly described Caerlaverock and in the next year a double-pronged campaign culminated only with the taking of Bothwell Castle, a meagre return for a massive investment.

Eventually the incessant English pressure began to take effect, and Robert Bruce, fearing papal or French intervention on behalf of Balliol, came over to Edward's side. In 1302 the French defeat by the Flemings at Courtrai ended the threat from France, while the conflict between Boniface VIII and Philip IV effectively neutralized the papacy. Early in 1304 the majority of Scottish leaders came to terms with Edward I. The garrison of Stirling Castle had held out for about three months, but was forced to capitulate after a massive show-piece siege. A special viewing-gallery was constructed for the ladies of the English court to watch the events. Gunpowder was used to make what was known as Greek fire; the man in charge, Jean de Lamouilly, a Frenchman, received £20 as a reward for his work, though his resentment at not receiving his wages in full was many years later to cause him to kidnap the Earl of

Pembroke. Many siege engines were used at Stirling – the greatest was the *Warwolf*; its engineer Thomas Greenfield was granted £40 by the king. In the following year William Wallace, who was hated and feared far more than any other Scot, was captured. He was sentenced to be hanged, disembowelled, executed, to have his innards burned and his body quartered, the various punishments reflecting his various alleged crimes of robbery, homicide, treason and sacrilege.

The English put immense effort into the war. Edward's successes were achieved as a result of well-organized logistics, not by tactical or strategic skill. The voluminous records of the royal wardrobe testify to the constant endeavours of hard-worked clerks to organize recruiting and supply food and materials for the huge armies. Victualling bases were set up at Berwick and Carlisle and fleets of ships brought supplies from as far away as the Isle of Wight: further flotillas carried them on to the armies and garrisons in Scotland. Careful estimates were made of probable requirements, and remarkably full records maintained. In 1303 prefabricated bridges were brought up the east coast for the crossing of the Firth of Forth, and in the next year elaborate arrangements were made to collect together all the siege engines and other equipment needed for the taking of Stirling Castle: Edward I possessed a highly skilled bureaucracy, and made full use of it.

Although the logistics of the campaigns were efficiently managed, with the system hardly ever faltering, finance was a constant worry. In the king's view it was lack of funds rather than the stubborn resistance of the Scots that delayed success. In 1301 he wrote to the exchequer, rebuking them for their failure to send the money he needed:

And you can be certain that if it had not been for a lack of money we would have finished the bridge which was started to cross the Scottish Sea [the Firth of Forth], and you must understand for sure that if we had been able to cross this season, we would have achieved such an exploit against our enemies that our business in these parts would have been brought to a good and honourable conclusion in a short time.[7]

It was in fact inadequacy of resources, rather than administrative incompetence, that led to the shortage of funds in Scotland. The effects were plain to see: Master James of St George was employed in Scotland as he had been in Wales, but financial stringency meant that he was able to construct little more than wooden palisades and earthen banks – a sad contrast to the imperial battlements of Caernarfon. The armies that marched north became steadily smaller and desertion by the infantry was a constant and insoluble problem – even the regular soldiers of the Berwick garrison mutinied over their pay.

The chronicler Peter Langtoft claimed that Edward would have established his position in Scotland securely had he shared out the land properly to English magnates. Although important estates were granted to his supporters – Aymer de Valence received Bothwell, the Earl of Hereford Annandale and the Stewart's estates went to the Earl of Lincoln – these men were never able to exercise effective lordship over them. The war did not promise substantial rewards to the participants. It was possible to persuade Scottish magnates to support the English cause, but their loyalty was liable to melt away 'as frost in May',[8] as one poem put it: whereas in Wales Edward had been able to recruit large numbers of ordinary Welshmen to his service, he was unable to win the ordinary people of Scotland to his side in any number.

In 1305 Edward I attempted a political settlement in Scotland as he had done in Wales in 1284. Superficially, the arrangements suggest a policy of statesmanlike moderation – the Scots were fully consulted, and although the king's nephew John of Brittany was appointed as royal lieutenant and warden, and other high positions were given to Englishmen, many local posts went to Scotsmen. The most important castles, however, were to remain in English hands. A sinister note was struck by the statement that the law was to be reformed and amended so that it would no longer contain anything 'clearly displeasing to God and to reason'[9] – this echoed the king's policy in Wales. Most significantly, Scotland was no longer termed a 'realm' or 'kingdom' – it was relegated to the status of a 'land'.

Edward, who had been treated to the traditional greetings accorded to kings of Scotland as he travelled through the country in 1304, had evidently determined that the Scottish crown should be no more.

The question of whether or not Edward I acted in good faith towards the Scots has been the subject of much debate. From the king's point of view there is no doubt that he was pursuing what he regarded as his legal rights, but it is also true that there was no general agreement as to what those rights were. While he behaved with propriety during the hearing of the Great Cause, his subsequent failure to adhere to the spirit of the promises he made at the outset of the proceedings is striking. The Pope in 1299 accused Edward of having subjected to his power a realm which lacked the support of a king, but in fact it was only after Balliol's enthronement that the English ruler really began to press the Scots. He had been thwarted by the death of the Maid of Norway in his attempts to establish control over Scotland through the marriage of his son to the Scottish heiress, but became increasingly determined to gain his ends by other means. He was certainly justified in intervening when Balliol entered into alliance with the French, but his effective abolition of the Scottish throne was remarkably arbitrary: there was an ample tradition which demonstrated how kings should be deposed, going back to Pope Gregory VII's actions against the Emperor Henry IV, but no lengthy charges were brought against Balliol, and no attempt was made to have him removed from office by the community of the realm of Scotland. The simple act of Balliol's resignation in the churchyard at Stracathro could not extinguish the long tradition of monarchy in a kingdom as cohesive as Scotland, particularly when there was in Robert Bruce a man determined to gain the throne for himself.

Edward I had made the mistake in Wales of not rewarding such allies as Prince Dafydd adequately for their service, and he repeated the error in Scotland. Robert Bruce may well have been led to turn to Edward early in 1302 in the hope of gaining the throne, but his expectations were dashed: as he complained in 1305, he was not even allowed possession of his hereditary lands in Annandale. It is hardly surprising that Bruce rebelled. In 1306 he murdered John Comyn at Dumfries when the latter refused to help him. He was then enthroned and crowned as King of Scotland at Scone by his supporters. At first, the English achieved remarkable success against their new enemy. Valence routed him at Methven in 1306, and he spent the next winter in hiding, his whereabouts eluding both his pursuers and later historians. In 1307 the tide began to turn: Methven was avenged at Loudoun Hill. The English reacted to the rising with a new degree of vindictiveness. Prisoners were sent south to be hanged, drawn and quartered, rather than to be imprisoned at the government's expense. Edward I realized too late that such policies were counter-productive – support for Bruce rose steadily, while there was little enthusiasm for the war in England. A group of knights closely associated with the heir to the throne deserted the campaign in 1306, and when the old king died on his way north in 1307 the expedition was promptly abandoned.

Edward II 'chicken-hearted and luckless in war',[10] did not share his father's single-minded commitment to the conquest of Scotland. Nevertheless, he was not prepared to surrender his claims to the overlordship of Scotland, or to recognize Robert Bruce as king. Military initiative passed firmly into the hands of the Scots. No royal campaign took place in the north between 1307 and 1310, and Bruce was able to establish his position firmly in the course of a brief civil war in Scotland. Then he turned to the capture of the English-held castles, using techniques of surprise attack. Major successes soon came; Perth was taken in 1313, when Bruce led the assault himself, wading through the icy waters of the moat; Dumfries was starved into surrender; Roxburgh and Edinburgh fell in 1314. The first of many raids into England was conducted in 1311; the Scots gained money and supplies with which to support their war effort.

Robert Bruce did not want to engage the English in pitched battle. The lesson of Falkirk had been a bitter one, and the power of the heavily-armoured mounted knights was feared by the Scots. In 1313, however, Bruce's brother Edward besieged Stirling Castle, and negotiated the surrender of the fortress with the constable – provided no relieving force appeared before Midsummer 1314, Stirling would be handed over to the Scots. The challenge was one which even Edward II could not ignore. A huge effort was made by the English – no pay rolls survive to give precise details of the army they raised, but it was probably on a par with the greatest sent north by Edward I, despite the absence of the Earl of Lancaster. Bruce had little alternative but to fight, and the set-piece battle took place on 23 and 24 June.

The battle of Bannockburn has been discussed at great length by historians. Medieval chronicles do not permit the accurate reconstruction of tactical manoeuvres in the field, and in this case there is even doubt about the exact site of the battle. The question of precisely which bog the battle was fought in is of less importance, however, than the fact that the Scots were able to choose their ground with care, ensuring that the English cavalry would flounder in unsuitable terrain. Although the English writs of summons show that there was some awareness of the problems they were likely to encounter, no proper preparations had been made.

There was always a danger in medieval warfare that enthusiasm for acts of chivalrous daring and a desire for individual glory would confound the discipline and order required for success. Edward II was no natural leader, and could not resolve the serious arguments between the Earls of Gloucester and Hereford as to who had the right to lead the vanguard. The battle began with the famous single combat between Robert Bruce and Henry de Bohun, still celebrated on some Scottish banknotes: this was the result of a chance encounter, but Bruce would probably not have risked his life had it not been for the feud between himself and the Bohun family over the possession of Annandale. The first day saw little more than skirmishing. On the second day battle was fully joined. Gloucester, trying to establish his rights to lead the army, charged suicidally into the enemy ranks – it was later said that he was deserted by Bartholomew Badlesmere, a man whose name subsequently became synonymous with treachery. The English fought on too narrow a front for their weight of numbers to be effective – charges against the schiltroms were initially ineffective and ultimately fatal. Edward 11 was led to safety, but the flower of the English army perished; many drowned in the Bannock burn itself. In the closing stages of the battle Giles d'Argentein, one of the most noted knights of the day, proved his chivalric courage and personal folly by charging the Scots single-handed. Gallantry was no substitute for generalship.

Edward 11 had no stomach for the war, but could not risk the ignominy entailed in making peace. New exemplars of the notarial records of the Great Cause were ordered in 1315 to help demonstrate the king's rights in Scotland. In military terms little could be done beyond largely futile attempts to defend the north of England. Royal accounts show castles as far south as County Durham being garrisoned by royal forces. In 1315 contracts were made with the Earl of Pembroke and other leading magnates to provide troops, but the king himself did not campaign. These were years of famine in England. At Berwick the garrison was reduced to such straits that the common soldiers acted against orders and raided enemy territory, only to suffer heavy losses. The constable reported to an apparently unconcerned government that of 300 men-at-arms only fifty could be mounted and armed, since so many horses had died, and so much equipment had been pawned by the men. The situation would have been still more serious for the English had not the Scots diverted much of their resources into an invasion of Ireland led by Edward Bruce, which eventually ended in his defeat and death.

It needed a major disaster to force Edward 11 to undertake another full-scale campaign. In 1318 the Scots took Berwick through treachery. An army over ten thousand strong was assembled in the following year to regain the town which was a vital military and administrative base. Instead of challenging this force directly, the Scots mounted a diversionary raid, which culminated in the defeat of a hastily-assembled and totally inadequate force under the Archbishop of York at Myton in Yorkshire. The news of this caused the abandonment of the siege of Berwick: the Earl of Lancaster, who may even have been in secret collusion with the Scots, was anxious to withdraw to ensure the security of his estates. A two-year truce followed. Then Edward, in buoyant mood after the defeat of his rival Lancaster at Boroughbridge, led his last expedition to Scotland. The army included the remarkable figure of John Harrington, a Rutland knight who insisted on mustering, even though he was over eighty years old. The 1322 campaign was a fiasco. The Scots withdrew in face of the large English host which marched through a denuded countryside to Edinburgh. It was said that they found only one cow in the whole of the Lothians. Edward was forced to withdraw by famine and disease. Insult was added to injury when the Scots retaliated with a massive raid into Yorkshire, and almost succeeded in capturing the English king.

By this time the mood of many in the north of England was defeatist. Local communities bought peace from Scottish raiding parties with payment of tribute, giving hostages if the sums demanded could not be raised. In 1317 William de Roos had handed over his castle of Wark to Edward II in exchange for lands safely situated to the south. In the same year Gilbert de Middleton in an act of rebellion had joined forces with the Scots. By 1322 the constables of Bamburgh, Warkworth, Alnwick and Dunstanburgh were being severely rebuked for their inactivity towards the enemy and the men of the western March complained that their situation was intolerable as a result of incessant Scottish attacks. Peace was clearly the most sensible policy. Andrew Harclay, recently made Earl of Carlisle, negotiated on his own initiative. In 1323 he recognized Bruce as King of Scotland and obtained peace terms. For this, he was found guilty of treason and executed. However, shortly afterwards Edward II agreed on a thirteen-year truce. The Scots had sought a period twice as long, but even after so many failures, the English had not wholly abandoned their ambitions. Edward II had the stubbornness sometimes to be seen in weak and stupid men, and he was not prepared to concede Bruce's right to the Scottish throne.

The truce ended with Edward III's accession in 1327. Although old and afflicted with the dreaded disease of leprosy, Robert Bruce decided that the time was right to consolidate his position. Edward III was under age, and the regime of his mother Isabella and her lover Roger Mortimer was none too secure. A major Scottish raid was countered by an English army under the nominal leadership of the young Edward; there is a superb eye-witness account of the campaign, written by a Hainaulter, Jean le Bel, who accompanied a small mercenary troop of his fellow-countrymen. The difficulties and frustrations of medieval warfare emerge very clearly: the immense English host – the last for which a traditional feudal summons was used, save for an antiquarian revival under Richard II – was divided into three battalions. The infantry could not march quickly enough to catch the swiftly-moving enemy, who were all mounted. The terrain of County Durham and Northumberland proved totally unsuitable for the heavy carts of the English baggage train – the cavalry eventually advanced alone. They had only bread to eat, and as the loaves were tied behind their saddles, they became soaked in the horses' sweat. The men had to spend the night in the open in full armour, holding their mounts' bridles, as there was nowhere to tie them up. Incessant rain exacerbated their problems. When contact was finally made with the Scots, they refused to come to battle on equal terms, but stayed put in a strong defensive position. A surprise night attack by James Douglas on the English camp nearly ended with the capture of the young King Edward. After a week the Scots slipped silently away by night, leaving a totally frustrated English army with no chance of catching them. The horses were hungry and worn out, the majority with no horseshoes and their harness in tatters; so many were lost on the campaign that it cost the crown just over £28,000 to compensate their owners.

It appeared to the English that Bruce initiated a new policy in the aftermath of the 1327 campaign – the conquest of Northumberland. An elaborate siege of Norham Castle emphasized the contrast with the earlier swift-moving raids. Isabella and Mortimer responded by negotiating the treaty of Northampton, which became known as the 'shameful peace'. Bruce's rights as king were fully acknowledged, and marriage between his son David and Edward III's sister Joan agreed upon. The Scots agreed to pay £20,000 to the English, who renounced all claims to sovereignty over Scotland. Peace undoubtedly made sense after so many years, but relatively few English magnates gave their consent to the treaty. Edward III himself expressed his displeasure by refusing to attend his sister's marriage, while the Londoners refused to release the Stone of Destiny to the Scots. The sum of £20,000 was paid over, but was simply appropriated for Isabella's private use.

After the treaty of Northampton, it was not easy to revive English claims to the overlordship of Scotland, but a new excuse for war was found in the person of John Balliol's son Edward. He had been invited to England from France in 1324, and his strong claim to the Scottish throne after the death of Robert Bruce in 1329 provided a rallying-point for the so-called disinherited – those with unsatisfied claims in Scotland. There were many who had been disappointed by the fortunes of war, and who were willing to take a desperate gamble in pursuit of profit.

Chief among the disinherited was Henry de Beaumont. He had a claim through marriage to the earldom of Buchan, and had indicated his anger at a policy of peace as early as 1323, when he had been removed from the royal council because he would not give his consent to the truce. Henry Percy and Thomas Wake also had important claims in Scotland, and Balliol's cause found support among those Scottish nobles who had sided with the English. Gilbert d'Umfraville had lost the earldom of Angus because of his family's consistent English allegiance, and David of Strathbogie had a claim to the earldom of Atholl. Only very limited steps had been taken in 1328 to settle such grievances. Robert Bruce had conceded that Henry Percy might enjoy his hereditary lands and rights in Scotland, and similar promises were probably made to Wake and Beaumont, though these were not implemented. The English for their part restored some lands which had been taken from William Douglas in 1296.

The disinherited acted in 1332. Beaumont raised money by leasing his lands, and the Archbishop of York, doubtless anxious to see his defeat at the battle of Myton avenged, advanced money. The little force gained the advantage of surprise by making a landing in Fife. At Dupplin Moor they met a far larger Scottish army, and defeated it resoundingly: Edward Balliol was then enthroned at Scone. He had already secretly performed homage to Edward III, who had turned a blind eye to the venture; he now promised full recognition of English sovereignty, and the surrender to Edward III of lands valued at £2,000 a year. His initial triumph was short-lived. He was speedily expelled from Scotland, and it became clear that further success could only be achieved with the full and open support of the English king.

Edward III was very anxious to fight; he had not forgotten the humiliation of the 1327 campaign, but he did not find it easy to transmit his own enthusiasm for a renewal of war to his subjects, for peace had brought advantages. He failed to obtain full parliamentary consent for his plans, but recruited an army in 1333 and proceeded to besiege Berwick. The Scots were now caught by a bargain similar to that which had led to Bannockburn: complex negotiations led to agreement that the town would surrender unless the Scots crossed the Tweed at a specified point, forced an entry to the town with two hundred armed men, or fought a pitched battle. The final option was selected, and at Halidon Hill the English won a resounding triumph. As at Dupplin, they fought from a strong defensive position on foot. As if in echo of Bannockburn, the battle was preceded by a single combat – a gigantic Scottish champion was worsted by Robert Benhale, a knight of the royal household who had been convicted two years earlier of 'divers trespasses and excesses contrary to the king's peace'.[11] As at Dupplin, the Scots were decimated by English archery as they struggled to reach the English lines; those who succeeded were cut to pieces by the men-at-arms.

Edward III had toyed with the idea of reasserting English claims to the direct lordship of Scotland, but in the aftermath of his triumph he accepted Balliol's homage. He was granted a vast tract of southern Scotland, the real value of which must have far exceeded the promised £2,000 a year. The settlement was not, however, a secure one: the young David II, Robert Bruce's heir, was given refuge by Philip VI of France, and French support did much to stiffen resistance in Scotland to the English and Edward Balliol. A pattern of warfare superficially similar to that of Edward I's day emerged; large English armies marched north every year, and as they withdrew, so the Scots reasserted themselves. Tenure of the main castles of southern Scotland failed to provide the English with effective control of the country, and payment of the garrisons proved highly expensive. The Scots, notably under Andrew Moray's leadership, reverted to the strategy that had served Robert Bruce so well – they avoided pitched battle, and picked off English garrisons one by one. Castles were destroyed so that they could not be used in future: at Bothwell half of the great keep was cast down. There was a severity to the war that had rarely been present under Edward I; English troops burned, pillaged and ravaged Scotland in an orgy of destruction. The king's brother, John of Eltham, is said to have consumed lands which had submitted to the English with fire and sword. One result was that the English were unable to raise much money in Scotland to pay for the war. The sheriff of Dumfries recorded a total receipt of a mere £18 in 1335–6, and the accounts of English officials are a dismal catalogue of the destruction caused by war.

The constant threat of French intervention meant that Edward III had no chance of success in Scotland unless Philip VI abandoned his ambitions there. The Scottish situation was an important element in the growing crisis between England and France that led to the outbreak of the Hundred Years War in 1337. The war with France diverted Edward III's energies from Scotland, although he led a campaign in the north in the winter of 1341–2 and conducted the destructive raid known as the Burnt Candlemas in 1356 after the Scots had taken Berwick. In the late 1330s the pattern of warfare began to change. The English were increasingly placed on the defensive, and the Scots began once again to launch their raids across the border. In 1341

David II returned to Scotland, and in the next year his troops took Stirling Castle.

In 1346 David II invaded England, hoping to take advantage of Edward III's preoccupation with war in France. Just outside Durham his army was met by a hastily-recruited force which won a famous victory at Neville's Cross. The soldiers were spurred on by the chanting of the Durham monks from a nearby church tower. Although the Lancashire archers received a £20 bonus for the campaign, one contemporary remarked that many of the English bowmen withdrew from the fight, which was won through the perseverance of the men-at-arms. David II, wounded by two arrows, was captured. The English had achieved a decisive advantage in the war.

Edward III had none of his grandfather's consistency of policy towards the Scots, and showed himself throughout willing to exchange his rights for territorial or financial advantage. There was clearly little to be gained by supporting the increasingly ineffectual Edward Balliol, who finally surrendered his rights to the Scottish throne to Edward III in 1356. The English king probably hoped to achieve mastery over Scotland in that year's campaign and establish direct rule, but his fleet was destroyed by a storm and the enemy could not be brought to battle. So negotiations were reopened with the captive David II, who was prepared to agree to severe peace terms in exchange for his freedom. Most important was the payment of a ransom of 100,000 marks, a sum which would help to finance Edward III's ambitions in France. A treaty was agreed in 1357, and although only two of the promised annual instalments of the ransom were made under this agreement, subsequent negotiations led to the payment of about three-quarters of the total sum by the time of Edward III's death in 1377. At long last the English had found a way to profit from the war with the Scots. The last twenty years of Edward III's reign saw peace between the two countries, though disturbances on the march in 1376 and 1377 showed that the patterns of hostility which had been established in the years since 1296 were far from broken.

The Scottish wars witnessed the forging of the weapons which the English were to use with such great effect in the Hundred Years War. The narrative of events does not disclose the way in which the armies were organized, nor when it was that the decisive changes took place in the military revolution which led to the English triumphs at Crécy and Poitiers. It is often argued that it was Edward I who remoulded the English army by the introduction of pay on a large scale, but in fact it was the defeats and difficulties of Edward II's reign that did more to compel the English to reform and reorganize the traditional structure of the army. The tactics that were later to prove so devastating in France were not used by Edward I at Falkirk in 1298, but they had been developed in time for Edward III to employ them at Halidon Hill in 1333. The first element in the army to consider is the cavalry, the second the infantry, while the important logistic achievements of the royal administration in organizing supplies for the campaigns also deserve attention.

The elite of a medieval army in the thirteenth and fourteenth centuries consisted of the bannerets, knights, squires and sergeants. All of these men were heavily armoured, and rode great war-horses which were expensive to buy and to feed. In a large army there might be as many as three thousand of these heavy cavalrymen. The host that Edward I led into Galloway in 1300 was described in a heraldic work:

> The king with his retinue set out immediately against the Scots. They were not in coats and surcoats, but were well armed and mounted, on costly great horses, so that they would not be taken by surprise. There were many rich trappings of embroidered silks and satins, many fine pennons on lances. The neighing of the horses could be heard from far away, and everywhere the mountains and valleys were filled with sumpter horses and carts bearing the provisions and equipment for the tents and pavilions. The days were fine and long, and they proceeded in short journeys, arranged in four battalions.[12]

Records show that one of the four battalions was largely composed of the troops of the royal household, totalling some 850 cavalry. The king's household was the hub of the

military machine, as well as being the heart of the administration, but the number of those permanently retained in
royal service varied considerably. In 1300 there was a large
establishment of eighty bannerets and knights, but in
Edward I's last years numbers fell. In 1317 there were about
sixty, but five years later the number had fallen by half. By
the late 1330s there were about fifty. These men would
bring their own retinues with them on campaign, so that in
time of need the royal household could quickly be
expanded to the size of a small army.

The great magnates also brought their own retinues of
knights and squires with them on campaign. In 1297 the
Earl of Norfolk agreed to provide a hundred and thirty
cavalry for the war in Scotland. Thomas of Lancaster's
retinue at the siege of Berwick in 1319 may have been five
hundred strong; his household rivalled that of the king in
size. Great men recruited their followers by means of
documents known as indentures. The earliest such agreement that is known was made in 1270, by Edward I before
his accession, and a number made by magnates survive
from his reign. Men might be retained for a single campaign, being promised payment of wages and compensation for loss of horses; where an indenture was for life, the
retainer would receive annual fees and robes, and perhaps
also shoes and saddles – he would be entitled to meals in his
lord's hall, and might be expected to serve at tournaments
and parliaments as well as in war.

It was a surprisingly long time before the crown came to
terms with the realities of military service in the way in
which it summoned magnates to fight. The traditional
means of raising an army was to issue a feudal summons.
This requested those who held their estates directly from
the king to appear with the unpaid service of a set quota of
men for forty days, in accordance with their vows of fealty
and homage. Edward I used such summonses for Wales in
1277 and 1282, and for three of his Scottish campaigns. The
hosts of 1310, 1314, 1322 and 1327 were mustered similarly.
The size of the feudal quotas had been radically reduced
since the twelfth century, and the best response to such a
summons under Edward I was the 522 men who appeared

in 1277. Numbers later were less, although almost five hundred men answered the summons in 1322. There was a ridiculous element to feudal service: in 1300 one man appeared in accordance with the terms of his tenure, equipped as an archer, with only one arrow. He fired it at the first Scot he saw, and promptly left for home; the man obliged to attend on a horse worth five shillings, carrying a stick with a bag on the end of it, was of little more use. Baronial conservatism provides one explanation for the continued use of these anachronistic feudal summonses – the system also provided certain financial benefits. The magnates were entitled to levy a tax – scutage – on their own lands on the occasion of a feudal muster, and the crown gained something from fines paid by those who did not wish to send soldiers to perform their service. In 1322 it cost the Bishop of Salisbury £100 to have the service of five knights performed, and it was often easier to make a payment to the crown in lieu.

The issue of a feudal summons served in part as a general invitation to fight. In 1300 the writs specifically asked the magnates to bring as many men as they decently could in addition to the formal quotas. If no feudal summons was issued, as in 1298 or 1301, the king would simply make a polite request to the magnates, asking them to come in accordance with their fealty. No mention was made of homage in such a writ. There was no formal obligation to answer such a summons, and no way in which the crown could determine how many would appear. In 1334 Edward III wrote furiously to fifty-six men who failed to respond to the summons, but there was little that he could do. The most effective way of securing the service of the magnates was to enter into firm agreements with them and pay them wages, but at first there was a strong reluctance to accept royal pay.

Edward I initially attempted to recruit a wholly paid army for the Welsh war of 1282, but he was forced to back down. It seems likely that the earls and barons resented the subordination that would follow from accepting wages, and that they feared that they would have no rights over lands they captured during the campaign. Such scruples did not extend to overseas expeditions or to winter operations, however; even Roger Bigod, that staunch opponent of Edward I, took pay for fighting in Scotland in the winter of 1297–8, though he served at his own expense the following summer. This enabled him to abandon the campaign when he, not the king, chose. In Edward II's reign the scruples of the magnates dissolved. Thomas of Lancaster never took wages for himself from the king, but in 1316 the Earl of Hereford agreed to serve with a hundred men-at-arms for a fee of 2,000 marks in wartime. In 1322 the Earls of Pembroke, Arundel, Warenne, Norfolk and Kent all received wages. Pay at the standard daily rates of 8s for an earl, 4s for a banneret, 2s for a knight and 1s for an ordinary man-at-arms was some inducement to fight, though it probably did not even cover expenses in full. From the crown's point of view it was important that by the end of Edward II's reign a more effective degree of control over the army had been achieved by the use of pay than had existed under Edward I.

The crown did not recruit cavalry solely by means of summonses directed to the earls and barons. Edward I and his son both tried to establish a direct obligation of the knightly class to serve, but success was limited. In 1295 and 1296 orders were issued that all who possessed at least forty-pounds-worth of land were to be ready to fight, and in 1297 the king unsuccessfully tried to obtain the service of all with twenty-pounds-worth of land. A summons of forty-pound men in 1300 provoked considerable resistance. Edward II unwisely tried to recruit fifty-pound men in 1316; this was one of the causes of his breach with the Earl of Lancaster in that year. In the final years of Edward II's reign there were attempts to reorganize the whole system of military service: in 1324 the sheriffs drew up lists of all the knights and men-at-arms resident in their counties; this was presumably the first stage of a general reform. The crown began to recruit the heavy cavalry by using specially appointed commissioners, just as was done with the infantry. This was a startling innovation, and inevitably provoked a conservative reaction in Edward III's first parliament. Nevertheless, there were occasions, notably for the Scottish war in 1346 and 1356 when both men-at-arms and archers were recruited by commissioners of array in the counties. For the most part, however, it was only lightly-armed horsemen, known as hobelars, who were raised in this way by Edward III.

A most effective means of recruitment was the use of contracts by the crown. Magnates would agree to serve with specified numbers of men in return for a previously-agreed sum. The system had its origins in Edward I's reign, and was used when the administrative machinery of the royal household was not available to supervise the regular issue of wages. The Earls of Lancaster and Lincoln were contracted for service in Gascony between 1294 and 1298. In the autumn of 1297, when the king was in Flanders, six magnates including Bigod made contracts for three months' service in Scotland. The system became more common under Edward II, with the arrangements made to defend the north of England when the king himself was not campaigning. In 1315 Pembroke and three other magnates contracted to provide a force of two hundred and forty men-at-arms, and in 1317 Arundel agreed to defend the March with a hundred men-at-arms for £3,000. It was not until 1337, however, that the contract system was employed to raise a whole army. In that year Edward III's personal attention was switched from Scotland to Flanders, and the wardrobe staff were not therefore available for the administration of the campaign in Scotland. Contracts were drawn up for the army led by the Earl of Warwick, and provided for a total of some five hundred and eighty heavy cavalry. The actual contingents produced did not fall far short of the numbers promised, and a highly satisfactory precedent was set for the use of contracts on a wide scale during the Hundred Years War.

The way in which the knights and men-at-arms fought was dramatically transformed in the course of the Scottish wars. In Edward I's day they fought on horseback with lance and sword in true chivalric fashion. The charge of heavily-armoured knights could be a most formidable weapon, which proved decisive at Dunbar in 1296 and at Methven ten years later. Cavalry can only operate on good terrain, however, and at Bannockburn the boggy ground proved disastrous. It was difficult to integrate the horsemen properly with the infantry who made up the bulk of the army. The claim that in Edward I's reign horse and foot had been effectively combined at such battles as Irfon Bridge and Maes Moydog in Wales is based on very inadequate evidence. It was only after Bannockburn that the English began to experiment with tactics that were to make effective use of both knights and archers. At the battle of Boroughbridge in 1322 Thomas of Lancaster was defeated when Andrew Harclay, schooled in the conflicts of the northern border, dismounted his men and made them fight on foot, drawn up in schiltroms in the Scottish manner. In 1327 a public proclamation stated that even magnates were to be prepared to fight on foot, and when the English army encountered the Scots on the campaign in that year, they were ordered to dismount, and were drawn up in line of battle on foot. The first major triumph for the new tactics came at Dupplin Moor. At first the English line was driven back by the weight of the enemy, but they recovered their ground when Ralph Stafford urged the soldiers to turn their shoulders to their lances. At Halidon Hill the English again dismounted to fight, 'contrary to the old habits of their fathers',[13] and again they triumphed. They were drawn up in lines, rather than schiltroms, with archers on the flanks, in a way that was to become only too familiar to the French in later years.

Other military techniques were learned in the north. Although the large armies of Edward I's reign marched slowly, encumbered by carts and baggage, some swift raids were mounted against the Scots. In 1298 one was planned from Edinburgh to Stirling, to consist of two hundred cavalry with no infantry. Supplies were to be taken by three hundred pack-horses. This was in imitation of the Scottish mounted raids, and the English were quick to copy their opponents' techniques of burning and plundering. The need for speed and mobility was increasingly appreciated as it became harder to force the enemy to fight. For an abortive campaign in 1323 the magnates were asked to bring sufficient saddles for pack-horses, as it had been decided to abandon the use of cumbersome carts for transport. In 1327 the cavalry left the infantry behind, and advanced rapidly to try to catch the Scots. In 1336 Edward III demonstrated the potential of the rapid raid when he appeared unexpectedly at Perth, and then rode at speed to rescue the Countess of Atholl who was besieged in the castle of Lochindorb. The scene was set for the *chevauchées* – the swift mounted expeditions of the Hundred Years War.

An increasingly decisive part in battle was played by the infantry, armed with the longbow. Edward I recruited large numbers of footsoldiers for his wars: in Wales in 1277 there were some fifteen thousand; for the war of 1294–5 he had more than double that number in pay at one time. Detailed pay-rolls show that there were about 25,700 footsoldiers at Falkirk, but numbers fell for the later Scottish campaigns. In 1303 the maximum was only about 7,500. In the early years of Edward I's reign many of the infantry were armed with spears, but by the time of the Scottish wars the majority were described as archers, with the remarkable exception of a corps of slingers from that legendary home of archery, Sherwood Forest. The records suggest that the infantry was ill-equipped and poorly disciplined. They were organized in platoons of twenty men and companies of a hundred, but desertion soon after the start of every campaign rapidly played havoc with the system. The crown made little effort to provide weapons or equipment, although the local communities from which the men were recruited were supposed to send them to war properly armed. Recruiting was the task of specially appointed commissioners of array, but they were open to bribes, and frequently the villagers themselves picked out the least valuable members of society to send to war. 'The strongest shall stay at home for ten or twelve shillings, and send forth a wretch that cannot help himself when he needs.'[14] Shakespeare's picture of recruiting procedures in *Henry IV part ii* was not far from the truth. There were many like Mouldy, Shadow, Wart and Feeble in Edward I's armies.

There was a growing awareness in Edward II's reign of the need for competent footsoldiers. Writs of summons for the Bannockburn campaign argued that because of the position taken up by the enemy, which could not be penetrated by cavalry, infantry skilled in the use of arms were needed. The problem facing arrayers is demonstrated by a letter from John Botetourt in 1315 in which he complained that the men recruited for his company were 'feeble chaps, not strong enough, not properly dressed, and lacking bows and arrows'.[15] When a grant was made in parliament in the next year of one footsoldier from every locality, or vill, it was laid down that they should have haketons (heavy jerkins), bacinets (helmets), swords, bows, crossbows, lances or other suitable equipment. The levy was abandoned, but in the subsequent campaigns of the reign it was normal to request that at least a proportion of the foot should be armoured. As a result, whereas it had cost about 5s to equip an infantryman under Edward I, the figure rose to over one pound in the next reign.

The policy of recruiting heavily-armoured infantry has been criticized, notably by J. E. Morris, the greatest historian of Edwardian armies. In his view, the disastrous 1322 campaign proved the futility of such forces, for they totally failed to engage the enemy. Yet the concept had some merits: the infantry had proved their value in battle in the past, and it was logical to demand that they should be properly equipped. It was obviously unsatisfactory that they should be reduced, as at Falkirk, to hurling stones found lying on the ground in the absence of sufficient quantities of proper ammunition. What needed to be solved was the problem of mobility, and this was done early in Edward III's reign. The archer was mounted so that he could ride with the army and dismount to fight.

Mounted archers first appear in the records in 1334, but they were almost certainly used in the previous year. The lightly-armed hobelars provide some precedent for them, although they had fought from horseback. Mounted archers were paid 6d or 4d a day: at least double the rate of an ordinary infantryman. With their mobility, they could be integrated into the retinues provided by the magnates – an important step in the co-ordination of the army. It now became possible to adopt far more systematic battle tactics.

At Falkirk in 1298 the infantry had been brought up quite separately from the cavalry, to attack the enemy schiltroms when the mounted charge failed. Now a properly combined force could be organized, with the archers providing the offensive fire-power and the men-at-arms the muscle for hand-to-hand conflict. By the 1330s a standard battle formation had been developed, with each battalion of dismounted men-at-arms flanked by wings of archers.

It was said that James Douglas, who died in 1330, had such a respect for the English longbow that he either cut off the right hand or gouged out the right eye of any English archer he captured. A legal record of Edward II's time describes three sorts of bow. One, the classic longbow, was two ells in length, or about seven feet six inches – it was the thickness of four thumbs, and fired a 'clotharrow' a yard long; then there was a turkish bow, one and a half ells long, which fired a barbed 'wolfarrow'. Both of these bows were made of imported Spanish yew, but native yew was also used. Lastly, there was an elm bow, which fired a barbed Scottish arrow a yard long. It is likely that the heaviest bows had a range of up to four hundred yards, though real accuracy was unlikely beyond two hundred. A rate of fire of ten flights a minute was possible; a constantly reiterated simile of fourteenth-century chroniclers is that arrows fell like snow on the battlefield; but unlike snow, arrows produce a terrifying noise, bewildering men and panicking horses. At Dupplin Moor and Halidon Hill the archers were able to decimate the Scottish troops before they even approached close to the English positions, so anticipating the later successes of Crécy and Poitiers.

Wars were not, however, won solely by means of efficient battle tactics, or skilful strategy. It required a highly-complex logistic exercise to send an army up to thirty thousand strong to fight in Scotland and to keep it adequately provisioned once it was there. Neither in Wales nor in Scotland could armies live off the land, and experience rapidly taught Edward I that it was not enough merely to encourage merchants to follow the army. Large victualling bases were set up, notably at Chester for the Welsh wars, and at Berwick and Carlisle for those in Scotland. The crown had a traditional right known as prise, which entitled it to buy up food supplies compulsorily. This was intended for the purposes of the royal household, but the system was extended under Edward I to cover provisioning for the whole army. Sheriffs were ordered to supply vast quantities of wheat, oats, barley, beans, salt-meat and fish. They sent officials round the county to buy up goods on credit, and to organize transport by cart or barge to collection points. The goods were then taken to a suitable port. There ships would be assembled by other officials, again using compulsory powers, loaded up and then sailed on to the victualling bases. The voyage was not always an easy one; on one occasion, a ship was blown off course and ended up in Norway.

The incidence of such levies of food supplies was not uniform; Yorkshire and East Anglia suffered particularly during the Scottish wars. On occasion huge quantities were demanded, such as the 63,200 quarters of grain requested in 1296. Accounts show that in 1300 the royal victuallers in Scotland had charge of about 12,000 quarters of grain, 38,000 herrings, over 1,300 tuns of wine and many other goods. In the year leading up to the débâcle of Bannockburn the victualling officer at Berwick had at his disposal almost 15,000 quarters of grain and over 3,700 quarters of beans and peas. The system rarely failed. The battle of Falkirk was fought on empty stomachs; horses died from want of fodder in the winter of 1301–2. The headlong chase after the Scots through Northumberland in 1327 put the cavalry out of touch for a time with the baggage train, leaving them at the mercy of profiteering merchants who charged six or seven pence for a badly-cooked loaf of bread not worth a twentieth of that. These were exceptional cases. Efficient victualling did much to make possible such success as the English achieved in their wars in Scotland. There was, however, a very striking contrast between their methods and those of the Scots. On their raids south the Scots relied solely on meat from animals they captured, and on oatcakes made from grain that they carried with them in saddlebags. Armies that could live off the land could move far faster than those, like the English, which were dependent on complex and extended supply routes. The administrative lessons learnt from the Scottish wars were to be important to the English in the Hundred Years War, but so too was the ability they acquired to feed themselves from the lands they plundered on their *chevauchées*, in the way that the Scots had done in the north of England.

The impact of the Scottish war upon England was considerable. Not only had troops to be recruited and supplies collected, but also funds had to be raised to finance the armies. War in Scotland was not as costly as expeditions overseas, as large numbers of sailors were not needed, but in 1301 war wages alone amounted to almost £25,000; they stood at a similar figure in 1335. With all the additional expenses of victualling, payment of compensation for horses lost, siege equipment and so forth, a single major campaign would cost some £50,000 or more. In 1316–17, a year when there was no royal expedition, garrisoning costs alone came to just over £17,000. Edward I's heavy indebtedness at the end of his reign was the result of war, and it is no coincidence that the crown only became fully solvent under Edward II once truce had been agreed after the 1322 campaign. The heavy costs of Edward III's Scottish wars in the 1330s were the worst possible precursor to the immense financial effort of the initial stages of the Hundred Years War.

The Scottish wars affected the whole country, but it was the north that bore the real impact. The Scots conducted a damaging raid south of the border as early as 1296, though their invasions only became an acute problem under Edward II. There is a great deal of evidence of the effects of their techniques of burning crops and houses, and of driving off cattle. The accounts of John Balliol's English manors in the 1290s, after they had been taken into royal hands, show widespread losses; some manors were said to be wholly deserted as a result of Scots raids. The evidence from Edward II's reign is striking. The tithe revenue received by Durham Priory from churches in Northumberland fell from £412 in 1313–14 to a mere £10 by 1319. The manor of Tarset in the same county, once worth £237 a year, yielded a mere £4 after the Scots had burned the buildings and driven off the cattle. A survey of Prudhoe taken in 1325 shows that a hundred and twenty acres of the lord's land lay waste, with no tenants available to work it – even the pigeons had been destroyed. Examples can easily be multiplied; as late as 1346 a commission recorded widespread devastation in Cumberland, with houses burned and lands laid waste in a wide swathe of territory around Carlisle. Losses from war were not easily made up. Not only were crops destroyed, but the whole economic system of the north was severely dislocated. In 1310 Corbridge had been worth almost £100, but by the early 1330s men had stopped coming to market there, and by 1352 the value had only built up again to just under £50.

Statistics of declining rents and falling land values show that nowhere was the expanding economy of the thirteenth century halted more rudely in its tracks than in the north of England, but they do not show the appalling extent of human misery caused by the wars. Contemporary petitions reveal something of this. In 1316 Robert de Raynes stated that he had fought in all the campaigns of the war, and had lost horses and armour to a value of £100. He put damage to his lands by the Scots at £1,000. He had been captured at Bannockburn, and ransomed for five hundred marks, but since he could not raise the money he had been compelled to leave his son as a hostage in Scotland. Robert de Blackburn served in Berwick and in the field for twenty-two years. He was badly wounded when Berwick was captured in 1318, but managed to lead twenty-two horses south to Newcastle. He had lost his brother and ten friends at Bannockburn, and had no sources of income left – 'He is in such debts in London and elsewhere, he knows not where to turn.'[16] The aristocracy was provided with some compensation for their losses in the war, but little was done for the common people. There is a striking contrast between the thousand marks granted to the Earl of Hereford to cover the costs that resulted from his capture at Bannockburn, or the similar sum paid to a French noble, Henry de Sully, taken by the Scots in 1322, and the meagre forty tuns of

wine allocated to aid the people of Northumberland in
1319. It is hardly surprising that many northerners began to
look to the Scots. Changes of side were not uncommon.
The case of Gilbert de Middleton has already been mentioned. Walter of Selby was an Englishman who fought for
the Scots in Edward II's reign. He was later pardoned by
Edward III and rejoined the English cause, only to be
executed for treason by the Scots when they captured him
in 1346. Many northern families had ties of blood or marriage across the border, and their lack of loyalty to Edward
II is hardly surprising, given the failure of the English
government to protect their lands and property.

The Scots did not plunder indiscriminately. It was possible to buy protection from their attentions at a heavy price.
The men of County Durham claimed that they paid out
£20,000 in all to the Scots, though that figure was an
exaggeration. Durham was exceptional, for a powerful
group of local magnates and gentry exercised sufficient
authority for them to be able to negotiate with the Scots on
behalf of the whole county. Elsewhere agreements were on
a more local basis, as when the town of Ripon promised
in 1318 to pay 1,000 marks as the price of security. The
unfortunate inhabitants of Bamburgh found themselves
squeezed between the Scots who demanded £270 for a
truce, and the constable of the castle who refused to let
them pay unless they made an equivalent sum over to him.
It was not always easy to raise the sums demanded; the
men of the vale of Pickering agreed to pay the Scots £400,
and handed over hostages as a guarantee. When the money
was not forthcoming, the hostages petitioned Edward II,
who ordered the sheriff to raise the money so that they
might be released. Food might be taken as well as cash. In
1322 the canons of Bridlington, who had prudently sent
their treasure south, used one of their own brethren who
was a Scot by birth to negotiate with the enemy. He
returned with nine Scots, and it was agreed to let them take
as much food and drink as their eighteen horses could
carry.

With the Scots laying such a heavy burden on the north
of England, the crown under Edward II was forced to

abandon the collection of taxes in the region. Robert Bruce, in contrast, was able to finance his war out of the proceeds of the raids into England. It was only after the conclusion of a truce in 1323 that he had to turn to his subjects for a grant of taxation. Archaeological finds of hoards of English coins in southern Scotland are perhaps another piece of evidence of the effectiveness of Scottish fund-raising in England. There is, unfortunately, no way of assessing the total sum amassed by the Scots in the course of their incursions, but it must have been far in excess of the £20,000 conceded by Robert Bruce in the shameful peace of 1328.

War has always brought profit to some, and even in the darkest days of Edward II's reign the Anglo-Scottish conflict was no exception. Most of those given military command were able to take advantage of their position. Andrew Harclay's rise, for instance, was meteoric; he held a series of posts on the western March, and benefited from royal patronage, booty gained from the Scots and extortion from the men of Cumberland. His service at the battle of Boroughbridge gained him the title of Earl of Carlisle and the promise of large estates – a promise not fulfilled since he was executed for treason in 1323. His rival and effective successor Anthony de Lucy retained his power in the western March through the political revolutions of 1327 and 1330, and he continued to hold a series of lucrative posts on the border until his death in 1343. Thomas Ughtred, a Yorkshireman, had his share of misfortune; he was captured in 1319, and surrendered Perth to the Scots in 1339. Yet he did well in the wars. After distinguished service under Edward II, he joined the disinherited and was later well rewarded for his continued employment in the north, though not as spectacularly as John of Coupland, who was awarded £500 a year for capturing David II at Neville's Cross. At a lower level, the near collapse of royal authority in the north so striking in Edward II's reign provided ample opportunities for rogues and ruffians. One such was Jack the Irishman, who assisted the constable of Bamburgh Castle in the exploitation of the local townspeople, and raped Lady Clifford at Barnard Castle. One chronicler considered that the oppression by English officials in the north 'was more injurious to the people than the persecution of their enemies'.[17]

The war changed the whole complexion of society in the north. Many of the old families failed to adjust to the new conditions; Robert FitzRoger, one of Edward I's opponents in 1297, fought valiantly in the north, but his son, John of Clavering, ran heavily into debt and surrendered his rights to the castle of Warkworth in 1311 much as William de Roos was to give up Wark six years later. The most striking example of a family which capitalized on the difficulties of others in the north is that of the Percies. In 1311 they negotiated for the purchase of Alnwick Castle, and in 1332 they acquired Warkworth. Among other acquisitions they gained the barony of Beanley in Northumberland in 1335 following the decision of Patrick of Dunbar, Earl of March, to withdraw his allegiance from Edward III. The old families were losing power and authority; they could not exercise as effective a lordship as those men who received royal military appointments. The wages that the latter were paid provided them with some compensation, perhaps, for the acute loss of revenue from agriculture.

There was some inevitable resentment against those men who were successful. John of Denton, a Newcastle merchant who profited by supplying English armies, and who was suspected of trading with the enemy as well as being deeply involved in Edward III's unpopular manipulation of the wool trade, was improperly imprisoned by a group of his fellow burgesses. He died after being subjected to a diet of bread and water, each being given on alternate days. John of Coupland, David II's captor, was murdered in 1363 by some of the Northumberland gentry. The north of England, with large tracts of land reduced by the ravages of war to a barren waste, was a violent, disturbed region, where the crown was incapable of maintaining a tight control over its subjects. The bleak square utilitarian tower houses, of which the Vicar's Pele at Corbridge is an early example, mark a new departure in the military architecture of the north in the fourteenth century, and reflect the tough realities of border society.

The war with the Scots was a bitter one, as contemporary

propaganda testifies. The invasions of England by the Scots provoked such horror stories as the slaughter of pregnant women and children, and of two hundred schoolboys burned alive in the church at Corbridge. William Wallace in particular became a feared bogey-man for the English. His kind of war had threatened the whole population in a way that was quite new; it was claimed at his trial that he would spare no one who spoke the English language. The English sank to low abuse of their enemies; an English poem written after the victory of Falkirk concluded: 'The filthy Scots attack England like a pig rising up against the valour of the lion. The king therefore reduced them to servitude.'[18] A soldiers' song began:

> The foot folk
> Put the Scots in the poke,
> And bared their buttocks.[19]

By Edward III's reign mention of the Scots in poems or chronicles was almost invariably accompanied by abuse of their faithless and deceiving ways. They were 'cursed caitiffs', 'full of treason, sooth to tell', and childish delight was taken in the tale that at his christening David II had excreted over the altar. Abuse was not one-sided, of course. The Scots taunted their opponents with the traditional medieval belief that all Englishmen had tails. In 1348 they rejoiced at the news that England had succumbed to the Black Death, though their joy did not last long when they in turn were afflicted by the disease.

Edward I had high hopes in 1290 for the eventual peaceful acquisition of Scotland for his dynasty. Events worked against him, but his ambitions were not to be stilled. The enterprise to which he committed his country with his claims of suzerainty over Scotland and his attempted seizure of the country in 1296 was, it appears with hindsight, an impossible one. There were moments, as in 1296, 1304 and 1333 when it must have appeared that the English had triumphed, but every victory proved illusory. In the official vocabulary of the 1330s, England was a realm – a nation – whereas Scotland was merely a land, and the Scots a people not worthy of the dignity of nationhood. Nothing could have been further from the truth, and the immortal words of the Declaration of Arbroath of 1320 have to be quoted:

As long as a hundred of us remain alive, we will never on any conditions be subjected to the lordship of the English. For we fight not for glory, nor riches, nor honours, but for freedom alone, which no good man gives up except with his life.[20]

A full explanation of the English failure requires far more discussion of the Scots and their achievement than is possible here. From the English point of view, however, the opportunities presented by war in Scotland were an inadequate inducement for men to fight with the consistent determination required for victory. Edward I's personal determination was not fully shared by his nobility, and was not passed on to his successors. Under Edward II political failure at home marched hand-in-hand with military failure in Scotland. Edward III had great military ambitions, but these found more fruitful outlets in France than in Scotland. He never possessed his grandfather's determination to maintain his legal rights as he interpreted them; Edward III was an opportunist, prepared to compromise. He brought a new savagery to the war in the north, but showed a far greater capacity to appreciate the realities of the situation than either of his two predecessors. The conflict with the Scots posed testing problems for the kings of England; it was also a proving ground for the development of English armies, from which they emerged to triumph on the battlefields of France.

3
Edward II

The Incompetent King

Edward II was one of the most unsuccessful kings ever to rule England. The domestic history of the reign is one of successive political failures punctuated by acts of horrific violence. The opposition achieved no more than the crown; Thomas of Lancaster, the king's chief antagonist, owed his position to his wealth rather than to his ability, and proved to be no statesman. Personal hatreds and jealousies were more important than constitutional principles, as was demonstrated in the final overthrow of the incompetent king by his queen, Isabella. Yet the reign has its fascination. The failures of a society often reveal its essential character better than the successes, and even this reign was not without its constructive achievements.

Although Edward II came to be regarded as wholly unsuitable to hold the throne, he had some regal qualities. He was tall, muscular and good-looking, and had not inherited his father's slight lisp; he was a good horseman in an age when this was important. He could appear decisive: in 1312 he addressed the citizens of London firmly, asking them to defend the city in his cause. During a meeting with the French king in 1320, Edward on his own initiative rejected a demand that he should perform fealty as well as homage. He personally composed a written notification of the return from exile of his favourite Piers Gaveston, and examples of oral instructions by the king to his ministers show that he had a considerable understanding of the workings of government.

Such merits as the king possessed easily went unnoticed. Edward's greatest failing, perhaps, lay in his relations with his favourites. Even before he came to the throne his friendship with the young Gascon Piers Gaveston, son of a royal household knight, caused problems. Such was his son's generosity towards him that Edward I ordered Gaveston to leave the country, and tore out handfuls of the prince's hair in a rage. It was possible for one man to dominate Edward II to such an extent that he would not accept advice from any other quarter, and his munificence towards his favourites unbalanced the whole system of royal patronage. Gaveston was less dangerous than the favourite of the last years of the reign, Hugh Despenser the younger, for while the Gascon had no great political ambitions, Despenser was a determined and grasping man of considerable ability.

Opinion as to whether the king's relationships with his favourites were homosexual has changed considerably in recent years, reflecting a change in modern attitudes rather than the discovery of fresh evidence. Contemporaries made the accusation in guarded terms. The well-informed author of the *Life of Edward II* made no more than allusions to David and Jonathan. It was rumoured in 1308 that the king loved Gaveston more than his queen, 'a most elegant lady and a beautiful woman'[1] – who was, it should be noted, only twelve. Edward had four children by Queen Isabella, and one bastard son, but it is hard to doubt a sexual element in his friendships with Gaveston and Despenser. Homosexuality was regarded with horror at this time; it was tantamount to heresy, as the trials of the Templars showed, but it was not until after Edward's death that the charge was openly brought against the king by the chroniclers.

Edward II's tastes were unkingly; he did not even share Gaveston's enthusiasm for tournaments. Rather, he enjoyed boating, swimming, and rustic crafts. Before his accession, there is a record of his injuring one Robert the Fool during boisterous games in the water. After Bannockburn, one royal messenger said that it was not surprising that the king did not win battles, as he spent his time hedging and ditching rather than hearing mass. One household account records quantities of iron and plaster bought 'for the private works of the king',[2] and while nineteenth- and twentieth-century statesmen were not ill-thought of for chopping down trees and building brick walls, similar activities were not acceptable in fourteenth-century kings. Accounts for the purchase of boats demonstrate Edward's love of the water. This was sufficiently well-known for the Scots to taunt the English after Bannockburn with a song mocking the oarsman's chant of 'Heavalow, Rumbalow':

Maidens of England, sore may you mourn,
For you have lost your men at Bannockburn with 'Heavalow'.
What, would the king of England have won Scotland with 'Rumbalow'?[3]

Edward also enjoyed hearing minstrels; his accounts show that he retained a small orchestra, with two trumpeters, a horn-player, a harpist and a drummer. It was said maliciously that Walter Reynolds, chancellor and Archbishop of Canterbury, won the king's favour because of his skill in arranging theatrical presentations.

The household accounts contain many examples of the king's generosity. He gave no less than £50 to a surgeon who cured a stable boy bitten by one of the king's valuable stallions and a curious entry records £1 given to a woman with whom he drank when on his way to Newcastle in 1310. There was a remarkable custom that if the king was caught in bed on Easter Monday, he would pay a ransom for his release. Edward I was discovered several times by the ladies of the queen's chamber, and paid between £6 13s 4d and £14; in 1311 Edward II was dragged from his bed by three knights, to whom he paid £20. It was not only on Easter Monday morning that he stayed late in bed; in 1320 the Bishop of Worcester noted with surprise that the king was rising early in the morning, contrary to his normal habits.

Edward II was lazy and incompetent, liable to outbursts of temper over unimportant issues, yet indecisive when it came to major issues. He was held in little respect by his people, and it is hardly surprising that there were rumours that he was a changeling and not the real son of Edward I. Fewer people came forward to be touched for the king's evil – scrofula – under Edward II than in his father's day; in one year Edward I had blessed over 1,700 sick men: the highest annual figure for Edward II is 214. Yet the king did not lack a sense of the majesty of his position; he even tried to boost his position as a sacerdotal king by asking the Pope's permission to be reconsecrated in 1318 with some newly-discovered oil, which the Virgin had allegedly given to Thomas Becket. The fact that Edward had ambition as a king made his weakness all the more dangerous.

The reign of Edward II divides into separate phases. From his accession until 1311 there was argument over the position of Piers Gaveston, and demands for reforms on similar lines to those requested in Edward I's later years. These culminated in the production of the Ordinances in 1311, which in turn imposed a pattern on politics up to 1322. The last years of the reign were dominated by the ambitions of the elder and younger Despenser, in a dominant position following the fall of Thomas of Lancaster, the king's leading opponent, in 1322.

At his accession, Edward II had many advantages. The two main lay opponents of the crown in 1297, Bigod and Bohun, were dead, and Archbishop Winchelsey was in exile. The king had close family ties with the greatest earls; Thomas of Lancaster was his cousin, and Gilbert of Gloucester his nephew. There was no immediate hostility to the return of Gaveston, nor even to his elevation to the earldom of Cornwall. The old king's unpopular minister, Walter Langton, was dismissed. Although a massive debt of some £200,000 was inherited from Edward I, it was easy in the atmosphere of goodwill at the start of a reign to negotiate a grant of taxation, and the abandonment of the Scottish campaign reduced expenditure.

It was early in 1308 that signs of unease appeared. At the time of the king's marriage to Isabella of France at Boulogne in January an important group of magnates, all former councillors of Edward I, entered into a written agreement. They stressed their loyalty to the crown, but stated the need to reform 'things which have been done before this time contrary to his [the king's] honour and the rights of his crown, and the oppressions which have been done and are still being done to his people.'[4] The phraseology was deliberately vague, but probably refers both to the question of Gaveston and to more general administrative abuses. When the coronation took place, a new clause in the king's oath made him promise to observe 'the rightful laws and customs which the community of the realm shall have chosen'.[5] Again this lacked precision, but the clause could be seen as an attempt to ensure that the king would not go back on any future concessions, in the way that Edward i had reneged upon his promises of 1297. Very soon the Earl of Lincoln was to use it in a demand for the exile of Gaveston, which was duly carried out.

There were evidently divergent opinions as to what was needed. For some, the expulsion of Gaveston was the main aim, while others were prepared to use the favourite as a means of forcing the king to make concessions. In 1309 Gaveston returned, and in exchange the king conceded many of the demands of the opposition. This settlement was not successful. Financial weakness compelled the king to agree to the appointment in 1310 of twenty-one Ordainers, who were to produce articles of reform. The failure of the king's Scottish campaign placed him firmly in their hands, and in 1311 the Ordinances were produced.

Many of the clauses of the Ordinances looked back to Edward i's reign – the long-standing abuse of prise (the compulsory purchase of foodstuffs); the payment of customs revenues to Italian merchants; the misuse of the privy seal in judicial matters; the lavish grants of pardons in return for service in war – none of these matters were new. The demand that the king should not leave the realm or make war without baronial consent might refer to Edward ii's Scottish expedition of 1310, but could also have been provoked by memories of the constitutional crisis of 1297. The Ordinances also stated that all royal revenues should be paid into the exchequer: this move attacked the financial independence of the wardrobe, which had developed under Edward i, and represented a traditional policy. The demand for Gaveston to be expelled once again from the realm, however, was an element in the Ordinances which did not refer back to Edward I's reign. For one chronicler, this was the only clause in a very lengthy document which was worth recording. An important request for the annulment of all royal grants made since the appointment of the Ordainers likewise reflected the new problems created by Edward II's ineffective rule.

Some of those involved in the production of the Ordinances were old opponents of Edward I, like Archbishop Winchelsey and Robert FitzRoger, who had accompanied Bigod to the exchequer in 1297. More significant, however, was the fact that many former royalists backed the new programme. The Earl of Lincoln had been utterly loyal to Edward I, and was now an Ordainer; John Botetourt, a household banneret of previously unswerving loyalty was another. Edward II had alienated much of the support which he had inherited from his father, and his misuse of patronage had meant that he had not built up any worthwhile backing of his own.

Edward II was not prepared to accept the renewed exile of his favourite Gaveston, and demands for the removal from his household of a number of knights and officials made in a later set of ordinances infuriated him further. He tried to strengthen his position by recalling his old enemy Walter Langton as treasurer – a highly unpopular move. Civil war was threatened, but when the crisis came, the royal forces were woefully unprepared. The king and his favourite moved to the north, where Gaveston was besieged in Scarborough Castle. Edward clearly thought he would be safe there, but the baronial forces were too strong. Gaveston surrendered on quite favourable terms. He was entrusted to the Earl of Pembroke, who guaranteed his safety. When he was being led south, however, the Earl of Warwick captured him. Unable to hold his waspish tongue, Gaveston jeered at the earl, whom he had nicknamed 'the black dog of Arden'.[6] Warwick retorted that he was no dog, and that Piers was a liar and a traitor. He was led off to Warwick Castle, where he was tried and convicted on the questionable grounds that the royal revocation of the Ordinances had not reached Warwickshire. He was then handed over to the Earls of Lancaster, Arundel and Hereford, and taken to Blacklow Hill, the nearest property owned by Lancaster. Amid scenes of mob enthusiasm, shouts of joy and blowing of horns, he was executed.

There are no signs that Gaveston had influenced royal policy to a marked extent, save that he had made no effort to curb Edward's generosity towards him. Much of the hostility towards him was of a very personal nature; he had incensed the magnates even before the coronation by worsting them in a series of tournaments, and at the ceremony he had behaved with blatant arrogance, wearing purple robes decorated with pearls rather than the conventional cloth of gold. He was said to have exported much of his wealth by using the services of the king's unpopular Italian bankers, the Frescobaldi, who were themselves expelled by the Ordainers. He hardly deserved his fate, but it was evident that only death could rid the king of the favourite.

Gaveston's death transformed the political situation. Although the king is said to have remarked lightly on hearing the news, 'By God's soul, he acted like a fool. If he had taken my advice he would never have fallen into the hands of the earls',[7] there is no doubt of his grief and determination for revenge. The act at Blacklow Hill divided the opposition. Pembroke and Warenne had guaranteed Gaveston's safety, and joined the royalist cause – Lancaster, who took responsibility for the favourite's death, now emerged clearly as the king's leading opponent. His father-in-law the Earl of Lincoln died in 1311, and after inheriting his lands, Lancaster was immeasurably the wealthiest of the earls. The French had given the opposition some support up to 1312; Queen Isabella clearly resented Gaveston, and had been in correspondence with Lancaster. Now she had no rival for the king's affections, and Edward received the full support of his father-in-law.

There were fears of civil war in the aftermath of Gaveston's death, but there were influential forces working for peace. The Earl of Gloucester told the king, according to one account: 'King, if you destroy your barons, you indeed make light of your own honour', to which Edward pathetically replied: 'There is no one who is sorry for me; none fights for my right against them.'[8] Protracted negotiations were complicated by the king's desire to recover Gaveston's treasure, which had been captured at Scarborough. Agreement was eventually reached in October 1313. Pardons were granted, and the magnates agreed that they would not appear armed in parliament. A grant of taxation considerably eased the king's difficult financial position.

The next year, 1314, brought the military disaster of Bannockburn. The defeat discredited the government, in which Pembroke had been a leading influence. Lancaster and three other earls had not taken part in the campaign, on the grounds that the terms of the Ordinances requiring parliamentary consent for the expedition had not been met. Gloucester's death in the battle meant the loss of a powerful influence for moderation, and Lancaster emerged in a dominant position.

Thomas of Lancaster was not a man of original political ideas. His aim was to secure a full adherence to the Ordinances of 1311. At parliament in September 1314 he instigated a purge of the administration; hated household officials were removed, and many sheriffs changed. The majority of the new ministers were not Lancastrian partisans, however, but were men of long service and experience in royal administration, like William Melton, who became keeper of the wardrobe. An upright and able man, 'although he had lived long at court, he had not been contaminated by this intercourse, but, escaping the greed of the English, by the grace of God remained always unpolluted.'[9] A systematic attempt was made to adhere to the Ordinances, and many royal grants were annulled. Lancaster's position was finally confirmed at the Lincoln parliament of 1316; after arriving late, he was offered the position of chief councillor. This he accepted, while the king agreed to maintain the Ordinances and to see to the reform of the royal household.

The regime dominated by Lancaster was no more

successful than that which it succeeded. Plans for a campaign in Scotland came to nothing. Lancaster claimed that
the king was not observing the Ordinances, while Edward
accused the earl of threatening the peace by recruiting
troops. At the Lincoln parliament it had been agreed that
the feudal host would be summoned for service in Scotland, but in August the king issued two military summonses of a novel type; in one he asked for the unpaid
service of fifty-pound landholders, and in the other asked
the magnates to provide as many men-at-arms as they
could, rather than the traditional quotas, in accordance
with their fealty and homage. There were echoes of 1297
here, and it is hardly surprising that the campaign did not
take place. The Earl of Lancaster went to Newcastle, but the
king remained in the south.

The politics of the period from 1316 to 1318, when agreement was again reached between the king and Lancaster in
the Treaty of Leake, were complex. Edward began to try to
build up his strength, and made agreements with various
magnates and knights for their service in return for substantial payments. The Earl of Hereford agreed to serve for
1,000 marks in peace, and 2,000 marks in time of war, with a
hundred men-at-arms. A new group of royal favourites
emerged. Hugh Audley, Roger Damory and William
Montague were important household knights: early in
1317 the king showed his favour to the first two by marrying them to two of the three heiresses to the great
Gloucester earldom; the third was already married to the
younger Despenser, who with his father began to associate
himself closely with the courtiers. Division of the Gloucester inheritance had long been delayed by the determined
protestations of Earl Gilbert's widow that she was pregnant, but after two years her arguments had lost their force.
The estates were duly divided between Audley, Damory
and Despenser.

Lancaster adopted a threatening attitude towards the
courtiers. He withdrew from the king, and by the middle of
1317 he was summoning armed assemblies in the north in a
show of strength. One of his concerns was a private war
with Earl Warenne: civil war, however, was averted. At

Leake in 1318 an agreement was reached to set up a permanent council of seventeen members, one of whom was to be nominated by Lancaster. These men were to provide consent for all matters which did not require parliamentary approval. Lancaster and his followers were pardoned, and the favourites Audley, Damory and Montague removed from court. All royal grants were to be reviewed, and a committee was to reform the royal household.

A powerful tradition of historical writing has attributed the treaty of Leake to the work of a 'middle party', thought to have consisted of the Earl of Pembroke, the Earl of Hereford, Bartholomew Badlesmere, various bishops and some royal officials. An agreement between Pembroke, Badlesmere and Roger Damory was seen as one of the foundations of this party. Recently, however, Pembroke's biographer, J. R. S. Phillips, has argued persuasively that this was not a compact between equals, but was an attempt by Pembroke and Badlesmere to restrain an irresponsible favourite, and gain some influence themselves. Though they may have had moderate inclinations, they were both staunch royalists, with a long tradition of loyalty broken only briefly by Pembroke's period as an Ordainer. They certainly did not occupy a middle ground between the king and Lancaster.

A detailed study of the negotiations leading up to the treaty of 1318 suggests that the bishops played the leading part together with two cardinals in England at the time, for they were able to win the trust of all parties. Several of the bishops, however, were former royal clerks, men unlikely to be sympathetic to radical views. The agreement is best seen as a triumph for moderate royalists. The new council contained no close associates of Lancaster, save for the one banneret he nominated, and he was evidently there to ensure that the earl could not claim that he had not been consulted or involved in important decisions. The review of royal grants did not result in the wholesale recovery of lands that Lancaster had hoped for. The earl, however, could take some comfort from the removal from court of the favourites, and from the financial settlement they reached with him. He also gained Warenne's lands in

North Wales and Yorkshire, so augmenting his already massive estates.

The stability achieved in 1318 was short-lived. The failure of the siege of Berwick in 1319 caused bitter argument, and discredited the government. More sinister was the emergence of a new favourite in the form of the younger Despenser. He had been a supporter of the Ordainers, but had subsequently seen that his ambition 'that Despenser may be rich and may attain his ends'[10] was best achieved by cultivating royal favour. In 1318 he became the king's chamberlain, and a succession of grants to him testify to his success in winning the king's affection.

Despenser's ambitions were centred on south Wales, where he wished to enlarge upon his share of the Gloucester inheritance. His methods of gaining lands incurred the anger of the Marcher lords, for he challenged their rights and privileges. He persuaded the king to confiscate the lordship of Gower on the grounds that John Mowbray had taken possession of it without royal licence. The case was complex, with the Marchers claiming that no such licence was needed, while Hugh 'took no heed of the law and custom of the March, and appeared to accuse the barons who alleged such things of talking treason'.[11] A recent case involving the Countess of Gloucester and the Earls of Pembroke and Norfolk had shown that the courts were capable of supporting the arguments of the Marchers, but where Despenser was involved, there could be no doubt of where the king's sympathies lay. A small household force under a royal sergeant, Guido Almantini, was sent to take possession of Gower, and was captured by the Marchers.

The Marchers were a powerful group, who included not only Mowbray, Clifford, the Mortimers and the Earl of Hereford, but also the former favourites, Audley and Damory, who were finding it hard to retain their shares of the Gloucester inheritance in the face of Despenser's ambitions. Lancaster was presented with a splendid opportunity, and made common cause with the Marchers. He failed, however, to forge an effective link between the Marchers and the northern magnates, and refused to co-operate with one unlikely opponent of the king, Bartholomew Badlesmere. The latter had family ties with the Marchers, and perhaps found his position at court, where he was steward of the household, threatened by Despenser's rise.

The Marchers had little difficulty in seizing Despenser's lands and castles in south Wales, and by the summer of 1321 the king and his favourite were in a weak position. In August Edward yielded, and agreed to the exile of the Despensers. He was not a man to accept such treatment lightly, however, and in the autumn began an intelligently worked out counter-offensive, which culminated in the complete and utter defeat of Lancaster and his allies.

The king's initial target was Badlesmere, and the *casus belli* was provided by the queen. Leeds Castle in Kent had been promised to Isabella, but in 1318 it was granted to Badlesmere. Now the queen was sent to Leeds to demand hospitality. This was, not surprisingly, refused; to admit her might be seen as a recognition of her claims to the castle. Edward then authorized a siege, in which the Earls of Pembroke, Richmond and Norfolk took part. Loathed as he was by Lancaster, Badlesmere found little support, and the castle was duly surrendered. Edward then turned his attention to the Marches. There was a great difference between taking up arms against the Despensers and engaging in warfare with an anointed king. The Mortimers and some of the other leaders surrendered without a fight, while the Earl of Hereford with Audley and Damory left the Marches to seek refuge with Lancaster. The strategy of moving in stages against the opposition was proving immensely successful.

The final stage in the brief civil war was the confrontation with Lancaster himself in 1322. The royal army moved north, and the two sides faced each other at Burton-on-Trent. There was no enthusiasm for battle on either side, and after some skirmishing the baronial forces fled northwards, it was thought to seek refuge in Scotland. At Boroughbridge their path was blocked by a royalist force under Andrew Harclay, which had marched from Carlisle. Lancaster's cause was substantially weakened before the

battle by the defection of his chief lieutenant, Robert Holland. The fight was dominated by Harclay's hardened
soldiers, who fought on foot in Scottish fashion. The Earl of
Hereford was killed in a suicidal bid to cross the bridge,
while Lancaster's men failed to force a way over the nearby
ford in face of a hail of arrows. A truce was agreed until the
next day, but so many of the Lancastrian forces deserted
overnight that there was no hope of resuming the fight.
When morning came, Lancaster, Clifford, Mowbray and
the others simply surrendered.

At Pontefract Lancaster was summarily tried and condemned as a traitor. He was then mounted on a 'lean white
palfry',[12] with an old hat, tattered and torn, placed on his
head. He was led out through a crowd which jeered and
threw snowballs at him, and executed. He was turned to
the north, since it was alleged that he had looked to the
Scots for aid. In deference to his royal blood he was
beheaded, rather than hanged, drawn and quartered, but
the cruelty of the spectacle evoked clear memories of
Gaveston's death.

In any explanation of the disastrous course of political
events the enigmatic figure of Thomas of Lancaster must
take an important place. Lancaster had great resources at
his disposal. He inherited five earldoms, and was in a far
better position than most baronial leaders to present an
effective challenge to an incompetent king: he could count
on the service of over fifty knights in his retinue, a force
equivalent to that of the royal household. His estates were
worth over £11,000 a year. He held powerful castles in the
midlands and the north, and spent lavishly on their fortification, as the great gatehouse at Dunstanburgh shows. Yet
Lancaster was sadly lacking in energy and ideas, and possessed no personal magnetism. His political programme
never advanced far beyond the Ordinances of 1311, and
his inflexibility blinded him to the realities of the political
situation.

The one element in Lancaster's schemes which had no
place in the Ordinances was the claim to his rights as
steward of England. This was a traditional office, like those

of the marshal and constable, and Simon de Montfort had made political use of his claim to it. If his demands were accepted, Lancaster would have gained real control over the royal household, the right to supervise the administration of the law, and power to intervene in the king's choice of councillors. The case, however, was not a strong one, and was unlikely to win the support of many other magnates. There is no indication that Lancaster showed any real appreciation of the need to try to build up a political following based on shared ideals; a bill demanding reforms drawn up on his behalf in 1321 displays a poverty of ideas. The evidence linking him with a remarkably advanced tract, the *Modus Tenendi Parliamentum*, which gives the commons a place of great importance in parliament, is very slender. The earl's view of how the country should be governed was, as his advocacy of the Ordinances suggests, essentially baronial and oligarchic.

Lancaster was unfortunate in that he faced insuperable problems during his period of dominance after Bannockburn. There was economic catastrophe in 1315 and 1316, with appalling famine. Scottish raids were devastating the north, and in Lancashire the earl faced the rebellion of one of his own men, Adam Banaster. In Wales there was revolt, and the citizens of Bristol, aggravated by the high-handed behaviour of Badlesmere as constable of the castle there, resisted every attempt of the government to restore order. Yet this does not explain the way in which Lancaster allowed power to slip from his grasp in 1316 and 1317. It may be that he was ill; it may be that he felt that his duty was to his own estates, rather than to the government of the country. Whatever the truth is, it is evident that he was unsuited to the political role that was forced on him as a consequence of his birth and wealth.

One of Lancaster's major errors was to negotiate with the Scots, so laying himself open to a charge of treason. There is no doubt that he did have dealings with Robert Bruce; a safe-conduct survives which provided for thirty horsemen – clearly Lancaster's – to come to Edinburgh. A policy of peace with Scotland made excellent sense, of course, but was not acceptable in England and for Lancaster to seek a political ally in Scotland for his struggle with Edward II was an act of folly. It is striking that in the final débâcle he was unable to win much support from the northern magnates, and that it was Harclay's northern forces that routed him at Boroughbridge.

The final campaign revealed Lancaster's weakness. The earl appeared to have as little stomach for a fight as Edward II, and showed himself to be no soldier. He did not involve himself in the revolt until a very late stage, and those who recruited men on his behalf had little success. Even his own retainers lacked loyalty; the desertion of Robert Holland was a fatal blow. No proper unity had been built up between the various elements of the opposition, and Lancaster's unwillingness to accept Badlesmere's support was most unwise. A more effective leader than Lancaster would have been able to deal with the incompetent Edward II long before 1322, but the earl was neither temperamentally nor intellectually suited to the part that circumstances compelled him to play. At the end it was the Earl of Hereford who displayed a bravery on the fatal bridge that Lancaster had never shown.

Edward II's victory at Boroughbridge marked the beginning of an unprecedented bloodbath. One chronicler lists twenty-five executions and a total of a hundred and eighteen either slain, imprisoned, or fled into exile. Many men were compelled to buy their freedom with massive fines. The contrast with the aftermath of Simon de Montfort's rebellion in the previous century is striking; then, former rebels had been allowed to buy the king's peace at clearly set-out rates. Edward II, with the advice of the Despensers, had decided that the political conflicts which had dogged him since his accession could only be resolved by the total destruction of his opponents. Their political programme, the Ordinances, was formally annulled in parliament at York.

Their success in 1322 revived the Despensers' appetite for lands and wealth: they had not learned their lesson from the previous rising against them. The years until their fall in 1326 were characterized by a more blatant self-seeking attitude on the part of those in control of the levers of power than was the case in perhaps any other period of English history. The death of the Earl of Pembroke, who was maliciously said to have been 'murdered suddenly on a privy seat',[13] in 1324 removed a potentially moderate influence, and there seemed no way in which the advance of the Despensers could be halted. The charter rolls record thirty-nine grants to the younger Despenser in these years, while his father received the title of Earl of Winchester. The great water defences and massive outer works at Caerfili are tangible evidence of the younger Despenser's continued ambitions in south Wales. In addition to the former Gloucester estates he also obtained Chepstow Castle from the Earl of Norfolk for much less than its true value.

The royal chamber accounts bear witness to the extent of the younger Despenser's power. Royal funds were used to buy armour for him, to munition and fortify his castles, and to pay for his wife's expenses. When a new royal ship was built, it was called *La Despenser*. The scale on which Despenser used his position of authority to build up his private wealth was unprecedented. His techniques for acquiring land were unscrupulous in the extreme although he usually kept to the letter of the law. Widows were a favourite target: Lancaster's estranged wife, Alice de Lacy, was forced to hand over many estates under duress, and Pembroke's widow was systematically harassed. Elizabeth Comyn, one of Pembroke's heirs, was imprisoned until she made out an obligation to the Despensers for £10,000 and surrendered two important estates to them. Roger Damory's widow, Despenser's sister-in-law, suffered similar treatment. The accounts of the Italian banking houses of the Bardi and the Peruzzi show that the younger Hugh was accumulating a fortune; by September 1324 he had placed £6,000 with them.

One favourite technique of the Despensers and their allies the Earl of Arundel and Robert Baldock was to compel men to acknowledge large fictitious debts to them. Edmund de Pinkeney, for example, made out a recognizance to the elder Despenser for £10,000, and in London a complex mesh of such deeds was used to blackmail men into supporting the government. William de Boghan lost some lands when payment was demanded after he had acknowledged a debt of £4,000. The Bishop of Winchester was not permitted to take over his lands until he made out a recognizance for £10,000, of which £2,000 was to be paid and the rest held over him as a guarantee of good conduct.

The period of Despenser rule, though corrupt, was not unconstructive. Much work of administrative reform had been started in 1318, but it was under the direction of the younger Despenser, the chancellor Robert Baldock and the treasurer Walter Stapledon that major changes took place. The exchequer records were reorganized in an attempt to simplify debt collection, and an experiment was made by which the exchequer was divided into two: a northern and a southern office. The policy of the Ordainers of reducing the financial independence of the wardrobe was carried further, but the chamber – which was under the younger Despenser's direct control – became more important even though it did not gain permanent control of all the estates of the 'contrariants', as the vanquished of 1322 were known. With the introduction in 1326 of a system of home staples – places where merchants should buy wool for export – an important experiment in commercial policy took place.

The reforms that took place between 1322 and 1326 were of a technical nature, designed to increase royal revenue, not to win popularity. Despite the totality of the king's triumph in 1322, there were some criticisms voiced. The request of the prelates in 1324 that the quartered bodies of the contrariants, still hanging in chains, should be delivered for burial, perhaps reflects horror at the severity with which the rebellion had been treated. In 1325 petitions in parliament asked for adherence to the terms of the Forest Charter; for the maintenance of the liberties of London; for proper answers to be given to parliamentary petitions; for due process of law to be applied to rebels; and for tenants on the estates confiscated in 1322 to be allowed their legal rights.

Popular veneration of Thomas of Lancaster also provides evidence of the hostility towards the government.

Rumours abounded of miracles performed at his tomb, and armed guards had to be posted to prevent anyone entering the church. Not all of the earl's supporters had been dealt with. Robert de Vere had escaped after Boroughbridge, and gathered an armed band; they terrorized Northamptonshire, and de Vere declared that no one dare indict him before royal justices, as there was no law in the land. Lancashire was in a state of virtual civil war between the former supporters of Adam Banaster and those of Lancaster. There was, however, no danger of former Lancastrians banding together to bring down the Despensers. Their position seemed impregnable.

The challenge to the Despensers came from a most unexpected quarter – Queen Isabella. Neither Edward nor the Despensers appreciated her growing disenchantment with her position. She had been abandoned by the king at Tynemouth priory on his retreat south from Scotland in 1322, and when war broke out with France in 1324 she was placed under suspicion; her lands were seized and her French servants dismissed. There was, however, little enthusiasm for the war, and Isabella seemed to be a highly suitable person to send to negotiate peace with Charles IV of France, her brother. Part of the terms that were agreed with the French were that Edward II should perform homage for Aquitaine, but the Despensers were reluctant to let the king go. Instead, the young Prince Edward went in his place. This was a disastrous move for the government. With the heir to the throne in her hands, Isabella refused to return unless the Despensers were removed from court. A visit from the Bishop of Exeter, Stapledon, failed to reconcile her, but instead hardened her attitude towards the ruling clique. Isabella began to associate with the influential group of exiles on the continent.

The most notable exile was Roger Mortimer. He had escaped from the Tower in 1323, by drugging the guards at a final banquet he gave for his jailers prior to his execution. He probably only became Isabella's lover while in France, so causing a major scandal. Many of the other exiles came to France like Isabella, as emissaries of the government they subsequently disavowed. They included the Earl of

Richmond, the king's half-brother the Earl of Kent, and the Bishops of Hereford, Winchester and Norwich. The latter had been a loyal servant of Edward II, but he had infuriated the king and the Despensers when he obtained his bishopric from the Pope, for it had been intended by them for Robert Baldock.

There was surprisingly little alarm in England at the situation. A letter from the Archbishop of Canterbury early in 1326 reported rumours that an invasion fleet was forming in Normandy and the Low Countries, but he argued confidently that the French would never permit such a force to sail. In fact, Isabella found her support not in France, but in Hainault. The young Prince Edward was betrothed to the count's daughter, and in return he provided a small force of mercenaries for the invasion. In September 1326 Isabella and Mortimer landed in Suffolk. The success of their gamble must have exceeded their wildest dreams, as support for the king and the Despensers melted away. Most important for Isabella was the wild enthusiasm of the Londoners for her cause. Edward II's relations with London had never been easy, and a major judicial inquiry in 1321 had incurred great hostility. The rights of the City to self-government had been curtailed. Now there were scenes of wild jubilation, and the revolution revealed its nastier side in the lynching of Bishop Stapledon, who was dragged from his horse by the mob and beheaded with a butcher's knife.

Edward II panicked. He was abandoned by the bulk of the administration, and by many members of his household. He fled to Wales with the Despensers and a diminishing body of supporters. The elder Despenser surrendered at Bristol; he was summarily convicted in a deliberate parody of Lancaster's trial. Edward himself and the younger Despenser set out by sea from Chepstow; it is not clear where they hoped to go, but they landed in Glamorgan, possibly hampered by contrary winds. They were captured by Henry of Lancaster, Thomas's brother. The king was sent into captivity at Kenilworth, and his favourite was tried and executed at Hereford. A horrific account tells how Despenser's genitals were cut off and burned in front of him, since he was alleged to be a heretic and a sodomite: the queen's triumph was marked by a bloodthirsty spirit similar to that which had characterized her husband's success in 1322.

There remained the problem of the king himself. The queen and her supporters had not made his deposition a part of their programme: the sermon preached by the Bishop of Hereford on the text 'I will put enmity between thee and the woman and between thy seed and her seed' was directed at the younger Despenser, not Edward II. Edward had twice been threatened with deposition, in 1310 and 1321, and there were ample continental precedents for removing an incompetent or incorrigible king from office, the most recent being the deposition of the German king Adolf of Nassau in 1298. Nearer home, Edward I had demonstrated with his treatment of John Balliol that kings could be both made and unmade.

The decisive steps were taken in January 1327. Edward refused to attend the parliament summoned in his name. It was clear that a further attempt to place him on a leading-rein could not succeed. The parliament was sitting under a constant threat of mob violence; many of those present were forced by the Londoners to swear to support Isabella's cause. Inflammatory sermons set the scene for deposition; even the Archbishop of Canterbury had turned against the king. Articles were drawn up, and the archbishop announced that by consent of the magnates, clergy and people Edward was no longer king. A deputation was sent to Kenilworth, where a pitiful scene was acted out. In a highly confused state Edward displayed the full weakness of his character, fainting with grief and begging for mercy. He appears to have resigned the throne, on condition that his son should succeed him. In the end, therefore, the procedure was a confusing mixture of deposition and abdication. Such problems as how parliament could act in the absence of the king, who was an essential element in any parliament, were slurred over and not fully resolved. Every effort was made to associate the whole of the political nation with what was done, and principles of both feudal and Roman law may be discerned in the procedures. It is striking that no attempt was made to alter the constitutional position of the monarchy, and it is clear that the task of deposing Edward II was greatly simplified by the fact that he was to be succeeded by his rightful heir.

The final chapter of Edward II's life has often been told, with the aid of an emotional and highly-coloured account written by the chronicler Geoffrey le Baker some thirty years later, which culminates in the disgusting scene in which Edward was murdered by means of a red-hot plumber's iron thrust up his anus. Much in this story belongs to the world of romance rather than of history, but the most remarkable story about Edward's fate is not Baker's, for all the chronicler's horrific accounts of the foul chamber in which Edward was confined. It is the account by a Genoese priest Manuel Fieschi who claimed to have heard confession from Edward. It tells the story of how Edward having been forewarned that his life was in danger, escaped from Berkeley Castle where he had been sent, killing a porter who was buried in his place. After a period in Ireland he went to France, where the Pope received him in Avignon. He then travelled to Cologne, and then to Italy where he became a hermit. The details of the story up to the escape from Berkeley are reliable. Fieschi was a papal notary, and such a man was not likely to fabricate a deliberate falsehood. He may have been deceived by an impostor, but the story is almost too surprising to have been invented. When Edward III was in Cologne in 1338 a man calling himself William le Galeys appeared, claiming to be the king's father, but there is no indication that this was taken seriously. Edward III may, however, have believed that his father was still alive; it would explain why his father's murderers were not hunted down after the mid-1330s. The truth of this matter can never be known, like the fate of the princes in the Tower. There is no doubt, however, that Edward's murder was planned with Mortimer's connivance and that a body generally believed to be his was buried at Gloucester. Even if Edward did not die at Berkeley, he played no further part in the history of the country he had misgoverned.

. . . . .

How can the disastrous events of Edward ɪɪ's reign be explained? One chronicler produced a splendidly implausible answer for the civil war of 1322:

It was no wonder, for the great lords of England were not all of one nation, but were muddled up with other nations, some Britons, some Saxons, some Danes, some Picts, some French, some Normans, some Spaniards, some Romans, some Hainaulters, some Flemings, and some other assorted nations, the which did not accord well with the kind blood of England.[14]

A contemporary poem condemned the period with a fierce morality. It claimed that falseness and pride were the cause of civil war; the knights of England should have been fighting in the Holy Land, and were unworthy 'lions in the hall, and hares in the field'.[15] Corruption was said to be rife. The most intelligent commentator was the author of the *Life of Edward II*. The English for him were characterized by the fatal qualities of pride, trickery and perjury. Evil doing was encouraged, as it was easy to obtain pardons if the court favourites were cultivated. 'It may be said that the whole evil originally proceeds from the court.'[16] Attempts to negotiate between the factions were doomed to fail, since 'peace between magnates is to be regarded with suspicion when the eminent princes have arrived at it not through love, but by force.'[17] There is clearly much truth in these observations, as there is in the same author's condemnation of Edward ɪɪ, who did nothing 'that ought to be preached in the market-place or upon the house-tops'.[18] The situation was, however, more complex than contemporaries could appreciate.

Two of the most distinguished historians of the period, T. F. Tout and J. Conway Davies, interpreted the political conflicts in terms of a clash of fundamental constitutional principles. Royal autocracy was challenged by demands for government with the consent and participation of the magnates. Particular stress was laid on baronial hostility to government through the king's household, and in particular the departments of the wardrobe and the chamber. It was suggested that the demand of the Ordainers that all the revenues of the land should be paid into the exchequer was intended to limit the independence of the household. It is unlikely, in fact, that the king and his opponents were so sharply divided over questions of administrative organization and of the responsibilities of individual departments. It was a generally accepted ideal that the exchequer should exercise a complete financial supervision, and it was only because of the pressures of war that the officials under Edward had failed to achieve this. It is striking that after 1322, when it would have been possible to create a strong, financially independent household, this was not done. Although many of the lands confiscated after 1322 were briefly handed over to the chamber, they were soon transferred to the exchequer. What the king objected to in the Ordinances was not questions of administrative detail, but the unacceptable limitation placed on his royal power. The matters that concerned him were his rights of patronage, his power to select his own ministers, to make grants of lands as he chose. It was unacceptable that he was bound to consult the baronage in parliament before he left the realm or made war. The question of household finance was far less important than that of household personnel.

Enough has already been said on the subject of the hated favourites, Gaveston and Despenser, but there were many others in the royal household who contributed to the widespread distrust and hatred of the court. John de Charlton, Despenser's predecessor as chamberlain, first appeared in royal service in the humble position of a constable leading infantry levies to Scotland in 1301. A Shropshire man, he rose rapidly in Edward II's service. In 1311 the Ordainers demanded his expulsion from the household, but he remained firmly in royal favour, and received custody of Builth Castle in 1314. Through his wife he had a claim to the lordship of Powys in Wales, but this was challenged by her uncle, Gruffydd de la Pole. This local issue became important on a national scale, for with Charlton receiving the king's support, Gruffydd obtained Lancaster's. The dispute bedevilled the negotiations between the king and his opponents that took place after Gaveston's death. Charlton had only obtained his bride through royal influence; his rise from relative obscurity to the status of a Marcher lord was bound to create jealousies, adding to the unpopularity of the king. Charlton's star waned, however, after 1318 when Despenser replaced him as chamberlain, and in 1321 he even joined the Marchers in their rebellion. In 1327 he won some favour with Isabella and Mortimer when he summarily executed the Earl of Arundel, a close associate of the Despensers.

The career of John de Charlton reveals something of the importance of patronage and local rivalries in this reign; that of a lesser household figure, Robert Lewer, demonstrates rather better the vicious and unprincipled character of the royal household. Lewer was another man who first appeared as an infantry constable under Edward I. He became a royal yeoman under Edward II, and although he was not of knightly rank he was given custody of Odiham Castle in 1311, holding it with a force of twenty-one squires and their pages, mainly drawn from the household. He, like Charlton, was singled out for expulsion from the household by the Ordainers: 'Item, Robert Lewer, archers, and such manner of ribaldry shall be removed from the king's pay, and not stay in his service except for war.'[19] Lewer did stay in the king's service, however, and began to build up an estate by questionable means. He deprived Isabella Bardolf of a manor by using a writ of privy seal in a manner prohibited under the Ordinances. His disaffection began when Odiham was taken from him and given to the younger Despenser. In 1320 he was arrested for 'trespasses, contempts and disobediences',[20] and he compounded his fault by threatening to cut up those responsible limb by limb – in the king's presence if necessary. He escaped from custody, and came back into favour in 1321, when the king needed experienced troops; he received Odiham back, and was put in command of the household infantry. He arrived late for the Scottish campaign of 1322, and left early. In the next year he revolted. He attacked the elder Despenser's estates, and ostentatiously gave some of his spoils as alms for those slain at Boroughbridge. He was eventually captured and as he refused to answer in court he was put to death by the appalling method of *peine forte et dure* – slowly squashed to death by heavy weights over a period of days. This was considered well-deserved by one writer, since Lewer had earlier murdered his mistress's husband.

Robert Lewer's career may have been exceptional, but the household contained other unsavoury characters. Gilbert de Middleton was a household knight, and in 1317 he committed one of the most notorious outrages of the reign, attacking and robbing the newly elected Bishop of Durham and two cardinals as they were going north for the consecration ceremony. Another household knight, John de Sapy, had been given custody of Durham during the vacancy. He was not anxious to give up his profitable charge, and was probably involved in the outrage. Robert de Sapy – probably John's brother, and another household knight – rebelled against the king after 1322. Roger Swynnerton who was admitted to the household in 1317 was a notorious criminal who earlier in the reign had forced the county court at Stafford to abandon its session: he had closed the doors and threatened to kill the sheriff. He was indicted for a murder in 1326.

The de la Beche family provided several household knights. William's career was uneventful, but Nicholas, having been loyal in 1322, was arrested in the next year. He recovered his lands after the collapse of the Despenser regime. John de la Beche, whose removal from the household had been requested in 1311, joined his father Philip in rebellion in 1322 and was only released from the Tower in 1326. The family were deeply implicated in the serious local rioting against Abingdon Abbey in 1327. It is not possible to work out all the cross-currents of intrigue and jealousy that permeated the royal household under Edward II, but it is evident that not only were many of those employed unpopular in their own right, but that Edward was also incapable of retaining the allegiance of men who owed a great deal to his patronage. The political instability of the country as a whole was mirrored within the household.

A study of the household reveals the immense importance of patronage. Successful rule in the Middle Ages, as in most periods, depended on establishing a proper system of rewards for service. In a period of military success, as under Edward I or Edward III, this did not present quite such acute problems as it did under Edward II, for rewards could be provided out of the profits of war, although there still remained the important questions of the allocation of ecclesiastical benefices, grants of wardships, constable-ships of royal castles and so forth. The system had to be balanced, and this Edward II was incapable of doing.

The scale of Edward's generosity towards Piers Gaveston was a major cause of the crisis that led to the appointment of the Ordainers in 1310. The provision in the Ordinances for the annulment of grants made since then was very import-ant. Cancellations of grants made to royal supporters, such as that ordered in 1316, made it hard for the king to reward his followers properly. In that autumn and in the following year the king made every effort to build up his support. Since grants of land were liable to be revoked, he made a series of indentures with magnates, granting them substan-tial annual fees in return for service. Twenty-three new household knights were created, bringing the total to sixty-three. This technique of buying support was expen-sive, however, and with the reforms following the treaty of Leake the strength of the household was reduced. In 1322 the knights numbered only thirty.

Edward was presented with some splendid oppor-tunities for the judicious exercise of patronage, but they were badly mismanaged. The division of the estates of the earldom of Gloucester might have been used to strengthen the position of the crown, but instead it provided a new element of dissension. Edward did not spread the net of patronage widely, and this was never more the case than in the years of Despenser dominance. In the forfeitures of the contrariants' lands Edward II had at his disposal the great-est territorial windfall that any medieval English monarch enjoyed. The estates could have been used to create a new loyal following: instead, the benefits of royal favour were shared out by the small clique of the Despensers and their cronies in a period of tyrannical rule. Edward lacked the political acumen to use patronage properly: the rebellions of such erstwhile favourites as Roger Damory, Hugh

Audley and Andrew Harclay are one demonstration of this.

Ecclesiastical patronage was also important. By elevating royal clerks to bishoprics a king could both reward his servants and create a loyal episcopal bench. Edward II achieved one striking success, when he obtained the elevation of Walter Reynolds, his former clerk, to Archbishop of Canterbury in 1313; his father had never managed to obtain the see for Burnell. At the end of the reign, however, he failed to provide for Robert Baldock. In 1323 the Pope nominated John Stratford as Bishop of Winchester and two years later he gave the see of Norwich to William Airmyn. Though Stratford and Airmyn were both royal clerks, the king was not pleased, and they, along with Adam Orleton, another royal servant nominated to a see by the Pope, supported Isabella in the final revolution of the reign. Edward's mismanagement of church appointments lost him the support of men who would normally have backed him fully. There had been some unseemly competition for ecclesiastical preferment among Edward I's clerks, but the problem reached a new dimension under his son, adding to the complex political divisions of the period.

Problems of patronage, along with the political vicissitudes of the reign, help to explain the many changes of personnel in the top echelons of the royal administration. In twenty years there were no less than fifteen changes of treasurer. John Walwyn, the putative author of the *Life of Edward II*, held the office for a mere five months before he was removed as a result of 'the importunity of sundry persons'.[21] There were ten keepers of the privy seal in the course of the reign, and eight of the wardrobe. In such a situation, there could be no dominant figures, like Burnell or Langton under Edward I; although Langton served Edward II for a time he never recaptured his former influence. There were many long-serving civil servants, like Walter of Norwich who was acceptable to all regimes, but there was an inevitable lack of continuity and cohesion in the administration.

The weakness of the government under Edward II should not be exaggerated. Edward I's reign had shown, with the crisis of 1297, that financial difficulties could have grave political consequences. In contrast, the well-informed *Life of Edward II* stated that Edward II was richer than any of his predecessors on the throne. In the earlier part of the reign there are certainly good reasons for linking the king's political difficulties with financial problems; Edward inherited a heavy debt from his father and had to depend on loans from the Frescobaldi, some towns, the Earl of Lincoln and even his own officials in the years leading to the Ordinances. Collection of the tax granted in 1309 was suspended for several months prior to the appointment of the Ordainers as a political weapon against the king. In 1312 the king's financial difficulties were such that he had recourse to the unpopular levy of tallage, an arbitrary tax imposed on the towns and royal demesnes. The Frescobaldi were expelled from the country by the Ordainers, and went bankrupt. A new lender emerged, however, in the form of the Genoese merchant Antonio Pessagno. He advanced £5,000 for the king's chamber expenses in December 1312, and within two years had lent some £111,000, of which £102,000 had been repaid. Included in this sum was £25,000 from Clement V, lent on the security of the English revenues in Gascony. Loans on this scale are indicative of real financial crisis in the years prior to Bannockburn, but they also show that the king was able to command some substantial independent financial resources. In 1315 the situation was so difficult that the magnates were asked to provide military service at their own expense and a new expedient in the form of loans from monastic houses was attempted.

A succession of grants began to ease the position; taxes were negotiated in 1313, 1315, 1316, 1319 and 1322. In addition aid was obtained from the clergy in 1315 and 1316, while in the later years of the reign the crown received substantial shares of the taxes imposed on the clergy by the papacy. In the absence of major campaigns in Scotland expenditure did not rise to the heights it had reached under Edward I and heavy deficits were avoided, partly as a result of more efficient control exercised by the exchequer. At the time of Lancaster's revolt in 1322 the crown was not in a state of financial crisis, and it can be argued that the earl and the Marchers had little option save rebellion, as they could not force the king into submission by withholding taxation as had been done in 1310. At the close of the Scottish campaign of 1322 the wardrobe officials were still in possession of £7,000 in cash, a situation inconceivable under Edward I. The acquisition of the contrariants' lands after Boroughbridge gave the crown a new financial strength; one estimate put their value at £12,000 a year. In addition, the last years of the reign saw a recovery in the wool trade, with a consequent rise in customs revenues. The government was in the exceptional position of possessing substantial reserves of cash. Of £7,000 received by the king at Porchester in 1325, intended for war with France, £4,000 was deposited in St Swithun's Priory, Winchester; the sheriff was ordered to take it back to Westminster a year later. The continued financial strength of the government at the very end of the reign is indicated by the discovery of £6,000 in Neath Abbey, not far from where the king was captured. Constitutional opposition would be effective against an impecunious king: rebellion was the only recourse available against a rich one.

The crown had considerable military resources. Certainly, the magnates were able to overawe the king on occasion with a show of strength, as they appeared in parliament with their armed retinues. Edward, however, could recruit troops by means of commissions of array in addition to relying on his household knights; in 1321–2 he did not face the same difficulties as Thomas of Lancaster in assembling an army. Further, the crown controlled a large network of castles. Civil war threatened in the weeks following the coronation in 1308, but the king entrusted a dozen castles to loyal household men, and gave instructions for new fortifications at the Tower. Orders went out for fifty-two royal castles to be put in a state of defence. Again in 1312 the victualling and garrisoning of various royal castles was ordered; £179 was spent on Bolsover and Horestone in Derbyshire. In 1317 twenty-two royal castles were given military garrisons and forty men were placed in Wallingford. In the crisis of 1321–2 no less than sixty-three castles were prepared for attack, and it is striking that while the royal forces managed to take a number of baronial strongholds, Lancaster's men had no success at Tickhill. In many cases the royal castles were in a dilapidated, almost ruined state – unfit to stand up to a serious siege – but their very existence was a deterrent to the king's enemies. In the final disaster in 1326 the government was caught unprepared. It was only two days after the queen's landing that the constable of Pleshey Castle was ordered to array troops in Essex. Without adequate preparations, the military resources of the crown were quite insufficient – but the final failure of the reign was essentially a political rather than a military one – many of those sent to raise troops simply refused to do so.

A study of the central government can provide only a partial understanding of the politics of Edward ii's reign. The complex cross-currents of magnate rivalry had part of their origins in local affairs. In 1311 the Earl of Gloucester was in dispute with Lancaster not over national issues but because of a feud between two of their retainers, Walter de Berningham and Henry de Segrave. Lancaster and Pembroke had a private dispute over the ownership of the manor of Thorpe Waterville which bedevilled relationships between the two men. Feud between Lancaster and Warenne erupted into private war in the north of England in 1317; Warenne had been involved in the abduction of Lancaster's wife Alice de Lacy – a deed which had the lady's apparent approval. The Berkeley family, major landowners in Gloucestershire, were long-standing clients of the Earl of Pembroke, but in 1318 they turned against him with a violent attack on one of his manors. They looked to the Mortimers for protection, and so became involved in the Marcher rising of 1321–2. Local disputes like this often became inextricably confused with national politics. Detailed study of the Marcher rising of 1321–2 has shown that opposition to the Despensers had considerable support from the gentry and small landowners, but that in many cases these men engaged in attacks on the property of others in a way which had little connection

with the issues of high politics. They simply took advantage
of the rising to pursue their own ends, so exacerbating the
situation.

Political loyalties were hard to retain in this confusing
world of local rivalries. Even family bonds of marriage or
kinship might divide as well as unite, as the feud between
John Charlton and Gruffydd de la Pole demonstrates. The
old patterns of feudal lordship had lost their force by the
fourteenth century: in their place, lords were retaining men
in their service by means of indentures, promising them
fees and robes. While this system enabled magnates to form
large retinues, it lacked stability, for it was not strongly
based on land as was the old feudalism. Robert Holland's
desertion of Thomas of Lancaster is but the most striking of
many examples of the bonds of lordship breaking down.

Various attempts were made to reinforce the tenuous
bonds between men. The Boulogne agreement of 1308 was
fortified by threats of excommunication to try to make it
more effective and binding. Those responsible for Gaveston's death swore oaths of mutual self-protection on the
gospels, and drew up formal documents to the same effect.
Increasingly, political agreements, like that between Pembroke, Badlesmere and Damory, included heavy financial
penalties. In 1322 Badlesmere forced Peter de Maulay,
when the latter was threatening to abandon the baronial
cause, to agree to the marriage of his eldest son with Robert
Clifford's daughter and to pay £20,000 if he went against the
terms of the agreement. The many recognizances of the
Despenser period of rule fit into this pattern. The necessity
for such agreements testifies to the weakness not the
strength of the political ties of this period. Agreements
amounting to little more than blackmail could not be a
substitute for genuine commitment to a cause.

The violence of politics mirrored the brutality of the age.
Edward II could look to the example of his father-in-law,
Philip IV of France, who punished two knights for adultery
with his daughters-in-law with every possible indignity,
culminating with being flayed alive. In England gang warfare in which the gentry and aristocracy participated was
depressingly common. Thomas of Lancaster had shown his

preference for gaining his own way by force rather than by recourse to the law as early as 1305, in a vicious feud with Tutbury Priory. Those who were supposed to enforce the law were regarded with some contempt:

And justices, sheriffs, mayors, bailiffs, if I shall read aright, They can out of the faire day make the dark night.[22]

It is impossible to quantify the breakdown of law and order, but it is plain that the whole equilibrium of society was fragile in this period. The lack of opportunities for advancement through war in Scotland or abroad, the severe economic crisis of the famine and the failure of the government to respond adequately to the situation, all contributed to the widespread malaise.

There was a creditable reluctance to engage in the ultimate act of civil war, yet the reign of Edward II saw a series of executions with few parallels. The violence of the times may provide part of the explanation for them, while it is plain that the king's incorrigibility left Lancaster and his associates little alternative to execution as a means of ridding the country of Gaveston. At the same time there is a legal explanation. The development and definition of the doctrine of treason provided a formal justification for much that was done. Edward I had treated his Welsh and Scottish opponents as traitors rather than as enemies and while his reign saw only one Englishman, Thomas Turberville, executed for treason since he had spied for the French, the precedents were set for the executions of the next reign. The crime of levying war against the king, with banners unfurled, was clearly defined as treason. The manner of trial derived from military law, and the simple rehearsal of the accused man's record by the king was sufficient to obtain conviction. There was no defence against a charge of notoriety. So, although according to Magna Carta all free men had the right to trial by peers, or by the law of the land, it was possible by Edward II's reign to try and execute even the highest in the land by a most arbitrary form of justice. Lancaster, Damory, Badlesmere, the Despensers; the list is a long one, and in all cases some legal justification could be found for their executions. Scarcely a major town did not have portions of an alleged traitor displayed over the main gate in the course of the reign.

There were major issues at stake in Edward II's reign, and some important constitutional developments took place, as will emerge in the discussion of parliament in chapter four. The main determinants of the political rivalries, however, were those of personal antipathies and private jealousies and ambitions, rather than constitutional principles. Questions of the financial independence of the royal household were hardly as significant as hostility to the royal favourites. It is a mistake to try to interpret the political history of the period in terms of the antagonisms of parties possessing clearly articulated views as to how the country should be ruled. In the final collapse Isabella and Mortimer triumphed not on a programme of reform, but on the simple platform of the quarrel with the Despensers and Robert Baldock.

Although Edward II's personal incompetence lay at the root of much that went wrong in his reign, his deposition could not transform the whole character of English politics at a stroke. In many ways the three years of Isabella and Mortimer's rule form a postscript to the reign of the unfortunate Edward II, rather than a prelude to the successes of Edward III.

The coronation of the fourteen-year-old Edward III saw no transformation in the formal position of the monarchy. John de Sulleye, a former household knight, asked if the new king would swear the same additional clause of the coronation oath as his father had done, and was firmly told that if he did not, he would not be crowned. As Edward was too young to rule directly, a regency council was set up. Initially, Mortimer stayed in the background, while the council was headed by Thomas of Lancaster's brother Henry. The acts of 1322 were revoked as far as possible, but there was no full revival of Earl Thomas's programme. The Ordinances were not disinterred, and Henry made no claim to the stewardship. He soon found it difficult to maintain his position in face of Mortimer's greedy and unscrupulous ambition. His son-in-law Thomas Wake, who had played an important part in the revolution of 1326–7, was replaced as keeper of the Tower, and his other supporters were steadily removed from their posts. The financial exactions of Queen Isabella were a matter for bitter complaint. She obtained the younger Despenser's personal wealth, while Mortimer took over the elder Despenser's lordship of Denbigh, and most of the Earl of Arundel's Marcher estates. His elevation to the brand-new title of Earl of March in 1328 must have been galling to many of the nobility. It was said that his arrogance was such that he refused to allow the king precedence, but that he kept pace with him, and even pushed his way in front. No one was allowed to refer to him save by his title. He established himself as a more powerful landowner in the Welsh Marches than the younger Despenser had been, and his wealth was estimated at £8,000 a year.

The failure of the campaign of 1327 against the Scots, and the consequent shameful peace, added fuel to the flames of discontent. In the autumn of 1328 Henry of Lancaster, Thomas Wake and their allies refused to attend parliament. John Stratford, Bishop of Winchester, with Wake, came to London and set out their political programme. The king should live of his own – that is, rely on his own financial resources – he should have sufficient treasure available for war, and should accept the advice of his council. Law and order should be maintained. These ideas did not owe much to the programme, such as it had been, of Thomas of Lancaster but were well attuned to the situation of the late 1320s. Rebellion was, however, unsuccessful. Mortimer counter-attacked early in 1329, and forced Henry of Lancaster, who was going blind, to come to terms. The king's uncles, the Earls of Kent and Norfolk, deserted Lancaster's cause. Kent's reward was to be arrested and executed for treason. Lancaster himself was far from safe, but it was clear that the prospects for a further rebellion against the strongly entrenched Mortimer were poor. The regime proved highly vulnerable, however, to a palace revolution.

The coup against Isabella and Mortimer was dramatic. Mortimer had tried to prevent the young king from achieving any independence. He had placed spies in his entourage, and even tried to poison his young queen's mind against him. Edward, however, had none of his father's weakness, and his ability to choose the right men to support his cause was evident even at this early stage of his career. Richard de Bury, a noted bibliophile, had long been in his service; William de Montague was the son of a household knight, and, like another of the king's confidants, Robert Ufford, had been a royal ward. The little group made careful preparations, even soliciting papal aid. Bury explained in a letter that only documents containing the words *pater sancte* should be taken as expressing the king's own wishes.

The coup took place at Nottingham, where a council was summoned to meet in October 1330. Mortimer was nervous; he ordered Lancaster to lodge a mile away from the castle. A tense situation was exacerbated by rumours that Mortimer intended to usurp the throne. Montague told the young king that it was better to *eat* dog than to be eaten *by* the dog, and the conspirators acted. Nottingham Castle stood on a rock honeycombed with underground passages and chambers. The constable, in league with the plotters, admitted them through a postern gate to a passage which led them straight to the keep. Hugh Turplington, steward of the household, was killed, but otherwise there was little resistance. Mortimer was seized and dragged down to the hall, with Isabella wailing 'Good son, good son, have pity on gentle Mortimer'.[23] Her words were in vain. Mortimer was taken to London and tried for treason before the peers of parliament. His death, which featured all the indignities accorded to the younger Despenser, was the last in that series of bloody executions of high-ranking men which began with the beheading of Gaveston. Queen Isabella retired from public life at Castle Rising, and the personal rule of Edward III began.

The dramatic events at Nottingham were directed solely at the persons of Isabella and Mortimer, and did not alter the constitutional role of the monarchy. Lancaster's opposition had tried to create a wide basis of support against Mortimer, and failed; Montague and the young Edward III succeeded with the backing of a mere two dozen armed men. Personalities mattered far more in this period than abstract principles of reform. It was dislike of Gaveston that had held the opposition together in the early years of Edward II's reign; after his death, the programme set out in the Ordinances did not attract sufficient loyalty to ensure continued unity. The Earl of Hereford found little difficulty in joining the royalist cause after Gaveston's murder, abandoning it again in 1321. Then, it was the Despensers' affront to the liberties of the Marcher lords, and their acquisitiveness that led to the outbreak of civil war, rather than any political convictions of an abstract kind. Historians have tried to impose a structure of party politics on Edward II's reign, and have seen a revival of 'Lancastrian' opposition in the later 1320s, but on close examination the politics of this period lose any clarity of outline, dissolving into a confused welter of complex criss-crossing allegiances dominated by selfish ambitions and hatred.

4

Counsel and Consent

The Development of Parliament

The early history of parliament has proved to be almost as dangerous a battleground for historians as the field of Bannockburn was for Edward II. Although there is no evidence to suggest that contemporaries were in any doubt as to what a parliament was, there are difficult problems of definition. The composition of early parliaments varied widely, from a relatively informal gathering of the king's councillors to a well-planned meeting including lay and ecclesiastical magnates, and representatives of shires, boroughs and lower clergy. The function of the assemblies varied widely, from the discussion of great affairs of state and the granting of taxation, to legislation, judicial business and the hearing of private petitions. There is no medieval Erskine May to serve as a reliable guide. The one early fourteenth-century text describing parliament gives a highly idealized picture which purports to describe the institution as it existed in the time of Edward the Confessor, when of course there was no such thing. The application of the logic of Occam's Razor, paring away at the inessentials, has led to some absurdities, with meetings clearly designated as parliaments in contemporary records being declared by historians to be nothing of the sort, since they fail to fulfil certain arbitrary definitions. The aim of this chapter is to examine parliament in its formative years up to the beginning of Edward III's reign, looking at both its functions and its composition. There were to be further important developments under Edward III, but these will emerge in the discussion of the domestic politics of his reign in chapter eight.

The earliest official parliamentary record which gives a reasonably full account of the proceedings in chronological order is the roll for the Lincoln Parliament of 1316. It reveals something of the scale and scope of parliament as it had evolved by the early fourteenth century. Writs ordering the attendance of the prelates, magnates and representatives of laity and clergy had been issued in October 1315; the assembly first met in the Dean of Lincoln's house on 28 January. William Inge, a royal justice, made the opening speech. He explained that it had been decided to delay discussion of the major issue of the Scottish war until the Earl of Lancaster arrived. In the meantime, the routine work of parliament was to proceed. While the king enjoyed himself rowing, the Bishops of Norwich and Exeter with the Earls of Pembroke and Richmond were nominated to act on his behalf. Men were appointed to hear the many petitions presented in parliament; for the most part these auditors were experienced officials. The complaints of the clergy which had been presented earlier were answered on the king's behalf by the Earl of Hereford.

The important business of the parliament began on 12 February, once Lancaster had arrived. The king had the reasons for the summoning of parliament recited before the magnates – the record makes no mention of the presence of the representatives. What Edward II wanted was advice and assistance with regard to Scotland. In fact, when the magnates met on the following day in the chapter-house, and on the next in the Carmelite Friary, they firstly agreed to repeal price regulations set up in the previous year, and secondly discussed a statute on the appointment of sheriffs. On 17 February the Bishop of Norwich in the presence of the full assembly summarized what had been done. He announced that the king wished to see both the Ordinances of 1311 and the forest boundaries agreed under Edward I fully observed. This concession was designed to pave the way for his next move. He turned to the Earl of Lancaster, declared the king's friendship for him, and asked to become the head of the royal council. The earl replied, setting out his conditions, and was duly sworn in as a councillor. Three days later the magnates and the knights of the shire made a grant of one footsoldier from each vill to fight in Scotland, and the urban representatives promised a tax of a fifteenth. The king, with the consent of the magnates, announced that the feudal host was to be summoned against the Scots.

Many other important issues came up in this parliament. There was the question of the division of the Gloucester inheritance following the death of the earl over eighteen months previously. His widow delayed matters by claiming to be pregnant, and the demands of Hugh Despenser the younger and his wife for their share of the lands were put off since they had not obtained the necessary writ ordering the countess's belly to be examined by discreet knights and ladies to see if her pregnancy was feigned. A learned committee set up to discuss the matter failed to produce an answer. Despenser was also involved in a brawl with John de Ros in Lincoln Cathedral. Such a breach of the peace was particularly serious in time of parliament, and damages of £10,000 were claimed for contempt of the king. Both men were handed over to the marshal of the household, and though they were soon released without paying fines, it was not until 1320 that Despenser was finally pardoned.

The feud between Bartholomew Badlesmere and the citizens of Bristol was also discussed in parliament, as was the long-standing dispute between John Charlton and Lancaster's retainer Gruffydd de la Pole. The Bishop of Durham raised the question of his financial rights; he objected to the recent invasion of his palatinate by the notorious Jack the Irishman. Hugh de Courtenay made one of his periodic attempts to gain his rightful inheritance of the earldom of Devon, which had been denied him by Edward I. There were many minor matters raised by petitioners. A German merchant sought satisfaction from the citizens of Ipswich who had defrauded him of his cargo of dried fish. A man asked that the exchequer cease pestering him for arrears of taxation for which he was not liable.

The Lincoln Parliament with its wide range of business and comprehensive composition provides a good example of an early parliament. It was not wholly typical, of course.

It was not normal to hasten the routine business through in advance of discussion of the great affairs of state, and the usual venue for parliaments was Westminster. How far is it possible to trace back the various elements which can be discerned in the proceedings of 1316 into the reign of Edward I?

The first parliament of Edward I's reign, in 1275, was almost as wide-ranging in composition as the Lincoln Parliament over forty years later, with prelates, lay magnates, knights of the shire and a large number of urban representatives taking part. This pattern was not followed on all occasions, however. An assembly might be termed parliament although only a limited number of prelates, earls and barons were present, and it was not until late in Edward II's reign that there was any real consistency in the membership. The one element that was invariably present was that of the officials of the king's council: the chancellor, the treasurer, the barons of the exchequer, the keeper of the wardrobe, and the justices. It is, however, initially the functions of parliament that must be examined, rather than the composition, if the nature of the assembly is to be revealed.

In 1280 Edward I made it plain that the most important matter to be discussed in parliament was 'the weighty business of his realm and of his foreign lands'.[1] The reported dialogue between the king and Roger Bigod at the Salisbury Parliament in 1297 over the proposed expedition to Gascony provides a rare glimpse of a debate on a major matter of state. Parliament was the best place to raise important questions so that they would receive maximum publicity. It was in parliament in 1305 that the new organization for the government of Scotland was revealed, and two years later the main item on the agenda was 'to treat of the ordinance and stability of Scotland'.[2] Yet it was not until the magnates drafted the Ordinances of 1311 that there was a definitive statement binding the king to obtain consent for foreign war from the baronage in parliament. Edward I certainly did not always discuss such issues in full parliament. The decision to make war on the Welsh in 1282 was reached at a council held at Devizes. In 1297 the king certainly never obtained full consent for his expedition to Flanders. Even as late as 1324, by which time the Ordinances had been repealed, it was specifically stated that discussion of the war in Gascony was to take place before the magnates in a council rather than in parliament. However, by 1332 when Edward III put the question of Scotland to a council at York, it was agreed that it was so important that it should only be discussed in parliament. No such parliamentary monopoly of debate on major issues had existed under Edward I.

The great affairs of state were the concern of the magnates, not of the representatives of shire and borough. The earls and barons alone could not, however, make grants of taxation, for their consent was not binding on the population as a whole. Taxes assessed on a valuation of movable property and paid by all save the very poorest required a general consent that could only be obtained through a system of representation. By Edward I's reign there were ample precedents for the summons of men who were to act on behalf of county and urban communities. In a classic article, J. G. Edwards examined the way in which the formulae of the writs of summons evolved. In 1283 the representatives were to have full powers – plena potestas – on behalf of their local communities. By 1290 the knights of the shire were to come with 'full powers for themselves and the whole community of the county, to give counsel and consent for themselves and the community to those matters which the earls, barons and magnates shall determine'.[3] For the so-called Model Parliament of 1295 they were to have full powers 'to do what shall be ordained by common counsel'.[4] The reason for demanding that they should have such powers was to ensure that there was no possibility of their constituents later claiming that they had not authorized the representatives to make grants of taxation. When knights were summoned to a second assembly in 1283, at which there was to be no request for taxation, no mention was made of full powers. Again, in 1294 when two sets of knights were summoned, one to give counsel and consent, the other 'to hear and do what shall be more fully explained to them',[5] it was only the first group who were to come with full powers.

The writs of summons, by referring to the consent to be provided by the representatives, seem to imply that royal requests for taxation might be refused. Yet recent arguments, which are not wholly convincing, have questioned this assumption. An American scholar, Gaines Post, developed the implication of Roman law for English parliamentary representation. When Edward I summoned the clergy to parliament in 1295 he used a maxim taken from Justinian, *quod omnes tangit ab omnibus approbetur* 'what touches all should be approved by all'.[6] For Post, this was 'a well-established rule of law, recognized in church and state, in Roman-law and common-law countries alike'.[7] It bound the king to summon representatives to consent to matters affecting the people, but this in no way amounted to popular sovereignty. Consent was 'not voluntary, but procedural', and in effect the representatives were bound to give their approval to decisions of the king and his council. Another historian, G. L. Harriss, has taken the argument further. Again according to Roman law, the king had an undoubted right to demand taxation in a case of urgent necessity. He would have to establish that a genuine emergency existed, and if the magnates agreed that it did, then the representatives would be bound to offer aid. Consent had to be obtained, but could not be refused when there was an acknowledged necessity. Such arguments reduce the role of representatives to little more than a rubber stamp.

What was the reality of the situation? By the time that the parliament rolls are reasonably explicit about grants of taxation – in Edward III's reign – necessity was stressed. In 1339 the commons replied to a request for a grant 'and as for the necessity which he [the king] is in to be aided by his people, the commons who do this know well that he should be greatly aided, and they are fully willing to do this, as they have always done in the past'.[8] Exceptionally, however, they said that on this occasion they could only agree on a tax after consultation with their local communities. In 1344 they agreed to a tax after 'the necessity of our lord the king was shown to the commons by his council'.[9] This situation should not necessarily be read back into Edward I's reign. In 1275 and 1290 grants were made even though no necessity existed, and in the critical year of 1297 a specific appeal to the doctrine of necessity was only made in the context of Archbishop Winchelsey's threats to use ecclesiastical sanctions, such as excommunication, against royal officials. The king's expositions of his need for money were not couched in terms of Roman law, but were straightforward statements of his position, sometimes using feudal terminology. He asked his subjects 'to do their duty towards their lord with goodwill, as good and loyal people ought, and are bound to do towards their liege lord in so great and high an affair'.[10] The Roman law phrase *quod omnes tangit* was only used once by Edward I. This was no principle binding the king; it was a tag which an intelligent chancery clerk thought would appeal to the clergy. It is hard to imagine the knights and burgesses in parliament, men of little theoretical learning but weighty practical experience, acting within a framework of Roman law.

On occasion there was a very real element of consent involved in the negotiation of taxes, although it has to be admitted that leadership lay with the magnates rather than with the representatives. In 1280 a request for a land tax of 4d from every ploughland was refused, and no grant made. The Earl of Gloucester in 1294 successfully led opposition to the king's demand for a tax of a third or sixth, and it was duly reduced to a tenth and sixth, with the higher rate paid by the towns and royal demesne. In 1300 the conditions set upon a grant of a twentieth were so severe that the king declined to accept it. Under Edward II, in the course of the negotiations after Gaveston's death, the barons promised to do all they could to ensure that the king received a suitable tax for the Scottish war, when they met with their peers and the commons. This suggests that it was not always easy to obtain a grant even for such an obvious necessity as war. The controversial tract known as the *Modus Tenendi Parliamentum*, written in the early 1320s, certainly assumed that the representatives could refuse taxes as well as grant them. In practice, however, they were normally in no position to reject the demands of the crown although they were increasingly able to use their power to grant taxes as an opportunity to demand redress of grievances. The representatives were not asked to parliament simply to record an automatic assent to decisions reached by king and council. They were themselves a part of the community of the realm, and as such participated in a genuine process of consultation and consent. Study of the parallel situation in France suggests that although royal lawyers made full use of the concepts of Roman law, notably those of necessity and *plena potestas*, those who paid taxes took a very practical view of the question of consent.

Not all taxes were granted in parliament. Although in 1275 a large number of urban representatives gave their consent in parliament to the new customs duty of 6s 8d on each sack of wool exported, the *maltolt* of 40s a sack was agreed with the merchants in 1294 with no reference to parliament. Although Edward promised in the Confirmation of the Charters of 1297 that he would not in future levy this or any other duty without the consent of the community of the realm, he negotiated an additional duty of 3s 4d in 1303 solely with the foreign merchants trading in England. It was presumably because this had not been done in parliament that it was abolished in the Ordinances of 1311. That was far from the end of the story of separate negotiations with the merchants, and it was not until 1362 that Edward III eventually conceded a statute giving parliament rights over the grant of all customs duties.

Although clerical representatives often attended parliament, taxes on the clergy were normally negotiated in separate assemblies, as in 1294. When Edward II tried to obtain a grant from them in parliament at Lincoln in 1316, they temporized, and the matter was put off to be determined in a purely ecclesiastical assembly. So it was only the general taxes on movable property that were normally granted in parliament; where a tax was paid only by a specific group of the king's subjects, separate negotiations often proved simpler. However, in 1303 when the king tried to obtain the agreement of the English merchants to an additional duty similar to that conceded by the foreign traders, he was met with an unexpected refusal.

At the Lincoln Parliament of 1316, much time was devoted to judicial business. For two of the most notable historians of parliament, H. G. Richardson and G. O. Sayles, the legal aspects of the institution were paramount. In its origins in Henry III's reign, parliament had been an occasion when the king and his council were present together with the chief administrative officials and the royal justices, so that cases could be heard and petitions attended to without difficulty. In about 1290 the author of *Fleta*, a legal treatise, described parliament:

> The king has his court in his council in his parliaments, when prelates, earls, barons and others learned in the law are present. And doubts are determined there regarding judgement, new remedies are devised for wrongs newly brought to light, and there also justice is dispensed to everyone according to his deserts.[11]

The surviving parliamentary records from Edward I's reign largely deal with the hearing of cases and petitions.

The king's council, largely consisting of his ministers and justices, dominated the judicial business of parliament. In major cases, however, judgement might be made by a wider group. When in 1292 the *cause célèbre* of the private war between the Earls of Hereford and Gloucester came up in parliament, judgement that Hereford should lose his liberty of Brecon was made 'by the archbishops, bishops, earls, barons and the whole of the council of the lord king'.[12] In another major case involving a magnate – the charge of treason against Nicholas Segrave in 1305 – the earls and barons formed part of the judicial tribunal. The bishops were not involved this time, since the judgement might be one of blood. By Edward II's reign, there was a greater degree of definition, with the great council of the magnates in parliament being distinguished from the normal royal council. On one occasion the latter body declared that matters placed before them were so important that they should go before the great council in parliament. The notion of a parliamentary peerage was developing fast.

In 1311 the Ordainers spoke of 'the common consent of the baronage, and that in parliament',[13] but in 1312 the earls responsible for Gaveston's death were referring to 'the common assent of peers'.[14] By 1312 it was the peers of the land, the magnates in parliament, by whose judgement the Despensers were exiled.

The fact that parliament was a court gave it a very special status. The normal course of the law came to a halt during the time that parliament was in session, and all those present were under a special protection. In 1290 Bogo de Clare was fined £1,000 for summoning the Earl of Cornwall to appear before the Archbishop of Canterbury during parliament. In 1315 when the Archdeacon of Norfolk cited the king's niece, the Countess of Warenne, to appear in a clerical court, and did so in parliament, this was said to be 'in manifest shame of the king and in contempt of him to the extent of twenty thousand pounds and in derogation of his crown and liberty'.[15]

Not only was parliament a place where cases were determined which could not be dealt with in lower courts, it was also there that wrongs could easily be brought to the king's attention by means of petitions. Anyone could present a petition; the view that in Edward I's reign the normal way of doing this was to use the services of the representatives has long been exploded. Indeed, in 1299 the City of London appointed four men to present the business of the city in parliament, although in that year there were no representatives elected in response to the royal summons. By Edward II's reign the knights of the shire were presenting petitions on behalf of their counties, but it was not until Edward III's time that it became clear that petitions put forward by MPs had a greater chance of success than those presented privately. The precise mechanism of petitioning is still mysterious; how, for example, did the garrison of Kirkintilloch in Scotland arrange to present a petition seeking payment of arrears of wages to the king in parliament in 1305?

It would be wrong to lay too much stress on the judicial aspects of parliament. Petitioning probably took place in every parliament until 1332, when there was none in the first parliament of the year. Yet as early as 1280 Edward I tried to have as many petitions as possible dealt with at lower levels, so as to clear the decks for the discussion of major issues. A decade later a change in the character of parliament was noted by the author of a curious work, the *Mirror of Justices*, whose remarks provide something of an antidote to the definition given by *Fleta*. He stated that:

It is an abuse that whereas parliaments ought to be held for the salvation of souls of trespassers, twice a year and at London, they are now held but rarely and at the king's will for the purpose of obtaining aids and collection of treasure.[16]

This writer identified sin with crime, and by the salvation of souls he meant the dispensing of justice. With the increasing pressure of war finance in the 1290s there was a shift in emphasis in parliamentary business. Representatives were attending with greater frequency in order to grant taxes, and although the judicial element was throughout an intrinsic and essential part of the institution, it was no more than a part of the whole.

One last, very important, function of parliament remains to be discussed – that of legislation. The preamble to Westminster I, drawn up in 1275, reads:

These are the establishments of King Edward, son of King Henry, made at Westminster in his first general parliament after his coronation after the close of Easter in the third year of his reign, by his council and by the assent of the archbishops, bishops, abbots, priors, earls, barons and the community of the land summoned there.[17]

This sounds as if parliament was firmly established as the place where legislation should be enacted by means of the widest possible consent. Unfortunately, matters were not so clear cut. Edward I's later statutes did not, for the most part, have similar preambles, and although parliament had an obvious convenience for the promulgation of legislation, it was not invariably used. In particular, in the doubtful ground between administrative pronouncement and statutory legislation, important enactments were certainly implemented without parliamentary consent. Clumsily drafted statutes might be modified with no reference back to parliament. In 1283 the statute of Acton Burnell was agreed in what can have been only a small gathering, consisting of those men who stayed on when parliament was transferred from Shrewsbury to the chancellor's nearby manor. Likewise the statute of Stepney of 1299, dealing with coinage questions, was formulated after parliament moved to Stepney from Westminster. Such meetings were termed parliaments, but consisted of little more than the king's immediate councillors. They were not large gatherings at which a substantial measure of consent could have been obtained.

In Edward II's reign there came closer definition of the legislative function of parliament. In 1312 the earls, led by Lancaster and Warwick, stated that if the laws and customs of the realm were inadequate, they should be changed after popular complaint: this should be done by the king and his prelates, earls and barons, and established by common assent. The council in 1318 declared that it required great deliberation in parliament to change the law, and in 1322 the statute of York concluded with a clause which, while attracting little attention from contemporaries, has generated much comment from historians:

But the matters which may be established for the estate of our lord the king or of his heirs, and for the estate of the realm and people, are to be treated, granted and established in parliament by our lord the king and with the assent of the prelates, earls and barons, and the community of the realm, as has been the custom in times past.[18]

The prime purpose of the statute of York was to annul the Ordinances of 1311, and turn the clock back. The Ordinances were said to have limited royal power wrongfully, and any similar provisions which might be made in future were to be null and void. It was not politic, even in the heady days after the victory of Boroughbridge, to produce a wholly negative statement which could be read as preventing any future change in the laws and customs of the realm, so this final clause set out the proper way in which legislation might be carried out in future. It is not easy to determine precisely to what matters the clause referred. The phraseology of 'the estate of our lord the king' and 'the estate of the realm and people' was intended to apply to the normal legislative and political functions of parliament; what was excluded from consideration was anything relating to 'the royal power' of the king or 'the estate of the crown'. Matters such as the appointment of royal officials, or the king's right to make war, which had featured in the Ordinances, would not come within the competence of parliament. There is no evidence to suggest that contemporaries had the difficulties in distinguishing between these various matters that have plagued historians; they were well aware of what questions should be put before parliament.

The term 'community of the realm' in the clause presents further thorny problems. Did its use imply that the representative element in parliament was being given a place in the legislative function of parliament, or was it merely synonymous with the peerage? The phrase 'as has been the custom in times past' might suggest the latter. When in 1312 Pembroke, Warenne and Percy made promises on behalf of 'the community of the realm', it is hard to imagine that they meant anything more than the magnates. In 1314 the 'archbishops, bishops, earls and barons'[19] asked for maximum prices to be imposed on various foodstuffs. They did not describe themselves as the community of the realm, but in the writs implementing the new regulations the royal chancery described the petition as the work of the magnates 'and others of the community of the realm'. In such terms, it is possible that the statute of York was not making any reference to the commons at all.

Yet in most cases where the term community is used in a parliamentary context in Edward II's reign, the representatives were involved. In 1314 a petition concerning legal abuses, directed against the magnates and clearly deriving from the representatives in parliament, was said to be from 'the community of England'. At Lincoln in 1316 when the magnates agreed to the issue of a feudal summons, they were not described as 'the community of the realm', but when the knights of the shire joined with them in making the grant of one footsoldier from each vill, the term was employed. Certainly it was possible for very unrepresentative groups to claim to act on behalf of the community: a striking example is a petition about road conditions in Stratford from 'the community of the land, namely those of east London'.[20] Far more significant, however, is a petition from the knights and burgesses in parliament in 1320, noted in the margin of the record as being from 'the whole community of the land'.

It was in the early 1320s that the *Modus Tenendi Parliamentum* was written, almost certainly by a royal clerk intimately concerned with the business of parliament. It included the remarkable statement that two knights of the shire should have a greater voice in granting or refusing taxation than the greatest earl in the land. Although this was not an official document, it is surely significant that such ideas were being voiced at about the time that the statute of York was being drafted. It is interesting to note that when in 1310 Edward had issued letters patent authorizing the Ordainers to act, he had addressed himself to 'the prelates, earls and barons of the realm',[21] but when a clerk came to copy this out in 1322 he added 'and commons' to the list, clearly thinking that they should have a place in such a document.

The statute of York of 1322 was not intended to be novel. Its wording does not look unusual when set against the preamble of the first statute of Westminster of 1275, and the conception it reveals of legislation differed little from that expressed by the magnates in 1312. However, changes had been taking place in parliament with regard to the role of the commons, which meant that the conventional phrases of the statute might be understood in a different sense from their meaning in Edward I's day. The purpose of the statute was to restore royal authority after Lancaster's rebellion. It did not aim to allocate a new position of power to the commons, but its final clause gave a measure of recognition to the gains that they had made.

The events of 1327 show far better than the statute of York the place that the commons had come to occupy. The deputation which went to see Edward II at Kenilworth included knights and burgesses as well as prelates, earls, barons and possibly representatives of the lower clergy. Still more significantly, in the first parliament of Edward III's reign a whole series of petitions were presented by the commons, describing themselves as 'the community of the land', to the king and council. Legislation was duly based on these articles. By now the role of the representatives was not simply to accede to demands for taxation and report back to their localities on the business transacted in parliament, but was also to petition for administrative action and legislative change. The basis of their authority was their control over the grant of taxation, but the fact that they alone in parliament could be considered to represent the whole realm should not be forgotten. The *Modus Tenendi Parliamentum* went so far as to argue that the king could hold parliament with the community of the realm in the absence of the magnates. The presence of the knights of the shire, burgesses, and clerical representatives was in his admittedly extreme view quite sufficient. An early fifteenth-century poem was to summarize the position of the elected members of parliament thus:

We are servants, sent from the shires to present grievances, and to speak for their profit, not to grant money wrongly, but only for war, and if we be false to those that we represent, we are not worthy of our hire.[22]

The argument of this chapter so far has concentrated upon the various functions performed by parliament: political, financial, judicial and legislative. No one of these should be regarded as having primacy over the others, but as the institution developed, so the emphasis changed. In the early stages of the evolution of parliament, the judicial elements were more obviously predominant. As the pressures of war intensified in the 1290s, and with them the crown's demands for financial aid, so the representative character of parliament became more significant. In time it was this which was to give the English parliament much of its unique character.

For a fuller picture of what parliament was like it is necessary to turn from its functions to look at the men who

attended. How regularly did they come? Was the composition of parliament confined to those who appeared in
response to a formal royal summons? What sort of
men were elected as representatives? To understand the
medieval parliament it is necessary to try to forget the
inevitable preconceptions that arise from the knowledge of
the assembly as it exists today.

The modern division of parliament into a House of Lords
and a House of Commons was slow to evolve. The author of
the *Modus Tenendi Parliamentum* talked of six grades: the
king, the prelates, the representatives of the lower clergy,
the magnates, the knights of the shire, and lastly the
burgesses. There was, however, a fundamental difference
between those who were summoned individually by writ –
the magnates – and the representatives who were elected in
response to writs sent to the communities of shire and
borough. In practice many of those asked to attend might
not come, while a multitude of others who were not invited
were often present during parliament, even though they
could not participate in much of the business.

The magnates were poor attenders. On occasion, some
were even ordered to stay away, as in 1302 when Latimer,
Clifford and four others were asked not to desert their posts
in Scotland. In 1307 none were excused attendance at the
Carlisle parliament, but at most fifty-seven out of the
hundred and sixty-seven individuals summoned actually
came. Even when three earls and twenty-four lay magnates
were threatened with forfeiture of their estates, only ten
appeared. In 1315 some petitions could not be answered in
parliament, because the few magnates present were not
prepared to accept the responsibility of judgement without
the assent of all their peers. When less than half the magnates answered the summons in 1332, all that could be done
was to advise Edward III to postpone the assembly. The
record of magnate attendance in parliament provides a
valuable corrective to the view that the magnates' aim was
to gain control of royal government; for many of them,
participation in the councils of the realm was an unwelcome
chore.

The magnates who did attend parliament did not come

alone: they brought a body of retainers with them. In 1303 Robert FitzPayn promised to serve Aymer de Valence with a small troop of men both in parliament and at tournaments. The political troubles of Edward ii's reign resulted in men bringing very large followings with them: Thomas of Lancaster is said to have come with a thousand horse and one thousand five hundred foot in 1312, while 'the retinue of the Earl of Hereford, strengthened by a crowd of Welsh, wild men from the woodlands, was neither paltry nor mean.'[23] Prohibitions on appearing armed at parliament were often ignored, and it was possible to support political demands with an impressive show of force. In 1321 the baronial opposition came to parliament to demand the exile of the Despensers with their retinues all identically clad in green coat-armour of which one quarter was yellow with white bends, which gave the assembly its name of 'the parliament of the white bend'.

In addition to the retainers of the magnates, large numbers of lawyers, petitioners and others with legal business at parliament must have been present. Obviously these men would not be involved in such business as the grant of taxation, but they would have been able to attend the ceremonial occasions which might take place in parliament, such as the marriages of Edward i's daughters Joan and Margaret in 1290. Important foreigners might be there, as in 1337 when two cardinals attended, and heard a knight of the shire challenge to single combat anyone prepared to maintain the accusation that the king's allies the Count of Guelders and the Margrave of Juliers had been involved in a plot to poison the King of France. A 'copious multitude' was present on that occasion. The special protection and privilege of parliament was not confined to those actually summoned to the assembly, but covered all those present, as the Archdeacon of Norfolk found out to his cost in 1315. So large, indeed, might parliament be that it was not always easy to ensure adequate food supplies. The accounts of the sheriff of Lincolnshire in 1301 showed that he had to scour the whole county to provide sufficient victuals when the king held his parliament at Lincoln. In 1312 no less than 1,600 quarters of wheat, 2,300 of malt and 2,600 of oats, along with 1,360 oxen, 5,500 sheep and 700 pigs were ordered in preparation for parliament at Westminster.

The attendance record of the representatives was better than that of the magnates, although they were frequently dismissed before parliament ended. Those who were elected had to find men to act as sureties to ensure their presence at parliament. An isolated case from Bedfordshire in 1298 shows that one knight would only serve after eight of his oxen and four of his horses had been seized by the sheriff. For the most part, men were not reluctant to serve, as the prevalence of re-election indicates. Analysis of the returns for Essex under Edward 1 has shown that the normal type of man to be chosen was a knight of middle age, no longer particularly active in war but knowledgeable in administration. Chaucer's picture of the franklin could easily be applied to a knight of the shire of an earlier generation:

> At sessiouns there was he lord and sire;
> Ful ofte tyme he was knyght of the shire.
> An anlaas and a gipser al of silk
> Heeng at his girdel, whit as morne milk.
> A shirreve hadde he been, and a contour,
> Was nowher swich a worthy vavasour.[24]

Little is known about the way in which elections were conducted. A record of one in London under Edward 1 shows that the choice lay in the hands of a limited body of aldermen, but evidence for other towns is lacking. The knights of the shire were elected in the county court, a body of variable composition. It was dominated by the magnates, as is shown by the declaration of the sheriff of Sussex in 1297 that no election could take place, since the Archbishop of Canterbury and others, bishops, earls, barons and knights, were not present. The sheriff of Oxfordshire made a note in 1322 that he should summon 'the magnates or their stewards for electing knights'.[25] There is no evidence of disputed elections of knights of the shire; it is probable that the names emerged by a consensus process, not by actual voting.

Once elected, the representatives would be rewarded for

their service in parliament by payment of expenses. Standard rates were first laid down in 1327, with knights to receive four shillings and burgesses two shillings a day. There was considerable variation earlier, with the London representatives receiving a princely twenty shillings a day in 1296. In contrast, a Dorset knight complained under Edward II that he was receiving only sixteen pence a day. When the county community of Lancashire complained in 1320 that the sheriff had simply nominated men to go to parliament on their behalf, rather than holding proper elections, their objection was not on the grounds of a loss of political influence, but to the fact that they were being charged with £20 expenses, when they could have found men willing to perform the task for half that sum.

It is a fruitless task to try to analyse the choice of representatives under Edward I or Edward II in political terms. Thomas of Lancaster made no efforts to have his retainers elected to parliament; why should he, when he could simply bring them to parliament in his entourage? The crown did not try to secure the attendance of its own household knights as elected representatives. It has been argued that this situation changed under Edward III, but the evidence is not convincing. In 1361 and 1362 the only household knights in parliament were the members for Gloucestershire, and it was highly exceptional that John of Ypres, controller of the household, should have attended a great council in 1371 as a Lancashire representative. Sheriffs sometimes secured their own election to parliament, but this was for personal rather than political advantage. Under Edward III there were to be objections raised to the return of both sheriffs and lawyers as MPs, since they tended to abuse their position.

What the representatives actually did in parliament, apart from give their consent to taxes, is far from clear. It is known that in 1301 Henry of Keighley, a Lancashire knight of the shire, was responsible for a bill imposing conditions on the grant of a tax of a fifteenth, an early example of the representatives using their muscle to demand reform, but his is an isolated case. The records reveal virtually nothing of the activities of the two hundred or so burgesses, who were numerically by far the largest group in parliament. The place of the clerical representatives is equally shrouded in mystery; they still continued to attend parliament in Edward III's reign, even though no clerical taxes were granted there. The great legal historian F. W. Maitland could find no evidence of the activities of the representatives in parliament in 1305, save for the presentation of three petitions, one of which was produced jointly with the magnates. Yet they were present at Westminster for three weeks. No doubt many 'slumbered and slept and said but a little', as was said of the commons a century later, when some were 'like a cipher in algebra, that marks a place and has no value in itself'.[26] The role of the commons should not be unduly glorified. They had an important function in linking the local communities of the shires to the crown; in 1339, for example, the knights of the shire for Cumberland brought news to the king in parliament of the state of the northern Marches. They carried back from parliament news of the decisions reached by central government. On the other hand, it was claimed early in Edward III's reign that many knights of the shire were men of bad company, maintainers of false disputes at law, who prevented the good people of the realm from putting forward their grievances. The most notable feature to emerge from a biographical study of MPs is, perhaps, their criminal records. Some may feel that matters have changed little since the fourteenth century.

Parliament had undergone great changes by the beginning of Edward III's reign. What had begun as an occasion of variable character, in which judicial matters were always important, was transformed by the attendance of representatives as well as of royal councillors and magnates, and by the admixture of political and financial business. The compelling force behind the evolution of parliament was not the doctrine of Roman law 'what touches all should be approved by all' – it was above all the situation in which the crown repeatedly found itself from the 1290s, where war could only be financed by means of taxation. Direct negotiations with the local county assemblies for aid were never wholly successful: as late as Edward III's reign individuals were to claim that decisions reached in the county court were not binding on all inhabitants of the shire. However, by evolving the formula for the summons of representatives to parliament which included the request that they should have 'full power', the crown created an effective mechanism for obtaining consent to taxation which all accepted as valid. This gave parliament part of its special character. At the same time, its judicial role gave it a unique, almost sacrosanct, quality.

Under Edward I, for all the financial weakness of the later years, parliament was very much a royal creation. It was for the most part the king who initiated legislation and determined the particular shape of each assembly to suit his needs. The list of magnates to be summoned might be altered from one parliament to the next, and specialists might be asked to attend if the business required them. The Norham Parliament of 1291 which met to determine the Great Cause was quite distinctive in its composition. In 1296, when the king wished to discuss the rebuilding of Berwick, twenty-four towns were asked to send men to parliament 'who know best how to devise, order and array a new town'.[27] The core of parliament consisted of the king and his councillors, but beyond that there was no necessary uniformity of composition.

With the weak Edward II on the throne, it became abundantly clear that the English parliament was not to go the way of the French *parlement*, and develop primarily as a court of lawyers and professional administrators. The magnates laid claim to their rights as peers of the realm, and the representatives attended with increasing regularity, establishing their claim to be part of, and to speak for, the community of the realm. By 1327 they were initiating legislation on a large scale. This period saw parliamentary record-keeping become more systematic, and the composition of the assembly was increasingly standardized. It was possible for the author of the *Modus Tenendi Parliamentum* to set out rules and procedures for the conduct of an ideal parliament; what had been an occasion was becoming an institution.

Many varied strands went to make up a highly complex whole, and it would be wrong to single out any one element, either of composition or of function, as being of paramount importance in the evolution of parliament. In the development of parliament as a national assembly of a representative character, however, the importance of war should be emphasized. It was not in order to gain information about the country he governed, or to receive petitions from the localities, that Edward I summoned the representatives of shire and borough to parliament. It was in order to obtain a more satisfactory form of consent to taxation than could be provided in any other way. At the same time, parliament served other purposes. Different people needed it for different reasons. It served as a political forum, where concessions could be exacted from the king, and as a place where redress could be obtained for private wrongs. The English parliament was a remarkable institution, and yet it should not be glorified too much with the aid of hindsight. Contemporaries did not always anticipate the high opinions of historians. The children who used to pull off the hats of those going to parliament at Westminster clearly had little respect for the institution. The comment of one chronicler on the parliaments of Edward II's early years is worth noting: he wrote that at that time there were held in England many ridiculous and deceitful parliaments, through which heavy, fraudulent taxes were raised, and from which wise men went away, failing to find the justice they sought.

5
The Nobility

The English upper classes have always taken their superiority to the rest of their fellow countrymen for granted. There was more justification for this attitude in the Middle Ages than in more recent periods. Today, relatively subtle idiosyncrasies distinguish upper-class speech, but in the thirteenth and fourteenth centuries the aristocracy spoke a different language from the common people: a dialect form of French. The great nobles spent much of the time travelling, for their estates were widely scattered, whereas relatively few of the rest of the populace regularly went far from their homes. Legislation even attempted to ensure that the lower orders did not ape their betters by imitating their clothing.

The aristocracy were usually physically superior as a result of a better diet and good living conditions. Archaeological evidence suggests that most people were arthritic, unhealthy and relatively short in stature. In contrast, examination of the skeleton of Bartholomew Burghersh, an illustrious knight and diplomat of Edward III's reign, has revealed a broad-shouldered man of elegant build, about five feet ten inches in height, whose bones show none of the ostio-arthritic indications of a life of heavy toil. There is ample evidence of his martial prowess. He had suffered the inevitable minor injuries of tourney and battle: cracked ribs, strained elbow joints, a twisted ankle from a bad fall. Strikingly, the use of the weapons appropriate to his status, the lance and the sword, gave his right arm a very heavy musculature and even made it grow longer than the left. At the time of his death in 1369, when he was in late middle age, Bartholomew still possessed all his teeth.

How can the nobility be defined? There is not as clear-cut an answer for England as there is for much of the continent, where legal privilege confirmed the social gradations conferred by birth. A number of different criteria combined in England in a way that presented few problems to contemporaries, but which have made difficulties for historians.

Perhaps the clearest sign of status was knighthood. A knight was entitled to a coat of arms, and would be addressed as *monsire*, or sir. Knighthood was not hereditary as it was on the continent, but was an honour which could be conferred on those worthy of it by king or magnate. By the thirteenth century the notion that all those who held a knight's fee – an estate owing the feudal military service of a knight – should themselves be knights was becoming out of date, for many such fees were simply not worth enough. Instead, the crown attempted to ensure that all those of a certain degree of wealth should become knights. The qualifying level varied, but by the end of the century was normally set at £40 a year in land. Status, however, cannot always be equated with wealth, and poorer men with ambition were not excluded the rank of knighthood. Early in Edward I's reign Roger d'Arcy agreed to make Ingram of Oldcotes a knight, to provide food and clothing for him, a squire and two grooms, and to maintain three horses for him for life. In return Ingram was to hand over all his lands, worth about a third of the normal level for a knight, to Roger in return for a nominal rent. It was more normal, however, for men to try to avoid becoming knights, as they were anxious to avoid the costs of maintaining the necessary equipment and the inevitable burden of local administration. The crown attempted some remarkable expedients to try to increase the number of knights, such as the mass knighting of some three hundred men in 1306, when Edward I knighted his own eldest son. The eve of battle was frequently an occasion for knighting ceremonies.

The number of knights in England fluctuated. The

mid-thirteenth century saw some knightly families forced to sell their estates, often to religious houses or royal officials. Under Edward I numbers rose, until there were probably over a thousand active knights in the country, and perhaps as many as one thousand five hundred. When the king summoned knights individually to serve in Scotland in 1301, the total number reached about nine hundred and sixty. A major inquiry into the military capabilities of the country took place in 1324, and the incomplete returns record about eight hundred and sixty knights. For Lincoln-shire, the sheriff listed sixty-two, excluding those who were old, gouty, or not resident in the county. This tallies well with the figure of fifty-six knights summoned from the county to fight in Scotland in 1334. The heady days of success in the French war under Edward III provided a powerful incentive for men to take up knighthood, and in 1346–7 almost a thousand knights served in France. By the end of the reign, however, the situation had changed. In 1360 the sheriff of Northumberland reported that there was only one knight in the county, and he was feeble and useless. The evidence of the composition of armies after the resumption of the war in 1369 strongly suggests a decline in the number of knights. There was a compensation for this, for in the late fourteenth century esquires were rising in social status. They began to wear coat-armour like the knights, and a new distinction was emerging; that of gentil-ity. To be a man-at-arms in the last years of Edward III's reign was also to be a gentleman.

In the military hierarchy, the rank superior to the knight was that of the banneret. Such a man bore a square or oblong banner, rather than the long pennon of the knight, and would be paid four shillings a day, not two shillings. He would have a substantial retinue appropriate to his station, perhaps numbering fifteen or twenty. The position was not hereditary, and had little significance save on cam-paign: it implied a position of military command, rather than of social superiority. A poor knight, however, would not possess the resources required of a banneret.

In more general terms, the grade of society above the knight was that of the baron. To be a baron was to hold land by a particular form of tenure, defined by the payment of relief – an inheritance duty – at the rate of £100 up to 1297, and 100 marks thereafter. As a result, however, of the process of division and subdivision of estates some barons were relatively insignificant men. There was a great disparity of wealth between men claiming baronial status, and the group were in no sense a clearly-defined class. In the course of the fourteenth century it was common for important barons to call themselves lords, as Ralph Basset in a deed of 1319 termed himself Lord of Drayton, and the Mortimers styled themselves Lords of Wigmore. Such territorial titles were a claim to status, and an expression of lordship.

The development of parliament led to the emergence of a clearly-defined noble group in the fourteenth century. There was no obvious criterion that the king could use in deciding which magnates to summon individually to appear at parliament. Of the fifty-three summoned in 1295, twenty-two did not hold their land by baronial tenure, and at least six were not even royal tenants-in-chief. These men were selected on the basis of their personal worth. For reasons of administrative convenience, the same lists were used to summon men to fight and to come to parliament. As a result of the military importance of the Welsh and Scottish Marches, there was a preponderance of men from these areas. The numbers summoned might vary considerably from one parliament to another, but from 1299 a standard list began to emerge. It became increasingly normal for a son to succeed his father in receipt of a parliamentary summons. The list underwent major changes as a result of the political upheavals of Edward II's reign, but under Edward III a more regular pattern was established. In 1337 ten earls and forty-eight others were summoned. New names were added as men achieved distinction in the Hundred Years War; by 1349 the total was fifty-six.

Attendance at parliament was a clear sign of social standing, and from Edward II's reign there was a growing assumption that those who received individual summonses formed an elite. The term 'peers' came into use in a parliamentary context from 1312. The peerage emerged as a result of a chance process of selection, but it rapidly developed as a distinct and separate estate. It was not until Richard II's reign, however, that the process of creating barons by letters patent, and giving them a seat among their peers in the House of Lords began.

Until 1337 the highest rank in secular society was that of the earl, whose title was hereditary. The title of itself conferred few real rights, as is shown by the creation of Henry of Grosmont as Earl of Lincoln in 1349, when, 'lest the said title be said to be wholly empty and useless',[1] the king granted him £20 a year as the traditional earl's third penny out of the county revenues. Yet the title had great significance. One contemporary commented that no earl accompanied Edward I on his Flanders campaign in 1297, and clearly regarded this as a reason for the king's failure. In 1338 the Bishop of Exeter complained of the behaviour of Hugh de Courtenay since his elevation to the earldom of Devon in 1335. The new earl was telling the ignorant Devon folk that he was the equal of the king; that he could make laws and judge all matters; that in his person lay the wisdom of the realm, and that the business of the kingdom depended chiefly on him. Roger Mortimer obviously greatly valued his title of Earl of March, since no one was permitted to address him in any other way.

In 1337 Edward III introduced a new title, that of duke, when his eldest son was made Duke of Cornwall. The novelty of this was minimized by an argument that there had been dukes of Cornwall in the distant past, while the king himself was Duke of Aquitaine in France. Like the comital title, that of duke carried no substantial rights with it, but its holders were the most exalted members of society after the king himself. The first non-royal duke was Henry of Grosmont, created Duke of Lancaster in 1351. In 1362 ducal titles were conferred on the king's sons Lionel and John.

Summonses to parliament and grants of titles were not the only ways in which the nobility were gaining a separate identity. Heraldry assisted in the process of definition. The bearing of coats of arms had an obvious practical purpose in providing a means of recognition in the heat of battle, but it was also a matter of family pride. Rolls of arms were compiled by heralds, which recorded the names of those present at particular events. The most remarkable heraldic work was the *Song of Caerlaverock*, which provided short character sketches of most of the bannerets present at the siege of the castle in 1300, as well as details of their blazons. A typical extract runs:

And William de Cantilupe, whom I for this reason praise, that he has at all times lived in honour. He had on a red shield a fess vair, with three fleur de lis of bright gold issuing from leopards' heads.[2]

The author expressed considerable surprise that two men, Brian FitzAlan and Hugh Poinz, both bore the same arms: by the 1380s such a coincidence in the case of the Scrope and Grosvenor families was to lead to a complex legal dispute. One of the witnesses, John Sulley, claimed to be a hundred and five years old, and to remember seeing the Scrope arms displayed at the battle of Halidon Hill in 1333.

Sumptuary legislation attempted to establish acceptable standards of consumption for men of different status. In 1316 the council tried to limit extravagant eating by the upper classes, in an attempt to ease the famine conditions of the time. The 'great lords of the land' were not to have more than two meat courses served in their households, with only four kinds of meat in all. Prelates, earls and greater magnates, however, could have an extra course if they wished. A far more elaborate scheme was set out in 1363: the populace was carefully graded into workers, merchants, yeomen, valets, esquires, knights and lords, with the food and clothing appropriate to each rank laid down. In practice, such legislation could not be enforced. Popular songs testify to the impossibility of confining rich fashions to the highest in the land; one of Edward II's day protested at the way in which a low-born woman would wear elaborate head-dresses and ear-rings, 'though she has not a smock to hide her foul arse'.[3]

The basis of aristocratic power and privilege was, of course, wealth, and wealth was firmly based on land. The exception was William de la Pole, who rose into the ranks of the aristocracy as a result of his profits from the wool trade and the financial services which he provided for Edward III. There were great variations in the wealth of even the highest nobles. Definitive figures are hard to provide, since few accounts have survived, but there are some indications. At the time of his death in 1314 the Earl of Gloucester enjoyed an income of about £6,000 a year. Thomas of Lancaster's income provides some justification for that much misused term, 'over-mighty subject': he was probably in receipt of about £11,000 annually. Under Edward III Henry Duke of Lancaster received over £8,000 a year from his lands in England and Wales, and in 1377 accounts of the receiver-general of John of Gaunt, Duke of Lancaster, show a receipt of £12,803. Almost half of this, however, consisted of arrears of war wages.

Most magnates did not enjoy such large revenues, although at his death in 1376 the Earl of Arundel possessed the astonishing sum of over £60,000 in cash and bullion. In Edward II's reign Aymer de Valence, Earl of Pembroke, held lands worth about £3,000 a year. The grants made by Edward II to Andrew Harclay, Earl of Carlisle, and by Edward III to the earls created in 1337, suggest that an income of 1,000 marks or perhaps £1,000 was considered sufficient to maintain the status of an earl. The contrast with the £40 qualification for knighthood is striking, though it should be noted that by 1363 a knight was expected, according to the sumptuary legislation, to be worth at least £133 6s 8d a year. The landed wealth of the magnates was considerable even when set against that of the crown: in 1324 the income from the counties was put at almost £12,500. The magnates, of course, lacked the crown's power to raise revenue by taxation, but their position was nevertheless very powerful.

The power of a magnate was expressed in various ways. He had rights over his feudal tenants, which followed from the act of homage which they performed. Military service by them was something of an anachronism by the thirteenth century, but scutage – or payment in lieu of service – could be important. Rights of wardship when a tenant was under-age were also highly profitable. Magnates possessed rights to appoint to ecclesiastical benefices, and would have powers of jurisdiction of various types. By Edward I's day, the system of feudal tenure had become primarily a legal one, which did not necessarily entail any close personal relationship between lord and tenant; a new system of lordship was developing alongside the old, which made up for some of the latter's deficiencies.

Bastard feudalism, as it is often termed, was a system by which lords made specific written agreements, known as indentures, with their followers. These might be for a limited term or for life. In return for paid service in war and attendance in the lord's household when required, the retainer would receive fees and robes and possibly other perquisites as well. By Edward II's reign he might well wear his lord's livery costume, and in Edward III's time badges were used to proclaim allegiance to a particular magnate. The system was not directly tied to land: a life retainer might well be granted revenues from a particular manor, or simply receive a fixed annual payment. In contrast to the old feudal tenure, these arrangements were not hereditary.

Relatively few early indentures for life survive. There are two from 1278, and a well-known one made by Roger Bigod with John de Segrave in 1297. The terms of service agreed by Maurice de Berkeley with a squire in 1273 are also known. He was to receive two robes a year and a fee of eight shillings along with food and allowances for his horse and servant, and he was to act as master of the hounds. Despite the paucity of surviving agreements, the prevalence of this system of retaining men can be seen from the composition of the retinues that magnates led on campaign. There was a small core of permanent retainers who appeared year after year, while the bulk of numbers was made up by men hired on a temporary basis. Some retainers were expected to serve in the lord's household in some official capacity; others only attended occasionally. They represented their lord's interests in their own localities, and in return received his support.

Wealthy magnates could afford very large retinues. A list of the following of Roger Bigod, Earl of Norfolk, in 1297 names five bannerets, nine knights, seventeen men-at-arms and seven clerks. Since one of the bannerets is known from his indenture to have contracted to serve with between sixteen and twenty fully-armed horsemen, this list hardly demonstrates the full scale of the earl's resources. Thomas of Lancaster had up to fifty-five knights in receipt of his fees and wages at any one time, and probably at least double that number of esquires. In the late fourteenth century John of Gaunt had up to two hundred retainers in his service. A more typical level was that of the twelve knights and twenty-four esquires permanently retained by Thomas de Berkeley in 1327. This was far from being the full size of his household, which would have included 'gadlings and grooms, Colin and Colle, harlots and horse-knaves',[4] as mentioned in a contemporary poem. The family historian estimated that including menials and domestic servants, the Berkeley household approached three hundred people in size. The travelling household of the Earl and Countess of Gloucester was over two hundred strong in 1293.

The retinue provided much more than military power. A pattern of clientage and local influence developed, with serious implications for the maintenance of law and order; royal justices often accepted fees on a regular basis from magnates. In Edward I's reign Edmund Earl of Lancaster had two such men as members of his council. Legislation against the practice in 1346 had little effect; an account shows that in 1367 the Earl of Salisbury paid annual fees to one royal justice and eleven lawyers and chancery clerks in what was no doubt a successful attempt to oil the wheels of justice in his interest. In 1330 it was alleged that the sheriff and all other royal officials and ministers of justice in Gloucestershire were in receipt of Thomas de Berkeley's livery and wages, so that no justice could be obtained against him.

The system of retaining men by means of indentures could break down. In 1297 Walter de Burnham agreed to serve in Flanders under Roger de Mowbray, but he failed to appear. The Berkeley family were retainers of long standing of the Earl of Pembroke, but in 1318 they turned against him, attacking his manor of Painswick. In 1322 political caution proved stronger in many cases than the bond of retainer for members of Thomas of Lancaster's following, as the desertions prior to the battle of Boroughbridge show. Yet despite the fact that agreements could be broken, and for all the abuses that retaining led to, the system worked well in general. The magnates were provided with large and splendid retinues which added greatly to their prestige, and the retainers themselves enjoyed the security that a great lord could give them. For the crown, the system simplified the problem of recruiting troops for the war, as the magnates could simply be asked to bring their retinues with them on campaign.

The history of England in the Middle Ages has often been seen as a constant struggle between the crown and the baronage. It makes more sense to see the normal pattern of political life as one of co-operation and collaboration between the two. It was only when the equilibrium was upset by, for example, the emergence of unsuitable favourites, that some of the magnates might be forced into rebellion. The attitude of the crown towards its greatest subjects was far from consistent, however, and an examination of the different policies adopted by the three Edwards reveals much about their respective styles of kingship. Edward I was firm, authoritarian, ungenerous and tricky; Edward II scarcely had a policy worth the name, while Edward III achieved a remarkable rapport with the nobility; the product of skilled political management and an undoubted personal magnetism.

Noble families were naturally prone to extinction and Edward I took advantage of this, manipulating the rules of inheritance unscrupulously in his own interests: he created no new earldoms, and could even be reluctant to permit succession to an existing title. On average a quarter died out in the male line every twenty-five years. Despite the examples of Cornwall and Gloucester under Edward II, this was not usually the result of execution or war, but reflected the problems of producing male heirs in an age of high mortality. In Edward I's reign the Earls of Norfolk and Cornwall and the Countesses of Aumâle and Devon all died childless. The king himself was the heir to the earldom of Cornwall, but in the other cases Edward took steps to ensure that the lands came to the crown, rather than to the closest relative. On the death of the Countess of Aumâle, he supported a bogus claimant in the courts, and then bought him out for a mere £100. Walter Langton arranged a death-bed bargain with the Countess of Devon, by which she surrendered the Isle of Wight and other estates to the king in return for £6,000, so effectively disinheriting her rightful heir, Hugh de Courtenay. In 1302 Roger Bigod, Earl of Norfolk, then aged sixty and childless, surrendered his lands to the crown and received them back on condition that they should be inherited only in the direct line of descent. The reversion of the estates to the crown on his death, at the expense of his brother, was almost inevitable.

Edward I made other arrangements to advance the interests of the royal family. When his daughter Joan of Acre married the Earl of Gloucester in 1290, the earl surren-dered his lands to the crown and received them back on terms which effectively disinherited his children by his first marriage. Future earls of Gloucester would be members of the royal family as a result. Similar arrangements made in 1302 when Edward's daughter Elizabeth married the Earl of Hereford ensured that the estates were entailed on their children, while if there were none, the majority of the estates would go to the crown. The clear purpose of Edward I's policy was to ensure that his own family would be well provided with lands; the Norfolk estates, for example, were used to provide the king's youngest son, Thomas of Brotherton, with the wealth appropriate to one of royal blood. This was not a statesmanlike policy intended to increase the financial resources of the crown by building up its estates.

Edward I was not uniformly hostile to those who claimed comital rank. Although he had been instrumental in depriv-ing Robert de Ferrers of his title of Earl of Derby before his accession, he allowed his friend William Beauchamp to inherit the Earldom of Warwick in 1268, though he was only the nephew of the last earl and received the title while his father was still alive. In the early 1290s he permitted the heir to the castle of Arundel to take the title of Earl of Arundel which had been in abeyance since 1243. He also granted the earldom of Richmond to his nephew John of Brittany in 1306, although he was only the second son of the previous earl. In addition, Edward was prepared to let Ralph de Monthermer, second husband of Joan of Acre, use the title of Earl of Gloucester from 1297. This was surprising, since Joan had married Ralph for love after the death of Earl Gilbert, contrary to the king's wishes. Edward's immediate irascible reaction had been to imprison Ralph and seize the lands, but his anger soon abated, and Ralph served him loyally in the wars in Scotland, in spite of his friendship with Robert Bruce. Despite these examples, Edward was conspicuously lacking in generosity as far as comital titles were concerned. Roger Mortimer of Wigmore, who died in 1282, was wealthy enough to be an earl, and such men as the Cliffords, Robert Tibetot or Otto de Grandson were fully deserving of the honour in terms of the services they rendered to the king.

Edward II did not share his father's conservatism and caution with regard to earldoms. At the outset of his reign he made Piers Gaveston Earl of Cornwall, a title previously enjoyed by Henry III's brother Richard and his son Edmund. Another startling addition to the list of earls was Andrew Harclay, who was made Earl of Carlisle in 1322. This was a brand new title, and Harclay was not rich enough to maintain the status of an earl. The king therefore promised him lands worth 1,000 marks a year, and it is a reflection of the remarkable nature of this creation that the preamble to the deed set out the personal merits of the new earl – something that had never been necessary before. The new earldom was, however, ill-fated, and did not survive its holder's execution. The title of Earl of Winchester had been defunct since 1264, and was revived in 1322 for the elder Despenser. Edward II's other creations were less controversial. His young half-brothers Thomas and Edmund were made Earls of Norfolk and Kent respectively; the latter title having been in abeyance since 1243.

Edward III did not react against his father's policy of reviving old earldoms and creating new ones, nor against his mother's generosity in making her lover Roger Mortimer Earl of March – a wholly new title. Instead of reverting to the attitude of Edward I, he consciously strove to build up the number of the earls. In 1335 Hugh de Courtenay was given the title of Earl of Devon, of which he had long despaired; two years later the king rewarded his associates in the revolution by which he had seized power from Isabella and Mortimer. The four leading members of his household were all given earldoms: William de Montague became Earl of Salisbury, Robert Ufford Earl of Suffolk, William Clinton Earl of Huntingdon and William Bohun Earl of Northampton. Clinton was a younger son of a man who had once sat as a knight of the shire in parliament; Bohun the younger brother of the Earl of Hereford. At the same time Henry of Grosmont, eldest son of the Earl of Lancaster, was made Earl of Derby, and Hugh Audley Earl of Gloucester. Audley was the husband of one of the heiresses to the earldom which had been dismembered after the death of Earl Gilbert in 1314. Edward III explained his motive thus:

Among the marks of royalty we consider it to be the chief that, through a due distribution of positions, dignities and offices, it is buttressed by wise counsels and fortified by mighty powers. Yet because many hereditary ranks have come into the hands of the king, partly by hereditary descent to co-heirs and co-parceners according to our laws, and partly through failure of issues and other events, this realm has long suffered a serious decline in names, honours and ranks of dignity.[5]

The new Earls of Salisbury, Suffolk, Huntingdon and Northampton all received substantial grants to ensure that their powers were indeed mighty. These might be criticized on the grounds that they reduced the landed endowment of the crown, but Edward III used only lands which had come into his hands as a result of the death of the previous holder, rather than established royal estates. The grants could easily be justified in terms of the value of the service that the new earls gave to the king.

It was no coincidence that the appointment of six new earls came when Edward III needed to bolster his position at the outset of the war with France. He never again made so spectacular an addition to the ranks of the higher nobility. He did continue to make new earls, however. In 1340 his ally the Margrave of Juliers became Earl of Cambridge; Ralph Stafford was made Earl of Stafford in 1351; and in 1354 Roger Mortimer's grandson was given the title of Earl of March – a striking example of Edward's refusal to bear grudges against families. The king's son-in-law Enguerrand de Coucy was made Earl of Bedford in 1366. In addition, all his sons received titles with the exception of the youngest, Thomas of Woodstock.

The severity of Edward I's attitude towards the greater magnates in contrast to that of Edward II and Edward III is reflected in his approach to their legal rights and privileges. The years from 1278 to 1294 saw the jurisdictional rights of the magnates challenged by means of the *quo warranto* inquiries. There is a famous story, which is usually told of Earl Warenne, but which can be more plausibly attributed to the Earl of Gloucester since he was singled out for special treatment in the early stages of the proceedings. When he was asked by what warrant he held his lands, he produced a rusty sword from behind an altar and declared to the justices, 'Here, my lords, is my warrant',[6] and he claimed that it was with this weapon that his ancestors had taken his lands at the time of the Norman Conquest. The story goes to the heart of the problem. In many cases magnates did not have written charters to justify their claims, but they could justifiably point out that their forbears had, from time immemorial, always exercised the rights that were now being challenged. The inquiries went slowly, with difficult cases being postponed and referred to parliament. In 1290 a compromise was reached, which permitted men to exercise powers which their ancestors had possessed since 1189, even if no charter could be produced. The proceedings were deeply resented, and in 1297 the opposition claimed that men were no longer allowed to enjoy their customary franchisal rights, but had been arbitrarily deprived of them.

The *quo warranto* inquiries did not extend to the Welsh Marches, but Edward I used other methods there to try to limit the rights of the magnates. In 1290 he intervened to prevent the Earls of Gloucester and Hereford from settling their disputes by the traditional and accepted means of private war. In 1297 he lent a very sympathetic ear to the complaints of Hereford's tenants against their lord, though on that occasion he failed to curb the earl's powers. In 1299 the lordship of Oswestry was taken into the king's hands for a time and the rights of the Lord of Gower were considerably limited when he was forced to grant his tenants a charter. Such examples can be multiplied. Edward was not universally hostile to Marcher customs, as was shown in 1305 when he refused to abolish the lord's right to the property of tenants who died intestate, but he sought a new degree of definition which often effectively limited Marcher authority. Events in the Welsh March were paralleled by those in Durham, where the palatinate was twice taken into the king's hands, and the bishop compelled to grant his tenants a charter. The king's attitude to the exercise of franchisal rights by magnates was well expressed in 1306. After granting his close associate the Earl of Lincoln the right of return of writ (that of executing royal writs) in two hundreds he held, Edward declared that in future such grants could only be made to his own children.

Edward II had no real policy towards the rights of the magnates. The one threat to Marcher liberties in his reign was presented by the younger Despenser. He argued that John Mowbray had received the lordship of Gower from his father-in-law William de Braose without royal licence, but the Marchers claimed that this was proper according to their customs. The issue was contrived to give Despenser an excuse for acquiring Gower himself; it was not part of a concerted attack on Marcher rights. Indeed, when Despenser was granted his lands in south Wales in 1318 the king, with the assent of the magnates, specified that he could exercise all the traditional liberties which the Earls of Gloucester had enjoyed. Any concessions made by the earls to Edward I could be ignored.

Edward III's generosity in granting new titles was matched by his beneficent attitude towards the privileges of the magnates. He had no wish to upset the harmonious relationship he enjoyed with his companions in arms. None of the legal campaigns that took place in the course of the reign threatened the position of franchise holders as *quo warranto* had done; they were intended to promote law and order and to help fill the royal coffers. Edward I's wishes with regard to the right of return of writ were not respected. In 1335 William Montague was granted the royal crest of an eagle and promised the reversion of various estates: from the date they came into his hands, he was entitled to return of writ as well as various other rights. Two years later John Moleyns, an influential household knight, received the same privilege for all his lands in Buckinghamshire and Oxfordshire. Certain magnates were granted sheriffdoms for life, a policy to which the commons took vigorous exception in 1346. The one issue on which the king was adamant was that of taxation; he was not prepared to allow any exemptions from the collection of taxes granted in parliament.

The case of the lordship of Gower, over which there had been contention under Edward I and Edward II, provides a good example of the royal attitude towards baronial liberties in Edward III's reign. In 1354 the Earl of Warwick successfully challenged John Mowbray's right to the lordship, on the grounds that one of his ancestors had held Gower in 1184. The status of the lordship was then challenged by the Black Prince, whose aggressive attitude towards Marcher rights was reminiscent of Edward I. He was anxious to extend the jurisdiction of his courts at Carmarthen, and since Warwick could not show that he or his ancestors had enjoyed Marcher privileges in Gower within the period of legal memory – which began in 1189 – the council ruled in favour of the prince. Edward III valued Warwick's allegiance, and considered it far more important than his son's claims to exercise jurisdiction over Gower. He therefore granted the earl the full status and rights of a Marcher lord. This was not the only time that the king had to step in to protect a Marcher from the Black Prince's ambition. In 1354 it had even been necessary to lay down by statute that the Marcher lords held their lands from the king, and were not answerable to the prince.

The financial relationship between the crown and the

magnates was another area of considerable change between the reigns of Edward I and Edward III. Under Edward I many magnates were heavily in debt to the crown, often for payments dating back many years, even to John's reign. In 1295 the king used the threat of the collection of such debts to force a group of reluctant magnates to go to Gascony; one of Roger Bigod's grievances against the king was the way in which pressure was put on him to repay old debts. Given the reluctance of many magnates to perform paid service in the king's wars, the crown was not itself incurring heavy debts towards them, despite the financial difficulties of the later years of the reign.

Under Edward II only the Earl of Lancaster steadfastly refused to accept royal wages. With the other magnates entering into contracts to serve in Scotland, and in some cases even accepting annual fees from the crown, the crown was becoming a debtor towards them. The Earl of Pembroke had to wait until 1321 to receive part payment of £2,240 owed him for his campaigns against Bruce in 1307, and it was only in 1319 that he accounted for almost £2,000 dating back to the first two years of Edward II's reign. On his death a bargain was struck to try to balance the king's debts to the earl with the earl's to the king, though the malign influence of the Despensers meant that Pembroke's widow and executors had the worst of the bargain. A list of war wages owing in 1323 for the recent Scottish campaign shows that even the Despensers were owed almost £500 by the crown, and another account reveals debts of over £2,500 to the elder Despenser from the wardrobe under Edward I and Edward II.

By Edward III's reign most magnates were owed money by the king. The old debts to the crown dating from before 1327 were cancelled, and the financial resources of the government were rarely such that war wages could be paid promptly. The offer of the Earls of Warwick and Arundel to serve at sea at their own cost in the early stages of the Hundred Years War did not form a precedent; paid service was almost universal. Arundel was owed £2,854 for the Scottish campaign of 1337, and did not receive full satisfaction for this sum until 1349. Through a mixture of skilful management and good fortune, he became the richest of the earls, and by the end of the reign was a crown creditor on a very large scale. In 1370 he lent the crown £20,000, and four years later a further £10,000. His was, admittedly, an exceptional case, but it does point to a radically changed situation. Instead of the magnates paying off their debts to the crown by instalments, as Bigod was forced to do by Edward I, they were now making concessions to the crown. In 1344 Gloucester agreed to make out a full acquittance for £560 owed to him, even though he only received half that sum.

The balance of power between the crown and the nobility was also affected by legal developments. Edward I took a strict view of the rules of inheritance and land tenure. Until 1294 a tight control was exercised over the granting away of lands by royal tenants-in-chief, and thereafter it was still necessary to obtain a licence. Only in 1327 with a new statute did tenants-in-chief in effect gain the right to alienate their holdings as they wished. Of course, some of Edward I's legislation was in the interests of the great magnates. In *de donis conditionalibus* a partially successful attempt was made to enable men to impose binding conditions on grants of land that they made on such occasions as the marriage of a daughter. By Edward III's reign the development of a legal device known as the 'use' enabled magnates and others to do much as they wished with their lands.

The concept of the use was essentially that of a trust. Lands would be granted to a group of men known as 'feoffees', who would hold the land to the use of the grantor. As the feoffees were the legal owners of the land, the estates could not be taken into wardship by the crown on the death of the grantor should his heir be under age, nor could they be forfeited for treason at this period. Edward III showed no reluctance to grant licences for enfeoffments to uses. He willingly co-operated with the magnates, rather than trying to twist inheritance customs to his own advantage. The new system of uses did not overthrow the basic principles of primogeniture, but it did permit men to make more satisfactory arrangements to ensure that on their death their family and dependents were properly provided for. Edward III was also generous in permitting magnates to entail their estates. This meant that it was possible, for example, to arrange that the inheritance could only pass to male heirs, which would avoid such a situation as occurred in the Gloucester case after 1314 when the lands were split between the three heiresses. These technical legal matters were of great importance in an age when land was the basis of wealth, and territorial rivalries were the stuff of magnate politics. Edward III's reign witnessed a clear decline of royal control in this sphere, but this was arguably offset by the gratitude of the magnates towards the king. The personal relationship of the king with his nobles was extremely important. The omens were not auspicious should a future king fail to establish as effective a rapport with the nobility as that built up by Edward III.

The question of relations with the crown was only part of the complex web of magnate politics. The ambition to gain more lands and wealth might in part be satisfied by loyal service to the crown, which brought rewards in the form of grants of lands, wardships, rights of jurisdiction and so forth, but the best route to riches was marriage to a wealthy heiress. The significance of a match such as that of Thomas of Lancaster and Alice de Lacy, heiress to the earldoms of Lincoln and Salisbury, was immense, for it made Lancaster by far the richest of the earls. William Bohun, first Earl of Northampton, was a younger son with few lands, but marriage to Elizabeth de Badlesmere brought him riches; not only was she an heiress in her own right, but she had also acquired estates through her first marriage to Edmund Mortimer. It would be easy, if tedious, to multiply examples of men who did well through good marriages.

On occasion marriage plans might misfire. Edmund Earl of Arundel made an apparently good match for his son Richard with Isabel, daughter of the younger Despenser, in 1321; the couple were then aged seven and eight. The destruction of the power of the Despensers sharply detracted from Isabel's financial attractions, and although she bore Richard a son and two daughters, he obtained annulment of the marriage in 1344. The ostensible grounds were remarkable, as Richard alleged that he and his wife had been forced to cohabit by blows. The real reason was that he wished to marry Eleanor, widow of John de Beaumont and sister of Henry of Grosmont, future Duke of Lancaster, who had become his mistress during an embassy to Spain. Arundel was skilful in combining his amorous inclinations with his financial acumen.

Earl Warenne was far less fortunate in his marital adventures. He married Joan de Bar, a granddaughter of Edward I, in 1306 when she was about ten. The marriage was never successful, but Warenne's repeated attempts to obtain a divorce so that he could marry his mistress, Maud de Nerford, were doomed to failure. The earl eventually tired of Maud, and cancelled the arrangements he had made to endow their sons with land. Late in life he took a new mistress, Isabel de Holland, and again tried to divorce Joan. Warenne claimed that before his marriage he had slept with his wife's aunt, Edward I's daughter Mary, who was a nun. The case could not be proved, and in his will Warenne had to be content with describing Isabel as his companion. He left no legitimate heirs, and the bulk of his estates went on his death to Arundel, adding to that earl's already substantial fortune.

There are, perhaps, no historical incidents as dramatic and lurid as that in the romance of *Sir Bevis of Hamptoun*, in which Josian, who had given her love to Bevis, was forced to marry an earl. Rather than submit to his advances, she hanged him from their marriage bed. Alice de Lacy's marital career, however, was colourful enough for a work of fiction. In 1317 she was abducted from her husband, the Earl of Lancaster, by one of Warenne's knights, Richard de St Martin. He claimed to be her real husband, as he had slept with her before her marriage; a statement which Alice supported. In 1324 she married Eblo Lestrange in an undoubted love-match and on his death she took vows of chastity. Then in a dramatic scene in Bolingbroke Castle in 1336 she was again abducted, this time by Hugh de Frenes. He entered the castle with the complicity of some of her servants, and seized her in the hall. She was permitted to go up to her chamber to collect her things together, and when she came down was placed firmly on horseback. Only then did she realize the gravity of her situation, and she promptly fell off in an attempt to escape. She was put back, with a groom mounted behind her to hold her on, and led off to Somerton Castle. There, according to the record, Hugh raped her in breach of the king's peace. Since she was by then in her mid-fifties, it is likely that Hugh was attracted more by her vast estates than by her physical charms. As frequently happened in medieval cases of rape, the couple soon married; it is possible that she was not a wholly unwilling victim. With few exceptions, marriage for the medieval aristocracy was a matter of business and politics. Alice de Lacy was fortunate to have loved one of her three husbands; it was next to Eblo Lestrange that she chose to be buried.

It used to be fashionable to denigrate the nobility of later medieval England as boorish, ill-educated men 'of arrested mental development'.[7] As in any group of men, there were considerable contrasts. Thomas of Brotherton, Earl of Norfolk, had a wild and disagreeable temper, but on the other hand Henry of Grosmont, first Duke of Lancaster, was a highly civilized and cultured man. Generalization is hard, but it is perhaps possible to sketch some of the salient features of the aristocratic life-style of this period.

One chief concern of many of the nobles, particularly in Edward III's reign, was war; attitudes towards war, chivalry and tournaments will be discussed in chapter seven. At home, the complex business of running a great estate was a major preoccupation. A medieval estate was in some ways the equivalent of a major industrial enterprise today, and although magnates had councils to assist in the process of management, and a whole hierarchy of officials from stewards and receivers down to humble bailiffs and reeves, regular supervision by the lord was required. The surviving accounts of Henry de Lacy, Earl of Lincoln, show that a great lord would have at his disposal an administrative staff quite as capable and competent as the civil service. Men like Adam Stratton under Edward I, and John

Walwyn under Edward II, served as both private and royal officials. Estate management was not simply a matter of the supervision of manors and efficient accounting; much legal business was involved, to protect existing lands from encroachment and to acquire new ones.

Public affairs, too, must have occupied much time. Appointment to judicial commissions, attendance at the county court, recruiting of archers; such activities in the counties were shared between the magnates and the local gentry. The great men would attend parliaments and great councils, and might be employed on lengthy diplomatic missions. Some magnates, naturally, spent far more time in government employ than others. A comparison between the itineraries of the Earls of Pembroke and Lancaster under Edward II shows that the former spent surprisingly little time on his own estates, whereas Lancaster spent long periods in his castle at Pontefract.

Hunting and hawking were among the chief pleasures of the aristocracy and great parks were created to preserve the game. Thomas de Berkeley removed the old thorn hedges round his park at Whitecliff, and stocked it with a special strain of white deer which he acquired from the Earl of Salisbury. It was recorded that on one occasion this lord with his brothers stayed out four whole days and nights foxhunting. Henry of Grosmont's interest in the sport can be seen from the enthusiasm with which he set out instructions on how to force foxes from their earths.

Some members at least of the aristocracy had literary tastes. Guy de Beauchamp, Earl of Warwick, who died in 1315, was described as eminently well-lettered. He possessed a large library, and in 1305 gave a number of books to Bordesly Abbey, including some French romances about Arthur and Alexander. James Audley, one of the heroes of Poitiers, owned at least four romances, while the Bohun earls of Hereford in Edward III's reign were both book collectors and literary patrons. They played an important part in the literary revival characterized by alliterative poetry. Nor was such activity confined to the highest ranks of the aristocracy. A copy of a Grail romance once owned by a knight of Edward I's reign survives, and it was an Oxford-

shire knight, Thomas de la More, who commissioned Geoffrey le Baker, parish priest of Swinbrook, to write his
chronicle. The widespread employment of minstrels shows
that the literary works of the day found an audience largely
by means of recitation and song, but there is no doubt of the
literacy of the magnates. The fact that their letters were
written by scribes is no more an indication of illiteracy than
is the use of secretaries by modern businessmen.

An interesting reference survives, provided by John de
Champvent for his clerk Edmund de Martlesham, who was
leaving his service for that of Aymer de Valence. Edmund
was commended for his secretarial skills in French and
Latin, and for his ability to draw up accounts. He was also
'chaste of body, of good manners, and good company'.[8]
Even allowing for the professional skills of these men, there
is no reason to doubt the authorship of such letters as those
sent by Bartholomew Bughersh to the Archbishop of Canterbury announcing news of the Crécy campaign in 1346.
John, Lord Bourchier, wrote two letters home in his own
hand after his capture by the French in 1374. There were
even books written by members of the upper classes.
Thomas de la More wrote a memoir in French which was
used by le Baker. Thomas Grey of Heton, a northern knight
of some importance, wrote the *Scalacronica* while in a Scottish prison; it is a work which stands up well in comparison
to the monastic chronicles of the day. Most remarkable was
the work of Henry Duke of Lancaster. He composed two
treatises, one on the laws of war which has not survived,
and a devotional book in allegorical style, the *Livre des
Seyntz Medicines*. Parts of this contain a degree of self-
denigration highly unattractive to a modern reader, with a
description of the seven festering wounds caused by the
seven deadly sins to which Henry claimed to be addicted,
but there is some real sensibility and feeling. The book
contains some of the revealing personal comments so rare
in this period. The duke admitted a revulsion for the stench
of the poor and sick; he enjoyed the scent of fine ladies, but
preferred kissing the lower-born, for they were more
responsive. War, of course, limited the literary activities of
the nobility considerably, and it is perhaps significant that

the earls of Hereford, the most important patrons, were also the most inactive of the earls in campaigning.

The fourteenth century was an age of conspicuous consumption and display by the nobility. Dress was often extravagant. The Scots taunted the English:

> Long berde hertles,
> Peynted hode witles,
> Gay cote graceles,
> Maketh Englissheman thriftles.[9]

One chronicler commented on the way in which fashions changed constantly; long and wide one year, short and narrow-waisted another, with extravagant sleeves and huge hoods. Densely embroidered clothes were highly prized, like the 'summer vestment powdered with leopards',[10] bequeathed by the Earl of Suffolk to his son in 1369. Gold and silver plate, often encrusted with jewels, were another form of ostentation. The will of the Earl of Warwick, who also died in the plague year 1369, contained a long list of gold cups, rings, and such items as 'a cross of gold, wherein part of the very cross of our Saviour is contained, enamelled with the arms of England'.[11] Plate could be used for surprisingly mundane purposes: the Earl of Hereford bequeathed 'a basin, in which we are accustomed to wash our head'.[12]

English food in the fourteenth century enjoyed a better reputation than it does today. Jean le Bel, who went on the 1327 campaign against the Scots, was highly impressed. He was surprised to be able to buy a good fat capon for three or four pence, and a dozen fresh herrings for a penny, and was amazed that despite the lack of vineyards there was plenty of wine to be had, imported from Gascony or the Rhineland. His descriptive powers failed him when it came to a feast given by Queen Isabella at York. 'There you could see the great nobility well served with great plenty of dishes and side plates, so remarkable that I could not name or describe them.'[13] Food on such occasions was served with at least as much attention to appearance as to flavour. The alliterative poem *Morte Arthure* describes boars' heads burnished with silver, peacocks and plovers in platters of gold, swans on silver chargers, pastries, dainties, and a whole range of other delicacies. Henry of Lancaster's *Livre des Seyntz Medicines* bears witness to the pleasure that the great man took in food, both in eating it and in ordering rich meats and devising sauces. Unfortunately, the only two recipes he gave reflected his subject matter, and were for the preparation of rose-water and chicken broth for invalids.

The great feasts with their heavily-spiced and flavoured dishes were, of course, exceptional occasions. An idea of everyday aristocratic diet is provided by the entry for 24 June 1319 in a household account of Elizabeth de Burgh and her husband Roger Damory. There was half a carcase of salt beef, a small side of bacon, half a pig and a quantity of mutton. Forty herrings, two salt stockfish, two ling, half a salmon, whiting and eels provided fish courses. For poultry, there were two ducks, six hens and thirteen pullets, with a hundred and fifty eggs and a pennyworth of milk. A large quantity of bread was provided, with forty gallons of ale and eight of wine to wash the food down. The total cost was just over £1, and probably over fifty people were fed. Fruit also featured in the diet of the period, particularly apples and pears, with occasional luxuries like pomegranates. Expensive imports like sugar and rice feature on some accounts. One of the side-effects of a medieval diet can be seen from the examination of Bartholomew Burghersh's teeth: they were ground down practically flat, as a result of eating large quantities of roughly ground, gritty bread.

By modern standards, the nobles of the late thirteenth and fourteenth centuries endured very considerable discomfort and privation in their living conditions, which were cold, draughty, smelly and lacking in privacy. However, considerable improvements were taking place. In Edward I's reign there was a strong emphasis on defence in castle-building, as for example at Caerfili, built by the earls of Gloucester. By the end of Edward III's reign John of Gaunt was building a sumptuous and elegant range of buildings at Kenilworth which added nothing to the military strength of the castle. Thomas of Lancaster's

Dunstanburgh, with its great twin-towered gatehouse and extensive curtain walls, can perhaps be seen as marking the end of the tradition of which Edward I's castles in north Wales are the most striking examples. Domestic buildings were increasingly built as an integral part of the castle. The Valence castle of Goodrich, dating from the turn of the thirteenth and fourteenth centuries, provides an early example. Late in Edward III's reign the Scrope family built Bolton at Wensleydale. There, the whole courtyard was surrounded by halls, chambers and rooms, all forming a unified whole. Typically for a north-country castle, the towers were square, a shape less efficient from a military point of view than round towers, but providing much more convenient accommodation.

Castles and great manor houses had to meet several needs, providing both for a small permanent staff and for the occasional visits of the lord with his household. Sometimes duplicate sets of accommodation were provided to meet this problem. At Chepstow, Roger Bigod gave the castle two halls, each with its buttery and pantry; an early example of an increasingly common practice. A growing desire for privacy led to the construction of chambers, to which the lord could retire away from the hubbub of the hall. Thomas of Lancaster's accounts reveal the existence of five separate chambers at Kenilworth Castle, while at Tutbury a fenced garden gave privacy out-of-doors. At his birthplace, Grosmont, Henry Duke of Lancaster added two new blocks of accommodation, each three stories high, well provided with windows and fire-places. One finely decorated chimney still stands, incongruously modern in contrast to the solid mass of twelfth and thirteenth-century stonework.

Sanitation was considerably improved. In some castles all the privies were concentrated into one area, to reduce the stench elsewhere. At Goodrich a fine latrine tower features three parallel shafts discharging into the moat. Later in the fourteenth century a tower was built at Langley in Northumberland containing three tiers of four privies. Arrangements for water supply were often complex, though as far as is known, Edward III was the only person of his day to enjoy the luxury of a bath fitted with hot and cold running water.

The buildings of the fourteenth century testify to the richness and complexity of magnate life, rather than to the unease and insecurity of a violent age. The many castles reflect a desire to display wealth rather than suggesting a need for defence. A castle like Nunney, built by John de la Mare in the 1370s out of the profits of campaigns in France, may look formidable enough with its machicolated towers in the latest French fashion, but the fine double lancet windows tell a different story. Courtly ceremonial rather than military discipline characterized the way of life of those who lived in fourteenth-century English castles.

The century of the three Edwards was one of important change for the English nobility. Society was becoming more consciously stratified. The development of the House of Lords gave the upper ranks of the aristocracy a new sense of identity, and by the end of Edward III's reign there was a far clearer sense of order, from the royal dukes down through the earls, barons and bannerets to the knights and squires, than there had been in his grandfather's day. This was not, however, a society of rigid castes. The established nobility resented such additions to their ranks as Piers Gaveston, but the new creations of 1337, which were made with the full support of the parliamentary peerage, met with no hostility.

Perhaps the greatest change was in the attitude of the crown towards the nobility. Edward I had tried to set strict bounds upon the jurisdictional rights of the magnates, and he intervened where he could to turn the patterns of inheritance to his advantage, often using questionable methods. He faced some opposition, notably from the Earls of Hereford and Norfolk in 1297, but it was his son's reign which witnessed the acute political difficulties that could result from a breakdown of co-operation between the crown and the magnates. There is a remarkable contrast between the career of Edward II's bitter opponent Thomas of Lancaster and that of his nephew Henry of Grosmont, Earl and then Duke of Lancaster under Edward III. For in

Edward III's reign past positions were strikingly reversed. No longer were magnates in debt to the king; they were owed money by him. The king assisted the nobles in their manipulation of the laws of inheritance, and protected their rights of jurisdiction rather than challenging them. Edward was generous to those who served him well, and showed no lack of enthusiasm in adding to the ranks of the English earls. His policies arguably weakened the position of the crown in the long term, but as far as he was concerned, they paid a handsome dividend both in domestic politics and in the war with France. It is not surprising that his reign should have witnessed an evident increased sophistication in the life of the upper classes.

The nobles of the fourteenth century lived grandly, but their ostentation did not always extend to their obsequies. Otto de Grandson asked in his will that no armed horse or armed men should precede his coffin. His corpse was not to be covered in rich fabric, but only with a simple white cloth marked with the red cross of a crusader. Guy, Earl of Warwick, requested in 1315 that he should be buried with no funeral pomp, while Richard, Earl of Arundel, showed his financial sagacity to the last, and specified that no more than 500 marks be spent on his funeral. It is perhaps fitting that this chapter should end where it began; with Bartholomew Burghersh. He would have been appalled to find that his tomb and skeleton were to be the subject of an archaeological excavation: he wished to be treated with proper respect and dignity after death. His body was to be taken with all speed to Walsingham, and he asked:

That two torches be carried along, one on one side and the other on the other side, which are to be lighted at passing through every town, and then given to the church where it shall rest at night. Likewise I will that the chariot in which it be carried shall be covered with red cendall [a rich cloth], with the lion of my arms thereon, and my helmet at the head; and to every church wherein it may rest all night the like cloth of cendall with arms thereon to be left. . . . On the day of my funeral no other cover to be laid on my body than that of red cendall, with the lion of my arms, with my helmet, and also a taper at the head and another at the feet, and on every side a torch.[14]

6

'Our Just Quarrel'

The Hundred Years War

Edward III was one of the greatest of English war leaders and his fame rests on the achievements of the armies he deployed in his struggle with the Valois kings of France. Edward was in fact much more than a heroic soldier; he was politically adept, and showed himself to be a man of some cultural sensitivity. It is not possible, however, to make sense of the domestic history of his reign without establishing an understanding of the king's main enterprise; the war with France.

England and France were old enemies, but ever since the loss of Normandy under King John in 1204 the English had shown themselves to be unenthusiastic and ineffective in overseas campaigns, until they were inspired with a new enthusiasm by Edward III. Campaigning then took place in northern France, in Brittany and in Gascony; the conflict even spilled over into Spain. Everywhere English armies proved their mastery of military techniques, and it was only in Edward III's final years that it became apparent that they were not wholly invincible.

The origins of the Hundred Years War can be traced back many years. Both Edward I and Edward II fought wars against the French, and their failure to resolve the problems that arose from their position as vassals of the King of France for the duchy of Aquitaine, or Gascony, forms part of the background of Edward III's conflict with the Valois kings. Just as Edward I claimed rights of jurisdiction over Scotland by virtue of the homage he claimed from the

Scottish kings, so Philip IV laid claims to intervene in Gascon affairs. In 1294 Gascon involvement in a private naval war between English and Norman sailors provided Philip IV with the opportunity to summon Edward to appear before the *parlement* of Paris. The English did not want a war, and tried without success to negotiate a marriage alliance but conflict was not to be avoided. The war was extremely costly for both parties. Each side sought allies in the Low Countries and in Germany at great expense and with scanty results. English forces held on gallantly in Gascony, but the campaign Edward I planned for 1297, which was to consist of an invasion of France from the north with the aid of his allies, fizzled out miserably in truce negotiations. The bitterest fighting was that between the men of the Cinque Ports and those of Yarmouth; the riots between English troops and their Flemish allies ran it a close second. The French held their distance, and Edward, his financial resources exhausted, came to terms.

Although Edward II was married to a French princess, arguments continued over the question of the homage owed to the King of France. The matter came to a head after the accession of Charles IV in 1322. A dispute occurred over the construction of a new fortified town on the Gascon border at St Sardos; the English hanged a French official from the stake planted to mark the site. When it became evident in the course of negotiations that Edward II was reluctant to perform homage, Charles declared Gascony confiscate. However, Queen Isabella was sent to France to negotiate, and the matter was settled when the young Prince Edward did homage to Charles. The English promised to pay a massive relief, or feudal inheritance due, of £60,000, and lost the territory of the Agenais.

Throughout Edward III's reign the French insisted that the problem of Gascony was at the root of their dispute with the English. In fact, Edward performed homage twice to Philip VI, in 1329 and in more elaborate terms two years later. On the second occasion he slipped out of England in disguise, and the two kings agreed to try to settle all outstanding differences between them. The many problems of boundary disputes, claims for reparations, demands of merchants for compensation for war losses and so forth were not easily resolved. In the Processes of Montreuil and Périgeux commissions had sat at great length in Edward I's and Edward II's reigns, to little effect. In the Process of Agen set up in 1331 the endless quibbles of the skilled diplomats served to divide rather than unite the two countries. There was trouble over the Agenais and a clear incompatibility between the French position and English efforts to deny the full implications of the liege homage that Edward III had performed to Philip.

Gascony was certainly worth fighting for. An estimate of 1324 put the receipts from the duchy at £13,000 a year, while the wine trade was important to England, with perhaps twenty-five thousand tuns a year imported. Such economic considerations were probably less important, however, to Edward III than his honour. He was obliged to defend his inheritance, and must have known that the charges against his father included the alleged loss of Scotland, Gascony and Ireland. In the past, the French had displayed an utter determination to drive the English from Gascony, but as the first representative of the new Valois dynasty, it is possible that Philip VI was anxious to establish his right to the throne with a decisive triumph. In 1329 he drew up an elaborate invasion plan for Gascony. It is more likely, however, that he intended to use the threat of confiscation as a means of putting pressure on the English should their policies elsewhere threaten French interests. In the 1330s there were far more reasons for war between England and France than had existed in the 1290s or 1320s, and it is these which explain why the struggle which began in 1337 was so much more serious than the earlier conflicts.

One element of rivalry has already been discussed. In 1334 the young King David of Scotland was established at Château-Gaillard, and Philip VI made it clear that any settlement with Edward III must include Scotland. There was very real alarm in England. One letter estimated that should the Scots join with the French in an invasion, their joint army would number forty thousand men. It was plain to Edward that his ambitions in the north could not be realized as long as the Scots could rely on French support.

Just as the English felt threatened by French diplomatic moves towards Scotland, so the French resented Edward III's activities in the Low Countries. The complex world of the rivalries of the various princes there, some of whom were vassals of the French king, and some of the German Empire, provided many opportunities for intervention. In 1328 the French had won a striking victory over the Flemish townspeople at Cassel, but they could not destroy the strong English economic interests in the region. The Low Countries formed the most heavily industrialized part of northern Europe, and the weavers there were almost wholly dependent on the import of English wool. An English embargo on wool exports to Flanders in 1336 made it clear to the townspeople that links with England were highly desirable, even though their count was an ally of Philip VI. Edward further threatened French interests by creating a network of alliances with the rulers of Hainault, Guelders, Juliers and elsewhere. The gains that Philip had achieved with his victory at Cassel were considerably eroded by 1337.

Control of the sea was another important issue. In the 1290s the English had begun to develop a theory of their command of the sea; in 1320 some Flemish envoys even appealed to Edward II 'as he is lord of the sea'[1]. In 1336 Edward III declared that 'our progenitors, kings of England, were lords of the English sea on every side'[1], but repeated acts of piracy, particularly by the sailors of Calais and Wissant, showed that the claim was an empty one. Naval rivalry grew in 1337, and can be seen as a cause of the war rather as it had been in 1294. The English felt their position to be particularly threatened because after the postponement of a planned crusade the French fleet was moved round from the Mediterranean to the Channel. The crusade was to have been led by Philip VI, and Edward III had intended to take part; bickering over the plans contributed to sour relations between the two rulers.

The actual breach between Edward III and Philip VI came over yet another issue. Philip confiscated Gascony on the grounds that the English king had given refuge to his enemy Robert of Artois. Robert had initially been a staunch supporter of Philip, but in 1332 he was disgraced when he tried to bolster his claim to the county of Artois with forged documents. There were suspicions that he had poisoned his aunt who had held Artois until 1332, but the violence of Philip's feelings towards him is hard to explain. The French king was undoubtedly very angry when Robert found his way to the English court in 1336.

For contemporaries, Robert of Artois's importance in promoting the war extended further. It was thought that it was he who persuaded Edward III to lay claim to the French throne. This claim was to be constantly stressed by English ambassadors in reply to the French arguments that the central issue in the war was that of Gascony. The direct line of the Capetian dynasty which had ruled France since 987 died out in 1328. The throne then went to Philip of Valois, who was the son of a younger brother of Philip IV. Through his mother Isabella, daughter of Philip IV, Edward III was nearer in blood to the throne, but as the French were quick to point out, his claim was inherited through a female, whereas Philip's lay in the male line. The English had made a formal claim on Edward III's behalf in 1328, but no serious challenge to Philip VI had been mounted. Edward III's homage to the French king could be read as an effective recognition of Philip's right to the throne.

The story was that after his arrival in England Robert of Artois placed a heron before the king at a great feast, taunting him that this most cowardly of birds was a suitable dish for a man who did not dare claim his rightful inheritance. The poem that tells of the incident is a satirical piece of anti-English propaganda, but it may have been based on a genuine incident. Edward laid claim to the French throne in 1337, and in 1340 formally assumed the title of King of France. The claim was not important as a cause of the war, but it soon emerged as an important weapon in the English armoury of propaganda and of diplomatic argument.

In the 1330s Edward employed an impressive group of diplomatic experts, some of whom had even been professors of civil law. They were well versed in the precedents of the past, but, as various memoranda show, they found the framework of feudal relations that had governed Anglo-

French diplomacy to be a strait-jacket. One of them, Elias Jonestone, recommended that the traditional arguments should be used only until they were corrected by the king and council, or until better ones appeared. The claim to the French throne transformed the whole basis of disputes between the rival sovereigns. No longer would Edward III appear as a rebellious vassal, disregarding the terms of his homage; rather, as a claimant to the throne he was the equal of Philip VI. It was possible for Edward to try, not without some success, to win support in France by promising to return to the good government of St Louis and to abandon such unpopular financial techniques as the debasement of the coinage. One Norman was imprisoned for six years for asserting that Edward III should have the French throne, since he was better than Philip at exercising the traditional royal power of touching for the king's evil, or scrofula. For Edward's allies the claim was particularly important. The formal assumption of the title of King of France in 1340 took place largely at the request of the Flemings, for it permitted them to take up arms against Philip VI while still in theory remaining subject to the French crown. It would be wrong, however, to see the claim simply as a diplomatic bargaining counter. Edward III had seen three highly improbable coups succeed: that of Isabella and Mortimer in 1327, his own in 1330, and Edward Balliol's in 1332. It was surely within the bounds of possibility that he might one day be crowned at Rheims.

Major wars rarely have simple causes, and the Hundred Years War was no exception. The complexities of feudal relationships; the clash of economic and political rivalries in the Low Countries; the question of Scotland; the control of the Channel – all these combined with an intricate dynastic situation to make the war virtually inevitable. In addition, neither Edward nor Philip was absolutely secure at home. Success in a foreign war was a good recipe for strengthening a political position, while Edward certainly had a personal enthusiasm for war which the difficulties he had encountered in Scotland had not dashed. With his great campaigns in France, he appears in retrospect as the undoubted aggressor, but in the early stages the French

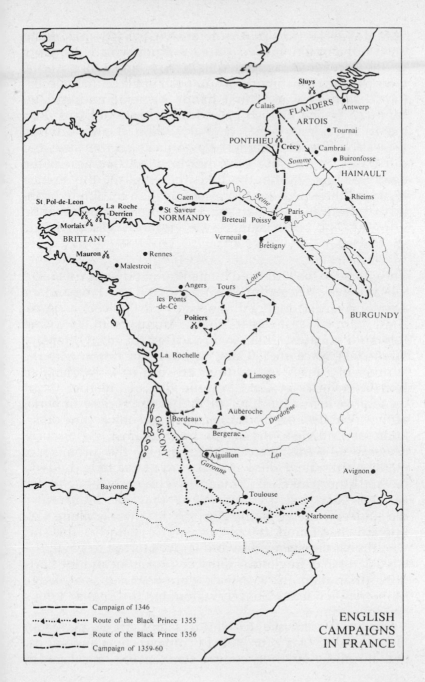

ENGLISH
CAMPAIGNS
IN FRANCE

- –––––– Campaign of 1346
- ····◄····◄····◄···· Route of the Black Prince 1355
- ◄––◄––◄–– Route of the Black Prince 1356
- –·––·––·– Campaign of 1359-60

attitude was far from purely defensive. In 1338 a major raid on Southampton caused damage from which the town hardly recovered, as rent rolls testify, and other coastal raids gave the inhabitants of southern England an unaccustomed taste of war at first hand. A memorandum later captured by the English provides evidence of plans for a major invasion in 1338. In 1339 Philip VI was advised to destroy English commerce by attacks on the wine and salt trade, and on the great herring fleet that assembled every year at Yarmouth. Like the English, the French regarded the war as far more serious than the limited conflict of the war of St Sardos. The complex concatenation of events and circumstances was not to be resolved by a short war.

The course of the Hundred Years War in Edward III's reign falls into well-defined phases. In the first, the king and his advisers were strongly influenced by past precedent. As in King John's war against Philip Augustus in 1214 and Edward I's against Philip IV in 1294–7, the main offensive was to take place not in Gascony but in the north, with the support of a massive coalition. Edward III even obtained from Ludwig IV of Germany the title of Imperial Vicar-General, which gave him full rights to exercise imperial authority in the Low Countries. He could enforce the obligation of Ludwig's vassals to fight against the French. Theoretical rights were backed up by the promise of massive subsidies, following Edward I's example. Ludwig IV and the Duke of Brabant were each bought for £60,000; surviving accounts show that the Brabantines did indeed receive some £30,000 in 1338–9 alone. As Edward I had found, the cost of a grand alliance of this sort was almost disastrous: Edward III was forced to pawn the Great Crown of England. Henry of Grosmont and the Earls of Northampton and Warwick were detained as a pledge for money-lenders who rightly doubted the English king's creditworthiness.

Edward III crossed to Flanders in 1338. A period of 'phoney war' was occupied by diplomatic manoeuvres. One chronicler unkindly commented that the king stayed at

Antwerp doing nothing save 'jousting and leading a jolly life'.[2] When the allied army advanced into France in 1339 it achieved little. The siege of Cambrai failed, and the first of a long series of challenges between Edward III and Philip VI aimed at settling their dispute by means of single combat came to nothing. The two armies confronted each other in full battle array at Buironfosse, but neither made an attacking move. Edward could not afford further subsidies to his allies, and was forced to withdraw.

In the next year the English achieved their first great success. The French had assembled a large fleet at Sluys, so as to prevent an English landing and possibly in the hope of invading England themselves. On 24 June, with sun and wind behind them, the English ships crashed into the dense mass of the enemy fleet whose vessels were chained together. The English archers caused a great deal of damage, and in a fierce mêlée of hand-to-hand fighting the men-at-arms achieved a victory. So many of the enemy were drowned that it was said that if the fish could have spoken, they would have learned French.

Edward lacked sufficient financial resources to follow up the victory at sea. The land campaign of 1340 followed a dismal course, very like that of the previous year. A truce was agreed after the failure of the siege of Tournai; again the armies failed to engage in battle. The English allies recovered some lost territory, but Edward could show little save empty coffers as his achievement. The strategy of the grand alliance had failed, and in 1341 Ludwig IV revoked the appointment of Edward as Imperial Vicar general. The Earl of Salisbury, who had argued in 1338 that the German alliance was unlikely to yield profitable results, and that the English would be unable to pay the promised subsidies in full, was proved right. The following years saw the steady decline of English influence in the Low Countries. In 1345 Edward was unable to press his wife's claim to part of the county of Hainault on the death of her father. The same year saw the assassination of Jacques van Artevelde, the leader of the Ghent commune who had done much to advance the English cause in Flanders.

In 1341, in Edward III's view, God presented him with a just cause for intervention in France, which changed the whole basis of English strategy. In that year Duke John III of Brittany died, and left his duchy to be disputed between his half-brother John de Montfort and his niece Joan of Penthièvre. She was married to Philip VI's nephew Charles of Blois, and obtained full French support for her claim. There was, however, a traditional connection between Brittany and England. Duke John had held the earldom of Richmond since 1334, and in a skilful balancing-act had maintained good relations with both Edward III and Philip VI. Now, Edward gave his backing to the Montfort claim, appealing to the provincial particularism of the Bretons who were resentful of a French government dominated by councillors drawn from the east of the country. The English king was easily persuaded that Brittany 'if he could conquer it, would be the best start that he could have for the conquest of the realm of France'.[3]

A small expedition sailed early in 1342 under the command of the Hainaulter Walter Mauny, the man who had conducted the first English raid on the continent in 1337. He was joined by the Earl of Northampton, and in the battle of Morlaix the French were given a sharp taste of the effectiveness of English men-at-arms fighting on foot with the support of archers. In the autumn Edward III himself sailed with a large force. His adversary of France, as the English termed Philip VI, also took the field, but as in the past made no move to attack. Following papal intervention, a truce was agreed at Malestroit. The English had firmly established their presence in Brittany, and both sides perhaps felt that they had too much to lose from a major engagement.

The events of 1341 marked merely the beginning of many years of civil conflict in Brittany. Agreement in the succession dispute was reached only in 1365, after John de Montfort's son John had finally defeated Charles of Blois. Until then, the situation in the duchy was a confused one of sieges, skirmishes and truces, with the Montfortian party relying firmly on English aid. Brittany was a constant problem for the French, diverting badly-needed resources. For the English, control of castles and towns on the Breton coast did much to assure the safety of the important sea-routes from England to Gascony. The Breton problem added a significant new dimension to the issues already dividing England and France.

Abortive peace negotiations at Avignon followed the truce of Malestroit. English insistence on the validity of Edward III's claim to the French throne was the main stumbling-block. The French insisted on the maintenance of the feudal relationship between Edward III and Philip VI, and were not prepared to concede that the English should hold the duchy of Gascony in full sovereignty. Following the diplomatic failure, Edward broke the truce in 1345, after some provocation from the French.

Edward's plans in 1345 were ambitious. Three fleets were prepared for a triple-pronged attack on France, via Flanders, Brittany and Gascony. The king himself went to Flanders, but events there merely underlined the startling decline in English influence in the Low Countries, and he achieved little. In Brittany, however, the Earl of Northampton and Thomas Dagworth had some striking successes. In 1346 a small force defeated Charles of Blois at St Pol de Léon, and in the next year Dagworth with a small troop made an astonishing night march, completely surprised Charles and took him prisoner at La Roche-Derrien.

Gascony formed the third prong of Edward's strategy. In the early stages of the war English policy had been that the war in the south-west should be financed out of Gascon resources. This had resulted in the accumulation of large debts and the near breakdown of the local administration. It proved impossible to control Gascon affairs effectively from Westminster, and in 1344 the Earl of Arundel and Henry of Grosmont were given full powers to act on the king's behalf in the duchy. In the next year Henry was appointed to lead a force of two thousand men to Gascony, and for the first time the English took the initiative in the war there.

Henry of Grosmont, who became Earl of Lancaster in 1345, was one of Edward III's greatest commanders. His first Gascon campaign was astonishingly successful.

Bergerac was taken, and a major French army defeated in a surprise attack at Auberoche. English control was re-established over much territory which had been lost earlier in the war. Then in 1346 Lancaster raided deep into French-held lands to the north. The army, a mere one thousand strong according to a newsletter from the earl, pillaged and burned its way to Poitiers, which it captured: 'We stormed it on the Wednesday next after Michaelmas, and it was won by force, and all those in the city were taken or slain.'[4]

The French were not inactive in the face of English success, and in April 1346 they began the siege of Aiguillon with a large army. Lancaster needed assistance, and a major expedition was prepared in England under the command of the king himself. Medieval ships with their broad beams and inefficient square sails could not tack into the wind, and the fleet was initially forced to return to port by contrary winds. It set sail again early in July, and on the eve of departure the king wrote:

All the lords are of one accord and good will to go with us, and by their common assent we have decided to leave on the next tide, with God's help, and to make our way and arrive where God gives us grace, and according to the way the wind blows, to avoid a long time at sea.[5]

The landing in fact took place on the Cotentin peninsula in Normandy. It is possible that Edward's strategy was deliberate, and that, like the Allied commanders in 1944, he kept the plan for an invasion of Normandy secret. It was said that a renegade Norman noble, Godfrey de Harcourt, had advised him that the Norman countryside was rich and plentiful, and that there was much to be gained by campaigning there. It is more likely, however, that the king's letter was truthful. Bartholomew Burghersh explained in a newsletter that Edward could make no headway towards Gascony, 'and since it pleased not God that he should go that way, he turned to the land where God should give him grace, and arrived well in good case, with all the fleet, in a country which is called Cotentin.'[6]

As Edward landed, he stumbled: blood poured from his

Edward I.

Edward I returning from Gascony.

Caernarfon Castle. Built by Edward 1 in imitation of Constantinople it was unusual in having polygonal towers, patterned with bands of different coloured stone.

The Eleanor Cross at Geddington, Northamptonshire.

The coronation of John Balliol in 1292. Edward I was not in fact present at Balliol's enthronement, although the artist shows him placing the crown on Balliol's head.

John Balliol does homage to Edward I, December, 1292.

Edward 1 (*on the left*), confronting Philip IV of France in 1297. A sketch on an exchequer memoranda roll.

The preparation of a medieval feast.

Edward 1 ordering the exchequer to observe all the clauses of Magna Carta, 1300. A sketch on an exchequer memoranda roll.

Medieval bankers at work.

Scarborough Castle, where Piers Gaveston was besieged in 1312.

The unsuccessful siege of Carlisle by the Scots in 1315. Andrew Harclay is shown leading the defence of the city.

Donc se partirent
nouuelles par le
pais tant quelles
puruindrent

Queen Isabella and her
forces welcomed by the
people of Bristol, 1326.

The execution of the Younger
Despenser at Hereford, 1326.

The effigy of Edward Despenser (d. 1375), grandson of Hugh Despenser the Younger at Tewkesbury.

Berkeley Castle, scene of Edward II's imprisonment.

The coronation of Edward III, 1327.

Sir Geoffrey Luttrell with his wife and daughter-in-law. His armour and equipment is typical of that of English knights in the initial years of the Hundred Years War.

Hawking.

A fourteenth-century naval battle.

ABOVE LEFT
A gold noble. Edward III began to mint gold coins in 1344. He is
shown on board ship, in celebration of his victory at Sluys in 1340.

ABOVE RIGHT
A guiennois, minted in Gascony, showing the Black Prince armed to
fight on foot, rather than horseback, as was normal on coins and seals.

Edward III and David II of Scotland.

The capture of David II of Scotland at Neville's Cross, 1346. The artist
has erroneously placed the battle outside Newcastle, rather than
Durham.

Death reaching out for his victim.

Edward III, from a
misericord in
Tewkesbury Abbey.

Edward III outside the
walls of Rheims in
1359.

Windsor Castle, extensively rebuilt by Edward III.

The Bassett Stall in St George's Chapel, Windsor; the earliest arms of a garter knight.

Jousting, from a misericord in Gloucester Cathedral.

Edward III in old age from the Great East Window in York Minster.

The funeral effigy of Edward III, probably based on his death mask.

nose after his fall, but rebuking those who saw this as a bad
omen, he claimed that it was a sign that the land welcomed
him. The army marched on a wide front towards Caen,
burning and looting as it went. The French were caught
completely by surprise. When the news reached Aiguillon,
the siege was promptly lifted, and the French army under
the Duke of Normandy hurried north, but it was too late.
The English took Caen after bitter fighting: 'And then were
taken the constable and the chamberlain, and to the
number of a hundred knights, and six or seven score
squires, and many knights, squires and other people of the
town were killed, in the streets, houses and gardens'[7], as
one eyewitness put it. Burghersh put the death toll at about
five thousand, 'so that, praise be our Lord, our business has
gone as favourably as it could.'[8]

From Caen, Edward III decided to press on inland, even
though he would no longer have the support of his fleet. He
claimed that he wanted to meet his adversary Philip in
battle, but in practice his aim was to conduct a ravaging raid
that would put pressure on the French, impoverishing their
country and reducing their faith in their ruler. His major
problem was how to cross the Seine. Shadowed by the
enemy, finding the bridges either guarded or broken, the
English marched almost as far as Paris. Repeated challenges from Philip asking to meet Edward in single combat
met with ambiguous replies. The French were diverted by
the English destruction of villages and even suburbs of
Paris while the bridge at Poissy was hastily repaired. The
army slipped across away from the unsuspecting French
and marched rapidly north only to meet a fresh obstacle in
the form of the river Somme. The French seemed to have
them trapped, but a ford was discovered at Blanche-Taque.
One version has it that its existence was revealed by a
prisoner when Edward offered a reward; another, that an
English resident in the area provided the vital information.
English archers forced the French who were guarding
the crossing into flight and the army again escaped its
pursuers.

Edward III had been very fortunate, but the French were
close on his heels and further retreat was difficult. At Crécy

he decided to stand and fight. He felt in a strong moral position as Crécy was on home ground in the county of Ponthieu – an English possession since 1279. The tactics of the battle will be discussed in the next chapter; for the present, it is enough to note that, although his forces were considerably smaller than the French, Edward won a resounding victory. He supervised the fight from a windmill in the rear of the lines; his eldest son, the sixteen-year-old Black Prince, fought in the thick of the mêlée. According to Froissart's famous story, the king declared that his son should take pains to win his spurs, 'For I wish, if God has so ordained it, that the day should be his, and that the honour shall be with him and with those to whose care I have entrusted him.'[9] This was one of the first battles at which cannon were used, but the real responsibility for the victory lay with the king's generalship and with the fighting skill of the English men-at-arms and archers.

After Crécy the English host moved on to blockade Calais. Many reinforcements were summoned for the lengthy siege. The inhabitants held out stubbornly, and must have thought their privations worth-while when in July 1347 a large French army appeared to relieve the town. Edward hoped for a battle, and wrote:

> Our adversary of France has encamped near Mountjoye, which is not three French leagues from our host, and we can see the tents and lodges from our said host, and we hope with the aid of our lord Jesus Christ that we will soon have a good tourney according to our just quarrel, to the honour of us and of all our realm, so we ask you to pray devoutly for us.[10]

Agreement was almost reached for a carefully staged battle, but when the French received the English offer, they 'began to vary their terms and to raise the question of the town again, as if putting off the battle'.[11] The marshy terrain was unsuitable for an attack on the English positions, and Philip did not want to suffer another defeat; he withdrew his army in haste, burning the tents and equipment. Calais was left at Edward's mercy, and the townspeople surrendered in the scene immortalized by Rodin's statue of the seven burghers. All who lived in the town were ordered to leave it, and were given a meal by the English which must have come as a considerable relief after the diet of dogs, cats and rats to which they had been reduced. Calais was repopulated by English settlers, and developed into a strong base for offensive operations. The convenience of the short sea-crossing was great, and the possession of Calais more than compensated for the decline of English influence in the Low Countries.

Two years of campaigning in 1346–7 had transformed the war. Astonishing successes had been achieved in Gascony, Brittany and northern France. In addition, the Scots had been defeated at Neville's Cross in 1346 and their king taken prisoner. The costs of war had been high; the wardrobe accounts alone show expenditure of £242,162 from 1344 to 1347. There would have been difficulties in following up the successes even had the appearance of the Black Death in 1348 not made further campaigning impossible for a time. In 1350 Edward III won what was probably his least glorious battle, the sea-fight of Les Espagnols sur Mer, the product of an unprovoked attack on a Castilian merchant fleet. In Brittany Walter Bentley's victory at Mauron ensured continued English dominance in the duchy for a decade. Negotiations in the early 1350s followed a similar course to those ten years earlier. The English refused to ratify an agreement reached at Guines in 1353, which would have given Edward extensive lands in France in full sovereignty. It is probable that at the last minute they refused to abandon the claim to the French throne, since they were tempted to reopen the war with the aid of a new ally, the maverick Charles, King of Navarre.

Grandiose plans were made for the campaigns of 1354, with expeditions planned for Calais, Normandy and Gascony. Lancaster's Norman venture was rendered abortive by Charles of Navarre, who deserted the English cause. The king's own raid from Calais was abruptly terminated when news came of the capture of Berwick by the Scots. In the south, however, the Black Prince, on his first independent command, conducted a highly successful march from Gascony right across to Narbonne on the Mediterranean coast.

His men raided and pillaged almost at will on the four-hundred-mile journey. The technique of the *chevauchée*, as this type of raid was termed, became a standard English instrument of war. It was less risky than engaging the enemy in battle, yet it put them under considerable pressure. 'And know for certain that, since this war began against the king of France, there was never such loss nor such destruction as there has been in this raid. For the lands and good towns which have been destroyed in this raid found for the King of France more to maintain his war than did half the kingdom'[12], was one report. Contemporaries found little difficulty in inflicting the full horrors of war on a defenceless civilian population while simultaneously aspiring to follow a high ideal of chivalric conduct.

The success of the 1355 raid pales in comparison with the achievement of 1356. The English strategy was to launch a double attack, with Lancaster moving south from Normandy and the Black Prince advancing northwards from Gascony. Lancaster began with a highly successful *chevauchée* in Normandy with almost two thousand five hundred men. Pont-Audemer was relieved, Breteuil revictualled, and Verneuil captured. The French challenged him to battle, but he gave an ambiguous reply and retreated at remarkable speed, making fifty-five miles in one day. He then moved south to Brittany, where he was appointed as captain and royal lieutenant. From there, he had hopes of making contact with the Black Prince, as had been arranged.

The Black Prince marched northwards, plundering as he went, but found that the river Loire was in flood, and the bridge at Les Ponts-de-Cé destroyed. He was forced to retreat without joining Lancaster, and instead of continuing with an enjoyable raid, found himself involved in a headlong race with the French army under King John. Laden with booty, the prince's men could not match the speed Lancaster had shown earlier in the year. Near Poitiers it became clear that there was no option but to fight. The army was tired and short of food, but many present were anxious for a battle. Attempts by two cardinals to negotiate were futile. The apparent weakness of the English position can be gauged by the fact that even an offer by the prince not to fight the French for seven years, and to return all the prisoners he had taken, was unacceptable.

The battle of Poitiers was hard fought. One writer noted that, whereas experienced archers could usually tell after the first four, or at most six, volleys which side would be victorious, on this occasion there was no telling after a hundred. One French battalion, however, left the field without apparent cause; it was commanded by the in-experienced twenty-year-old Duke of Orleans. King John's leadership was ineffective, and in the final mêlée the English were victorious. John was captured, and the shout of 'Guyenne! St George!' rose in triumph from the battlefield. Then 'you might see many an archer, many a knight, many a squire running in every direction to take prisoners on all sides'.[13] Ransoms were one of the main profits of war, and at Poitiers the English reaped a far richer reward than at Crécy, for there many French nobles had been slain, and Edward III had forbidden an undisciplined pursuit for fear of renewed enemy attack. There was much confusion in the aftermath of Poitiers. One French count gave his word to be the prisoner of no less than three different men, whose claims eventually had to be settled in court. There was even argument over who had captured King John himself. The honour was given to Denis de Morbeke, a renegade French knight, but his royal captive was soon entrusted to the Black Prince, and treated with great honour.

The capture of the French king put the English into an extremely strong position. What was now needed was to capitalize on the triumph of arms with diplomatic success. In 1359 an agreement was imposed on John in London. The French were to hand over to Edward an enormous swathe of territory from Calais in the north to Gascony in the south, to be held in full sovereignty. A ransom of four million écus, almost £700,000 in sterling, was agreed. Just as Edward had been prepared to give up his claims to direct lordship in Scotland in return for a massive grant of lands from Edward Bruce, so he was ready to abandon his claim to the French throne in return for almost half of France. The English king's cupidity was too great. The treaty was totally unacceptable to the French council and to the dauphin, the future Charles v. John remained in comfortable captivity, and a fresh campaign was planned for the autumn of 1359.

France by this date was in a dire condition. Although there had been no fresh English expeditionary forces invading since 1356, the country was ravaged by English companies, whose acts of brigandage continued unabated in spite of the nominal truce. There was revolution in Paris, and in the countryside the peasantry rose in the savage and apparently mindless brutality of the *Jacquerie*, as their rebellion was called. It must have seemed to the English that their cause must finally triumph with the king's campaign of 1359.

The strategy of the 1359 expedition was designed to place Edward III on the French throne. Instead of the familiar attacks on several fronts, one huge army set out from Calais to besiege Rheims, the traditional site for crowning kings of France. The city did not open its gates and welcome Edward as a deliverer from the anarchy afflicting France, as he clearly hoped. Instead, he had to blockade it. He did not want to gain the throne by such brutal means as those the crusaders had used in 1204 to place Baldwin on the Imperial throne at Constantinople, and held back from direct assault. Supplies ran short, and in January the siege was lifted. The wet and demoralized army marched eastwards into Burgundy, and then turned to encircle Paris. The dauphin made no move to attack, and Edward was forced to move on, as fodder for the horses ran short. A terrible storm caused considerable damage, and at Brétigny negotiations were reopened. Agreement was reached with surprising ease.

The terms of the treaty of Brétigny marked for the English a considerable retreat from those they had tried to extract in 1358. The ransom was cut to three million écus. An enlarged Gascony along with Ponthieu, Calais and the county of Guines were to be held in full sovereignty by the English. It was agreed that the exchange of territory should take place by June 1361, and that the final renunciations should take place by the following November. In the event, the transfer of lands was not completed until 1362, and the treaty was never fully implemented. Edward III stopped using the title of King of France, but he did not formally give it up. Whether it was English duplicity or ingenuity, or joint miscalculations that caused the treaty to fail cannot be determined. The truth may be that both sides found it unsatisfactory, but were content with what amounted to a truce which left the ultimate issues still unresolved.

The story of the war in Edward III's last years makes a sad anti-climax to the glorious tale of Crécy and Poitiers. Open hostilities with France were not resumed until 1369, but the continued rivalry between the two countries found expression in a conflict in Spain. Many of the great captains and soldiers of fortune found employment either in the service of Pedro the Cruel of Castile, or of his half-brother and rival for the throne Henry of Trastamara. The French backed Henry, and his initial success invited English intervention from the Black Prince, who won a resounding victory at Nájera in 1367. This, the last great triumph of Edward III's reign, was won at high cost, for the successful army was severely struck by dysentery. It was probably on this campaign that the Black Prince contracted the debilitating disease that was to leave him a mere husk of the former man. The high price that the prince demanded of Pedro, asking for both money and land in payment for his assistance, rendered the latter's position impossible. In 1369 Henry invaded, personally killed Pedro and once established on the throne, gave his full support to the French. With its powerful navy, Castile was a valuable ally. Had he taken a more politic approach, the Black Prince might have retained Castile for the English, but as it was, he threw away the victory achieved at Nájera. For him, war was a chivalric route to fame and fortune, rather than an instrument of statesmanship.

For all the romantic aura that surrounds his name, Edward the Black Prince had many failings. His rule in Gascony did not win him the affection of the local populace, and he had no answer to the interference of Charles v, who encouraged the lords of Albret and

Armagnac to present appeals to the *parlement* of Paris. When Charles announced that he was prepared to hear these appeals, he was denying English sovereignty over Gascony and committing himself to a renewal of the war. In 1369 Edward III resumed the title of King of France, and Charles V formally declared the confiscation of the English possessions in France.

The English could not recapture the mood of the great years of success. It is not easy to determine the direction of their strategy in the final years of Edward III's reign, for expeditions rarely succeeded in achieving their objectives. In Gascony, incessant French pressure steadily reduced their hold. In 1371 the Black Prince retaliated against the Bishop and populace of Limoges for their desertion of his cause with a brutality which, although technically justified by the laws of war, was suggestive of desperation. In the next year a fleet bringing reinforcements to the duchy, commanded by the Earl of Pembroke, was defeated at sea off La Rochelle by the Castilian navy. After this the English government virtually abandoned Gascony to its own devices. Few troops and scant financial aid were sent there, and as a result the French gradually took over almost the whole region with the exception of Bayonne and Bordeaux.

In the north a raid led by John of Gaunt in 1369, which cost some £75,000, achieved little: in the next year Robert Knollys, a man rich in experience but short of social standing, was appointed to command an army for two years. He was constantly harassed in his advance towards Paris and when he retreated towards Brittany his rearguard was caught and wiped out. The force broke up, disillusioned and torn by dissension, after only three months. Plans for a major expedition in 1372 were altered at a late stage, and instead of invading France, Edward III on his last active command determined on a naval campaign to repair the damage done at La Rochelle. Thwarted by contrary winds, the fleet achieved nothing. A new English alliance with the Duke of Brittany in the same year merely led to further French successes, and the exile of the duke in 1373.

A great expedition was planned for 1373, with John of Gaunt in command. The initial plan was to sail from

Plymouth to Brittany, but the port of embarkation was changed to Sandwich, and the destination to Calais. There has been much argument about Gaunt's aims. He marched east towards Rheims, but may have intended to turn his forces towards Brittany; it is suggestive that the Duke of Brittany was with him. French forces may have prevented him taking such a route, or alternatively Gaunt may have determined from the outset to march right through France to Gascony, and thence to Spain: through his second wife Constance he had a claim to the Castilian throne, which he wished to implement. The march was long and difficult. There was little food to be found during the winter months, and the raid achieved little save the loss of many of its participants and the exhaustion of the remainder. It did not distract the French from Brittany, and failed to revive English fortunes in Gascony. The cost was over £80,000. An expedition led by the Earl of Salisbury in 1373 sailed too late to achieve much in Brittany, and although further aid for the hard-pressed forces there was planned in 1374, the fleet did not sail until the following year, too late to save the fortresses of Bécherel and St Sauveur.

The case of John Menstreworth was indicative of the disillusion of the English in this phase of the war. He was one of those who accompanied Knollys on his *chevauchée* in 1370, and was responsible for much of the bickering that took place. He was held responsible for the defeat suffered on the retreat, and when his attempt to bring charges against his captain failed, he deserted to the French. It was later claimed that he had misappropriated his men's wages, and worse, that he had agreed to guide a Spanish fleet to England. However, he was captured in Spain and brought back to England to face the ignominious death of a traitor. It would have been inconceivable earlier in the reign that an English knight should join the enemy, but such incidents were an inevitable consequence of failure.

The war was proving very expensive, and was providing the government with few financial compensations in the form of ransoms or other profits. This fact, together with the military disasters, led the English to try to salvage what they could from the débâcle by diplomatic means. At

Bruges John of Gaunt negotiated a two-year truce in 1375. When the reign of Edward III closed in 1377, the war was on the verge of renewal. All that the English now held in France was Calais in the north, and a coastal strip of territory in Gascony stretching from Bordeaux to Bayonne; there were also some garrison forces in Brittany, where the duke was an increasingly discontented ally.

The English had achieved astonishing successes under Edward III in the years up to 1356. It was not that everything had gone their way: grandiose strategies had foundered upon the cost and unreliability of allies and the early stages of the war effectively bankrupted the English king. The English had intended to fight at Buironfosse in 1339, but had not done so; ironically, the victories of Crécy and Poitiers were both achieved when a pursuing French army managed to catch up with a retreating English host. Through their ravaging raids the English created many difficulties for their enemies, as well as winning profits for themselves, but it was the major victories in battle that made it seem that Edward might achieve his highest ambitions. He was above all an opportunist, however, and although many attempts to end the war by diplomacy foundered because of the English insistence on the validity of Edward's claim to the French throne, he was ultimately prepared to give this up in return for major territorial concessions. The English did not, however, gain much territory directly by conquest, in the way that Henry V was to do with his steady reduction of Norman towns and castles. Although Edward III did try in his propaganda to present himself before the French people as a true successor to St Louis, his only success was in appealing to the provincial particularism of people such as the Bretons, who resented the central government based in Paris. The achievement that was recognized in the treaty of Brétigny was to prove remarkably ephemeral in face of the resurgent French monarchy under Charles V.

The reversal of English fortunes in Edward III's declining years was almost as remarkable as the earlier successes. The lack of firm direction by the ageing king was revealed in a want of coherent planning. The earlier grand strategies of simultaneous attacks from various fronts had been abandoned in favour of what appeared to be aimless raids, often launched too late in the year to do much damage. The French had discovered, like the Scots under Edward I, the virtues of relative inactivity when faced with English attack. French commanders such as Bertrand du Guesclin, were ordered not to risk major battles, but English raids were diverted, and English-held territory steadily reduced by a combination of military and political pressure. By the end of his life, Edward III's fortune, which had served him so well in his prime, was at a very low ebb.

7
War, Profits and Chivalry

In his public pronouncements, Edward III found no difficulty in explaining his successes in the Hundred Years War. God had shown him his blessing, 'by his righteous judgement and of his lawful power .... out of respect for our right and according to our deserts'.[1] War was in theory a form of trial before God, in which divine intervention would ensure that victory went to the side whose cause was just. It was this concept of war as a trial which led to the repeated challenges between Edward III and Philip VI to settle their dispute by means of single combat, for in such a fight God could declare whose cause was just quite as easily as in a full-scale battle. Edward even suggested that the issue might be determined by Philip's testing divine approval by walking into a cage of lions, and by demonstrating his ability to cure scrofula. In practical terms, however, both Edward and his opponents placed more trust in the strength of their armies than in questionable manifestations of heavenly approbation. In order to resolve many of the problems posed by the war, it is necessary to analyse military organization and to investigate the motives that led men to fight. Traditional military history, with its stress on battles, and its maps with armies neatly depicted in coloured squares, provides few of the answers. The English war effort must be examined in a wide context, but initially the armies themselves need to be investigated.

Much of the credit for English success must go to the commanders of the armies. Edward III himself was a good leader of men. He had presence, charm, and an ability to inspire his followers. He showed his mettle on his first campaign in Scotland in 1327 when he addressed the troops from horseback. He asked them to do all they could for him and showed a significant concern for discipline when he forbade anyone to advance in front of the banners or to move before orders were given. There is no record to suggest that Edward I had ever made such a speech to his soldiers, but Edward III was to do so again before the battle of Crécy, while at Poitiers the Black Prince gave separate talks to the men-at-arms and to the archers. By their personal courage, the king and his eldest son set an important example. Edward could be rash, as his decision in 1346 to leave the coast and march up the Seine when he had no crossing assured shows, but he cannot be accused of foolhardiness. At Crécy he was able to control events by remaining in the rear; in contrast, Philip VI had little influence over his troops once battle was joined.

For the top positions of military command Edward was largely limited by convention to the highest ranks of society. Some of the earls were of course appointed to that dignity by the king himself, and men like Northampton who owed their eminence to ability rather than birth were well suited to serve as generals. In Henry of Grosmont Edward had a very able soldier and skilled diplomat on whom he could rely completely. Only in his obstinate and long drawn-out siege of Rennes in 1356–7 did Henry incur the king's displeasure. In his later years Edward was less well served by the English aristocracy. John of Gaunt and the king's other sons lacked the charisma of their elder brother the Black Prince, and men like the Earl of Pembroke lacked the outstanding ability of the commanders of the earlier phases of the war. Squabbles among the leaders of expeditions to France reveal a lack of the common purpose that had characterized the war effort in the years prior to the treaty of Brétigny.

Edward was fortunate that in appointing generals he did not have to deal with claims to military command based on hereditary right by men he distrusted. Edward I had been considerably inconvenienced by the demands of Bigod and

Bohun to exercise their rights as marshal and constable; in 1314 the dispute between Hereford and Gloucester as to who should lead the van at Bannockburn led to the latter's suicidal charge into the enemy ranks. According to later statements, the marshal and constable were responsible for such tasks as organizing billeting and sentry duty, maintaining order and keeping records, and were entitled to attend councils of war. They also claimed some of the booty won on campaign. In Edward III's Scottish wars these hereditary posts were still important. At Halidon Hill the first division of the army was commanded by the Earl Marshal and Edward Bohun, who represented his brother the constable. From 1338, however, the hereditary office of marshal was in the hands of a woman: the formidable Margaret, daughter of Thomas of Brotherton. Neither of her husbands was entrusted with the position, and instead Edward gave it to his trusted companion the Earl of Salisbury. On Salisbury's death the Earl of Warwick was appointed marshal; significantly this was only during the king's pleasure – not for life. At the end of the reign the post was held by the Earl of March, and then by Henry Percy. The earls of Hereford lacked military ambition, and made no claims to the constableship, although at the end of the reign Edward III's youngest son, Thomas of Woodstock, received the office because he was granted £1,000 worth of the last Bohun Earl of Hereford's lands. On his great expedition of 1346 the king was able to make his own choice of officers. He nominated Godfrey de Harcourt as marshal jointly with Warwick; his local knowledge of Normandy was of great value. Edward appointed the Earl of Arundel as constable. In 1359 the Earl of March was made constable, while Warwick shared the post of marshal with Suffolk. Edward was undoubtedly better served by such men than was Philip VI by the great nobles of France with their hereditary military posts.

It is sometimes argued that the Hundred Years War saw the rise of professional soldiers, as opposed to aristocrats, to positions of command. Edward III appointed such men as Thomas Dagworth and Walter Bentley to be in charge of the troops in Brittany; the Hainaulter Walter Mauny was another distinguished commander who was not of the highest social standing. Robert Knollys was of knightly rather than baronial rank – this was a factor in the difficulties which arose on his major *chevauchée* in 1370. Edward did not, however, give such men the most important positions, nor was their employment a complete innovation. John de Kingston, who led a substantial raid against the Scots in the autumn of 1298, was a knight and a professional soldier, and the commands given to Roger de Molis in the Welsh wars reflected his ability rather than his social standing. Yet when Edward I nominated Brian FitzAlan of Bedale for a major command in Scotland, he refused as he felt he was not wealthy enough. In the Hundred Years War men like Dagworth, Bentley and Knollys felt that they could win enough riches in war to be able to maintain the roles for which the king selected them. It should not, however, be supposed that such men were any more professional in their attitude to war than a great noble like the Earl of Warwick. High birth was not a concomitant of amateurism in the fourteenth century.

The soldiers who fought for Edward III in France were better equipped than those who had marched to Wales and Scotland under Edwards I and II. The chronicler Jean le Bel commented scathingly on the equipment of the English knights and squires in 1339: they wore outmoded padded hauberks, massive helmets of iron or hardened leather and flowing emblazoned surcoats. The French war provided a sharp incentive for the development of knightly equipment. In the 1320s armour had consisted primarily of a coat of mail, perhaps reinforced with plate to protect the legs, and with curious aillettes, or miniature decorative shields, on the shoulders. Plate armour developed rapidly in the following decades, and by the time of the treaty of Brétigny fitted suits of plate were the rule, with a tight *jupon* replacing the old loose surcoat. For battle, the bascinet with its movable visor and pointed peak was more practical than the old great helm, which was relegated to tournament use. Armour was sometimes covered with cloth; the Black Prince gave one of his followers some plate fitted over with black velvet, embroidered with feathers. The new fashion of fighting on foot influenced the development of armour: fuller protection and greater ease of movement was provided by the new style, which was lighter than the old-fashioned mail. Shields also became smaller and more manoeuvrable.

The archers were a different breed from the ill-organized infantry levies of Edward I's reign. The emergence of the mounted archer during Edward III's Scottish wars marked a profound change, for it meant that English armies were highly mobile and speedy, as Lancaster's hasty retreat in 1356 showed. There were usually similar numbers of mounted archers and men-at-arms in the armies that fought in France, in contrast to the vast hosts of Edward I's day. The only large army that Edward III raised was that for the static operation of the siege of Calais which numbered some thirty-two thousand men. Even the great invasion of 1359, which was exceptional in size totalled only about twelve thousand men. Relatively small forces could be much better equipped than large armies. The archers in Edward III's reign were often uniformed: the Earl of Arundel's men wore red and white suits, and the Black Prince's Cheshire archers sported green and white coats and hats. Much more was done than in the past to provide weapons. In 1341 the government ordered the collection of seven thousand seven hundred bows and a hundred and thirty thousand sheaves of arrows. The Tower of London was developed into a great central arsenal. So great was the demand in 1356, that critical year for the war, that supplies became hard to find: the chamberlain of Chester was told that no arrows could be found in all England, as the king had taken them all for his use. The Black Prince therefore ordered the arrest of all the fletchers in Cheshire, and forced them to work for him.

Many of the archers were provided by the magnates as part of their retinues, and this probably led to the recruitment of better soldiers than the traditional method of using commissions of array. In 1356 arrayers in Rutland could find no one fit to serve. They had discovered one man who could not fight, as he had been wounded in the Black

Prince's service, and had only arrayed two others, neither of whom had sufficient means to provide himself with equipment. The reason for their failure was that the Earl of Warwick and various other magnates had taken all the able-bodied men in the county for their retinues. The crown still persisted in recruiting criminals for the armies. At least one thousand eight hundred pardons were issued to criminals in return for their service at the siege of Calais. Not all were common offenders: the list was headed by the Earl of Warwick, but a more typical figure was Robert le White, guilty of 'homicides, felonies, robberies, rapes of women and trespasses'.[2] Such men could put their nefarious skills to good use in terrorizing the French populace.

The archers were organized in much the same way as in earlier periods, in units of twenty and a hundred, but the superiority of Edward III's forces is suggested by the way in which the Welsh levies came with a chaplain, an interpreter, a standard-bearer, a crier and a doctor for each contingent of a hundred men. Although some men left for home before the armies embarked for France, desertion was not the problem that it had been in the past – once overseas the English Channel provided a substantial deterrent. The evidence of their successes in battle shows that many of the archers must have been highly trained men, though curiously there is no indication that any formal training took place – practice with the longbow was probably on an individual basis. A well-known writ of 1363 regretted that archery was almost wholly neglected as a pastime in favour of such dishonest sports as football, hockey and cockfighting, and all were ordered to practise shooting on holidays. The corporate technique needed for a force of archers to be really effective in battle was probably acquired through practical experience in France, rather than through the formal drilling of recruits.

Historians have laid considerable emphasis on the widespread use of the contract system for recruiting the armies that fought in the Hundred Years War; it avoided the uncertainty involved in a traditional form of summons, when there was no way of knowing how many men would respond. The unpopular element of compulsion was not present when captains contracted to provide troops in return for a fixed lump sum. Contracts were undoubtedly important, but the system was not as new under Edward III as is sometimes suggested. It had been developed in the reigns of the first two Edwards, notably for operations when the king himself was not present. The English armies which fought in Gascony from 1294–8 were partly raised by contract, and there are several examples from the Scottish wars. If the royal administration, and notably the department of the wardrobe, was not available to organize a campaign, then the use of contracts was the simplest alternative. The first major contract army raised by Edward III was that sent to Scotland in 1337, when he himself, with the wardrobe, was engaged in the Low Countries. Contracts were certainly used on a very large scale in the Hundred Years War. In 1345 for example, Henry of Grosmont agreed to go to Gascony with five hundred men-at-arms, five hundred horse archers, and a thousand footsoldiers. On a smaller scale, two years later Thomas Ughtred contracted to serve for a year with twenty men-at-arms and the same number of mounted archers for a fee of £200 and payment of wages. No contracts were made, however, for the great army that the king led to triumph at Crécy and Calais, because that force was largely financed and organized by the household department of the wardrobe in the traditional way. Even as late as 1359–60, the army headed by the king was not raised as a contract force; one battalion was composed of the household knights with their retinues in very much the same way as the army Edward I had led to Scotland in 1300. The widespread use of contracts in the Hundred Years War was not the result of a revolution in military organization, but was a reflection of the fact that the king himself led only a minority of the many expeditions that sailed for France. The old systems of summons, and of appeals to traditional forms of military obligation were far from wholly obsolete as was very clear in 1346–7 and 1359. The fact that the contractual method of raising troops was neither new nor universally employed should not, however, lead to the conclusion that it was not effective. It was highly efficient both from a military and a financial point of view.

Recent work has laid stress less on the skill of the English in battle and more on the quality of their logistics. Edward III's government certainly took more care to plan campaigns than had been done in the past. In 1296 Edward I had ordered the exchequer to assemble sixty thousand troops at Newcastle – a quite impossible number. In contrast, a memorandum of the early 1340s, probably drawn up for the king's expedition to Brittany, gave detailed calculations of the precise number of troops to be raised by the royal household and by the magnates. The total was a highly plausible one of just over thirteen thousand five hundred with twelve thousand sailors in addition. Another document setting out the food requirements for an expedition contained a note: 'Item. Remember to speak with the king, to see if he wishes all the ships to be assembled at Portsmouth, or if some of them should be at other ports, and if so, which.'[3] The king's agreement to the plan for the whole fleet to gather at Portsmouth is recorded. Such evidence of close supervision of preparations by Edward III himself is impressive.

The armies that went to France were undoubtedly well equipped. Accounts show that ample quantities of horseshoes, bows, bowstrings, arrows and other military requirements were provided, while axes, sickles, hand mills and portable ovens ensured that the soldiers could live off the land. In 1359 there were even light leather boats carried in the baggage train, so that the monotonous diet of the army could be supplemented by fishing. The nineteenth-century historian, Sir George Wrottesley, commented that Edward III's army in 1346 was the best equipped of any to leave England prior to the Egyptian expedition of 1882. This important, but mundane, aspect of the war obviously did not attract much contemporary comment, but the process of loading the ships for an expedition to France was described in one poem, though the army embarking at Sandwich is King Arthur's, not Edward III's. The men

Bryngez blonkez on bourde and burlyche helmes;
Trussez in tristly trappyde stedes,
Tentez and othire toylez and targez full ryche,
Cabanes and clathe-sekkes and coferez full noble,
Hekes and haknays and horsez of armez;
Thus they stowe in the stuffe of full stern knyghtez.[4]

In some respects, however, the task of organizing the logistics of Edward III's armies in France was simpler than that for the earlier wars in Wales and Scotland. Forces were smaller in the Hundred Years War, and once in France could almost entirely live off the land. Supplies only had to be provided for the men prior to embarkation and for the start of any expedition. In 1346 the king's receiver of victuals at Portsmouth had charge of only about four thousand quarters of grain, far less than the officials at Berwick during Edward I's reign had been responsible for. The Calais garrison required a continued and ample supply of foodstuffs, but Edward III's reign never saw so concentrated and massive a demand for victuals as there had been between 1294 and 1298. It was possible for the crown to turn from the traditional method of purveyance by the sheriffs and their officials, which was always unpopular, to a system of contracts with merchants. An early example of this took place in 1339–40, when agreements were reached with traders to supply Edinburgh and Berwick, and from the 1350s the practice became increasingly common. Edward III's armies were never seriously hampered by any failures of the victualling arrangements made in England. Severe problems were encountered after the resumption of war in 1369 when it became increasingly difficult to live off the land, as the French deliberately wasted the countryside where the English were operating, and by harassment made the task of the foragers extremely hazardous.

Perhaps the least satisfactory part of the English military machine was the navy. Even the specially built or adapted royal ships were highly unmanoeuvrable, for their high fighting platforms, or castles, added considerably to the windage of a high freeboard. Contrary winds were a perpetual problem. On one occasion the return from Brittany took five weeks, with the fleet being driven right off course to the northern coast of Spain, though the voyage could be completed in less than three days in favourable conditions. Very large numbers of ships were needed, because not only had the soldiers to be transported, but also their mounts. In theory, each knight would have four horses, each squire three, and every mounted archer two. For the massive operation of transporting the forces needed for the Crécy campaign and the siege of Calais, some seven hundred and fifty vessels were required. Sailings were often delayed because of the difficulty of collecting the requisite number of ships together. The initial orders for the assembly of ships in 1346 set the date as the middle of February, but it was not until early June that the fleet finally sailed. It has often been suggested that the English victory at Sluys was important for the later successes in the war, for it assured control of the sea. Certainly it considerably weakened French naval power for a time, but the nature of medieval ships was such that all that could be achieved by any fleet was strictly localized control of a limited area during favourable weather. Nevertheless, it was not until the Earl of Pembroke's defeat off La Rochelle in 1372 that an English expedition was prevented from carrying out its task by enemy naval action, and the south coast of England was not as severely afflicted by enemy raids as was feared by the government and the local people, though the French attack on Winchelsea in 1360 came as a great shock.

Edward III and his commanders won their victories in France by the application and development of the tactics learned in the Scottish wars. The army would normally be divided into three battalions of dismounted men-at-arms, with archers placed on the flanks at an angle, so that they could fire at the advancing enemy from the side. The arrangement is clearly described by Jean le Bel in the case of the abortive battle at Buironfosse in 1339, and this pattern is almost certainly what Froissart meant when he said that at Crécy the English archers were organized *en herse*, – in harrow formation. The efficacy of the English archers was demonstrated at Morlaix in Brittany in 1342, and proved at Crécy four years later. There, they first routed the advancing Genoese crossbowmen, whose weapons could probably only fire one bolt to every five flights of English arrows. The hail of fire from the English bows then caused chaos among the French cavalry as they advanced. The English men-at-arms had taken up a strong defensive position which amply compensated for their inferiority of numbers, much as at Dupplin Moor in 1332. The French were compelled to fight on a narrow front, and were routed in the mêlée.

The best descriptions of the way in which the English men-at-arms fought come from Italy, where the techniques employed by the White Company which went there in 1361 caused evident surprise. Their method was to employ a formation of three men to every lance, two men-at-arms and one valet. The men-at-arms would hold the lance to meet the initial enemy onslaught, and would then fight back-to-back in the mêlée for mutual protection, with swords or other weapons. The valet would be in charge of the horses, held in an encampment at the rear of the lines, and he would bring them up when required, either for pursuit of a defeated enemy, or for flight.

The success of such tactics in the hands of the English caused the French to try to adopt them. In 1352 their men-at-arms fought on foot at Mauron in Brittany, and at Poitiers in 1356 the Scot William Douglas advised them to do the same. They lacked the support of experienced archers, however, and did not fight from a defensive position like the Black Prince's men. By the time the French had struggled through the English arrow-fire they were exhausted and in no fit state for the mêlée which then began.

The English were not invariably successful with their tactics. In 1359 a force under Eustace d'Aubrichecourt was routed at Nogent-sur-Seine, even though his forces were set out in the way which had proved so effective at Crécy and Poitiers. His archers were broken by the French infantry attack, and the field was then left open for the French knights to win the day on horseback. For the most part, however, the English had a decisive advantage on the field of battle in the years up to 1360, even when they fought in traditional knightly style on horseback as at Auberoche under Henry of Grosmont. In the years after 1369, when the French gave up trying to meet them in the open battle and devoted themselves to harassment and the reduction of English-held territory by sieges, the tide of war turned. The English could find no answer to the style of warfare practised by Bertrand du Guesclin under the direction of Charles v.

The English had learned more from the Scottish war than the art of fighting battles. They had discovered the efficacy of the plundering raid, the total war of the Middle Ages, with destruction of villages and crops, ransoming and slaying of the civilian population. In 1339 the English army engaged in a deliberate orgy of destruction around Cambrai. Geoffrey le Scrope led one of the cardinals who was trying to secure a truce to the top of a tall tower at night, to show him how the whole countryside was burning. Earlier the cardinal had declared 'The kingdom of France is surrounded by a silken thread which all the power in the kingdom of England will not suffice to break'.[5] Scrope now said 'Sir, does it not seem to you that the silken thread encompassing France is now broken?'[5] The Pope made a grant of six thousand florins to relieve the suffering, and records of how it was spent show that 174 parishes had been affected by the brief English operations. The operations of 1339 were a mere foretaste of the horrors that were to come.

The English excused their behaviour on the grounds that they were trying to force the French to do battle. It was even argued that the destruction of places around Paris in 1346 had this as its aim, although it was plainly an attempt to divert the French from the English attempt to cross the Seine at Poissy. By the time of the Black Prince's raid of 1355 it is clear that the English were using destruction of territory as a deliberate weapon, designed to reduce the resources available to the Valois monarchy and discredit it in the eyes of its subjects. A vivid description survives of the experiences of a French prior in 1358, a year when France was reduced to virtual anarchy by the actions of the English companies and the *Jacquerie*. English troops came to his town of Chantecocq in November, took the castle and burned the countryside. The inhabitants were then ordered to pay ransoms, either in money or kind. Many did so to avoid death by torture, but others fled to huts in the forest. The English made a thorough search, and most were discovered. The prior eventually made his terms with them, but no good came of it, for the English captain was soon captured by the French. The troops, said the prior, 'spoiled all the furniture of my house, drank four casks of my wine, carried off a peck of oats by Courtenay measure, took all my clothes and drove off the horses. On two occasions they stole all my money, and they ate up my pigeons.'[6] Such experiences were common in a savage war.

On occasion the English king tried to restrain his troops. In 1346 he was anxious to give a good impression during his march through Normandy, where he hoped to win local support, but his men looted and burned Carentan contrary to his orders. In Burgundy in 1360 there was widespread disregard of the specific orders that had been issued against looting. Commands that churches should be spared and that women and children not be harmed were consistently ignored: in battle the English were well disciplined, but on the march they were impossible to restrain.

One of the most important factors working for English success in France was the enthusiasm that existed for the war. There had been a striking reversal of attitudes since the thirteenth century, when – to use a contemporary metaphor which has survived the ages – the knights of England did not give a bean for all of France. Jean le Bel remarked with surprise on the willingness of the English to serve in 1339, even though their wages were not being paid. Records show that there were 416 archers in the army that year who had volunteered for service, rather than being recruited by arrayers or magnates. There was a consistent willingness to fight, at least until the last years of Edward III's reign, which was fuelled by a mixture of patriotism, desire for chivalric renown, and hope of financial gain.

Wages were one of the incentives that the crown used to encourage men to fight. In the initial stages of the war, in

1338–9, double rates were promised, even though there was such a scarcity of funds that payment itself was long delayed. For the rest of the reign, however, the only difference between overseas wage rates and those applying to the Scottish wars was that mounted archers in France received 6d a day, not 4d, and infantry 3d not 2d. Wages were a very substantial financial burden for the crown, but it must be doubted whether they provided any great inducement to men to serve, for payment was often heavily in arrears. Henry of Grosmont did not receive full satisfaction for his wages for the campaigns in the Low Countries until 1348. Debts, largely for war wages, in the wardrobe accounts for 1341–4 totalled almost £20,000. Although the financial situation was never again as acute as in the initial phases of the war, payment was often dilatory and inadequate. Thomas Dagworth was owed £6,350 for his Breton campaigns of 1346, but received only £2,790 from the crown. John of Gaunt and his companions in 1373 contracted to provide troops in return for various payments, including one of £12,000 to be sent out after six months. No money was sent to France, and very little was paid when the forces returned to England. Gaunt, however, did receive payment of some £6,000 arrears of wages during the last year of the reign, when he was, significantly, in a position of political authority.

Wages had never been intended to provide more than subsistence, and they did not move upwards in the wake of the Black Death, at a time when labourers' wages were rising as a result of the fall of the population. They were, it is true, often supplemented by the 'regard' – a form of bonus – but the financial rewards offered by the crown were always relatively unimportant as an inducement to fight. The agreement made by Robert Knollys for his *chevauchée* in 1370 shows this, for wages were only to be paid for thirteen weeks. After that the expedition was intended to be self-financing, from the booty and ransoms to be won in France.

While the war went well for the English, there were substantial gains to be made. The hope of gaining wealth through plunder was a major incentive. The chronicler Walsingham in a famous passage stated that, 'there were few women who did not have something from Caen, Calais and other overseas towns; clothing, furs, bedcovers, cutlery. Tablecloths and linen, bowls in wood and silver were to be seen in every English house.'[7] When Robert Knollys took Auxerre in 1359, it is said that goods worth five thousand *moutons d'or* (about £1,000) were taken, and the town ransomed for forty thousand pearls and forty thousand *moutons d'or*.

There were conventions for the way in which the spoils of war were divided up. In the early stages of the Hundred Years War it was normal for commanders to claim half of all booty, and the Black Prince continued to do so until the 1360s. Increasingly, however, the normal proportion was set at one-third, though of course much plunder must have been obtained surreptitiously and never declared. War was a business, and the aftermath of battle saw complex negotiations as men attempted to realize the assets they had gained in the form of prisoners. In 1340 Walter Mauny obtained £8,000 from the king for the prisoners he had taken. After Poitiers the Black Prince bought up the French king's son, the Count of Sancerre and the Lord of Craon. He then sold them to his father for £20,000. Thomas Dagworth's arrears of wages were amply offset by the £5,000 he received for Charles of Blois after he captured him. In theory, the sum demanded as a ransom should have been the same as a man's annual income, but in practice, much more was often asked. The great ransom of three million *écus*, or roughly £500,000, for King John gave the English crown a new financial stability in the 1360s and enabled the king to build lavishly at Windsor and elsewhere. The castles built by English magnates at the same period likewise testify to the profits they gained from the trade in prisoners.

Ransoms might be imposed on conquered territory as well as on prisoners. English occupation forces in Brittany and elsewhere were able to maintain themselves and make profits, by levying protection money. Walter Bentley, commanding in Brittany, complained of the number of men who fought for their own profit, and protested that the activities of the self-seeking soldiery were forcing the Bretons to turn to the French for help. The war could not be fully financed from England, however, and the accounts of the English treasurer in Brittany from 1359 to 1362 show an expected yield of almost £15,000 from local levies. In the Good Parliament of 1376 William Latimer was accused of raising £83,000 in ransoms and similar extortions, again in Brittany, without accounting for the money with the king. The English armies in France did not merely live off the land: they financed themselves from it as well.

Froissart gave full recognition to the material motives behind the war when he described his compatriot Eustace d'Aubrichecourt, who fought for Edward III: 'He acquired much wealth in ransoms, by the sale of towns and castles, through redemptions of the countryside and of houses, and the safe-conducts he provided.' In addition to operating a highly successful protection racket, however, Eustace performed 'many fine feats of arms, and often succeeded in knightly combat with noble men, nor could anyone stand up to him, because he was young, deeply in love, and full of enterprise.'[8] His lady love, Isabel de Juliers, widow of the Earl of Kent, sent him frequent letters and tokens which inspired him to further notable feats of arms. This was the language of chivalry, and in his wars in France Edward III was able to profit to the full from the knightly ethos of the day. The importance of those who, like Walter Mauny, 'loved honour more than silver'[9] should not be underestimated.

It is impossible to recapture fully that extraordinary mixture of personal bravado, religious ethic and class consciousness which went to make up the chivalry of the fourteenth century. Men would go to extraordinary lengths to prove themselves true knights, often by fulfilling foolhardy vows. A striking example took place in Edward II's reign, when William Marmion was presented with a helmet by his lady, and instructed to make it known in the most perilous place in Britain. He went at once to Norham Castle, then under siege, sallied forth single-handed, and was promptly engulfed by the Scots. He was fortunate enough to be rescued by the constable and garrison of the castle. In 1342 in Brittany Walter Mauny led a small force out of Hennebout after dinner to destroy a French siege engine. The enemy saw them, and Mauny promptly swore that he would never again kiss his mistress, or take refuge in a castle, unless he unhorsed one of his pursuers. He turned on them, and the flight for safety turned into an ugly skirmish, from which the English extricated themselves only with some difficulty. Mauny's reward of a kiss from the Countess of Brittany was hardly worth the danger in which he had placed his men. Another example is that of James Audley, who vowed to be in the van of any battle involving the king or his sons. As a result he plunged deep into the enemy ranks at Poitiers, not pausing to take any prisoners, and placing himself and his squires in quite unnecessary danger.

Edward III fully shared the chivalric enthusiasm of his followers, and successfully channelled it into the war. The poem of the *Vows of the Heron*, which records Robert of Artois's goading of the king to fight for the French throne, tells of the oaths all the magnates took to distinguish themselves in the war. The poem is satirical, but probably caricatures a real event. It tells of the Earl of Salisbury promising not to open one eye until he had fought in France, but omits to mention that he had already lost the use of an eye in an accident. In making his magnates swear to fight in France Edward III was following the example of his grandfather Edward I, who had used the same technique at the Feast of the Swans in 1306 to drum up enthusiasm for the Scottish war. Chaucer poked mild fun at these feasts when his squire described Cambuskan's banquets:

> I wol nat tellen of hir strange sewes,
> Ne of hir swannes, ne of hire heronsewes.
> Eek in that lond, as tellen knyghtes olde,
> Ther is som mete that is ful deynte holde,
> That in this lond men recche of it but smal;
> Ther nys no man that may reporten al.[10]

Edward III emulated his grandfather's cult of the Arthurian legend. At Winchester a round table still survives, which was probably constructed early in his reign, and in 1344 at a great tournament held at Windsor it was decided to build a round house to hold a similar table. The king was clearly contemplating the foundation of a knightly order on the Arthurian model, but for some reason the scheme was not carried out, although some of the building work was done. Four years later the Order of the Garter was founded as a select brotherhood of twenty-six knights, among whom was Sanchet d'Aubrichecourt. There is no contemporary warrant for the story of the ball at which the king picked up the beautiful Countess of Salisbury's garter, and declared to the jeering onlookers, 'Honi soit qui mal y pense' (He should be disgraced who thinks ill of it). It is, however, hard to imagine other circumstances in which an article of ladies' underwear might become an honoured symbol of a renowned order of chivalry.

Edward was a great patron of tournaments, the great festivals of chivalry. His attitude was in striking contrast to that of Edwards I and II, for they tried to limit and even prohibit tournaments for fear of political disturbance and because they distracted men from the business of war: much money was spent by Edward III on tournaments. In 1343 daily household expenditure was normally about £15 a day, but it rose to £317 for jousting at Dunstable. When his eldest son was made Prince of Wales in the next year, it only went up to £118. The king himself was no mean performer. In 1341 he participated as a simple knight in a gathering of over two hundred and fifty, when the contest went on into the night. Three years later he won the prize on three consecutive days of jousting as the best knight of the royal household. As late as 1359 he was still distinguishing himself, when in a tournament to celebrate the wedding of his son John of Gaunt he and his four eldest sons, with nineteen nobles, dressed up as the mayor and aldermen of London and held the field with honour. The masque-like element of some tournaments was even more evident three years later at a London tournament when seven knights dressed as the seven deadly sins challenged all comers.

So great was Edward III's chivalric reputation that in 1350 two soldiers of fortune, Giovanni Visconti and Thomas de la Marche – the latter a bastard son of Philip VI – agreed to submit their dispute to Edward for resolution by single combat. Edward presided over the fight, which Thomas won by raking his mailed gauntlet across his opponent's face, a blow which many considered to be a foul. In contrast, when a dispute between the Duke of Brunswick and Henry of Lancaster was, at the former's insistence, submitted to the French king John, the two men were forbidden to fight at the very last minute and a reconciliation was arranged. John was apparently not willing to risk an English triumph. His behaviour was similar to that of Richard II when he forbade the combat between Hereford and Norfolk in 1398, but it should be remembered that Edward I had also been unwilling to preside over the proposed single combat between Charles of Anjou and Peter of Aragon.

Jean le Bel regarded Edward III as the epitome of chivalry, particularly in contrast to the Valois kings. Such acts as King John's arrest of Charles of Navarre in 1356 and his arbitrary execution of the Norman nobles associated with him did nothing to enhance the prestige of the French monarchy. Edward's reputation enabled him to recruit many foreigners to his cause; men like Walter Mauny, Eustace d'Aubrichecourt and Enguerrand de Coucy. Although Edward's war was in some ways strongly nationalistic, he was able to appeal to the chivalric feelings of men of many countries.

Chivalrous attitudes affected not only men's willingness to fight, but also the way they fought. It may seem ironic to see a war characterized by looting, burning and rape, which was punctuated by such incidents as the French capture of an English messenger at Auberoche in 1345 and their hurling him into the castle from a siege engine, as chivalric. The knightly code, however, was largely applied only to other knights. There were practical reasons for treating upper-class opponents with respect and honour. It was said that Philip VI wished to execute the Earls of Salisbury and Suffolk when they were taken in 1340, but that the King of Bohemia objected, pointing out that they might usefully be exchanged should the English capture a French peer. It was also considered that to behave dishonourably towards a knight was to court disaster. The English regarded the defeat of the Scots at Neville's Cross as the result of the unjustified execution of Walter of Selby. Certainly there were instances of altruistic chivalry; at the sack of Caen Thomas Holland and his companions are said to have saved many women and girls from rape by the English soldiery. For the most part, however, chivalry was tempered by a considerable practicality.

The repeated challenges by the English and French rulers to resolve their differences by means of single combat fit well into the chivalric framework. Although it was in practice improbable that Edward III could have fought in an arranged hand-to-hand conflict with his Valois rivals, particularly since he was not prepared to concede his English kingdom should he be defeated, individual bouts were fought between members of opposing armies. After Edward crossed the Somme in 1346, a French knight begged the English that they send a knight to joust with him for the love of his lady. Thomas Colville accepted the challenge, and crossed the river on horseback. Two rounds were inconclusive: the French knight's shield was broken, however, and as a third round would have been dangerous, the joust was abandoned and the two men agreed to be friends for life. In 1359 another such incident took place, when a Frenchman calling himself the White Knight challenged the English to a fight of two against two, which culminated in an English victory. On a larger scale, there was an arranged battle between the French and the Bretons with two hundred on each side in 1341, and ten years later the famous 'fight of the thirty' in Brittany. This was a carefully staged battle, complete with a half-time interval for drinks. It is noticeable, however, that important issues were never determined by such means.

The widespread acceptance of the chivalric code meant that knightly opponents often treated each other with an almost exaggerated respect. After Poitiers the Black Prince served King John at dinner personally, and declared that he deserved the prize as the French knight who had displayed the most prowess in the battle. When Bartholomew Burghersh took a castle near Rheims in 1359, the French commander thanked him for his kindness, and remarked the *Jaques* – the peasant rebels who had been terrorizing the district – would have behaved far less generously. Mutual respect could go much further. In Spain the English captain Hugh Calvely joined forces for a time with Bertrand du Guesclin, and the two men even became brothers-in-arms, making a formal agreement of mutual support and profit-sharing. The extent to which knights behaved honourably should not be exaggerated, however. King John may have returned into his comfortable captivity when his ransom was not paid in full, but Simon Burley, tutor to the future Richard II, escaped from custody in France after he had given his word not to do so. Charles of Blois was dissuaded with great difficulty from executing two English knights, and one of the great experts of the day on chivalric matters, Geoffrey de Charny, was prepared to break a truce in order to recapture Calais in 1347: he was sternly rebuked by Edward III as a result.

There was a solid legal basis to chivalric behaviour. Both French and English recognized the validity of the laws of war, laws which were applied in military courts and which were based on Roman law concepts. They were refined and ordered by scholars, and dealt with such questions as the distribution of spoils, the ransoming of prisoners and the disciplining of armies. It was possible for an Englishman, Thomas de Uvedale, to bring a case successfully before the *parlement* of Paris for the payment of ransoms under this internationally recognized law. The religious element in the chivalric ethos was less clearly defined, although the writings of Henry of Grosmont and Geoffrey de Charny show that it was very important; for the latter, to accept the arms of a knight was to enter God's service. There was no reason, however, why the perfect knight should not, like Chaucer's, ride into battle 'as well in Christendom as in heathen lands',[11] and by the fourteenth century the canon lawyers had developed their doctrines of the just war, which meant that the kind of enthusiasm which had earlier inspired men to go on crusade could now be harnessed to the cause of the French war.

There was no element of sarcasm in the description of the Black Prince by the Chandos Herald as 'the perfect root of all honour and nobleness, of wisdom, valour and largesse',[12] despite such incidents as the sack of Limoges. The chivalric ethos had become distorted by the fourteenth century, but it undoubtedly helped to provide the participants in the Hundred Years War with both a moral inducement to fight, and a justification for many of the horrors of war. The dictates of chivalry might run counter to military common sense, as at the battle of Mauron in 1352: there, according to Jean le Bel, eighty-nine knights of the new French order of the Star were slain in an English ambush, because they had sworn a solemn oath never to retreat in battle. The English perhaps took their chivalry more practically. For many the hope of material profit must have been the main motive in going to war in Edward III's service, but even if the reality of the conflict was very different from the ideals of the contemporary romances, it still offered the chance to gain honour and renown.

How were the ordinary people of England encouraged to fight and to support the war effort? There was a far more consistent effort to inform those at home of the progress of the war than in the past. Newsletters are known from Edward I's day, but the plethora of despatches from the commanders and others on campaign during the triumphant years of Edward III's great enterprise was unprecedented. In 1346 Bartholomew Burghersh sent two letters to the Archbishop of Canterbury, designed for public consumption, telling of the events of the campaign as 'the king with his host advances into the land to conquer his right, as God shall give him grace.'[13] Another letter came from the chancellor of St Paul's Cathedral, who was with the army, and two clerks in the royal administration also sent back news.

The art of propaganda was fully understood in the fourteenth century. The myth – first invented by Edward I – that the French wished to extinguish the English language, was assiduously spread by his grandson, and much play was made with every threat of French invasion. At Caen in 1346 the English discovered in the archives an agreement made in 1338 between Philip VI and the Duke of Normandy for the conquest of England. This was brought home by the Earl of Huntingdon and read out publicly in the cemetery of St Paul's 'so as to rouse the people of the realm, that they might obediently show their esteem to the king, and pray devoutly for the prosperity and success of his expedition'.[14]

The government used all possible means to convey news and to build up support for the war. Public proclamations were made in every county court and major town in 1346 announcing the news of the victory at Crécy; merchants were asked at the same time to bring supplies to the army at Calais. Writs were frequently sent to the bishops asking them to have prayers said for the success of the king's enterprises and speeches at the opening of parliament were used to create enthusiasm for the war. The government's task was much easier while the war went well. Few can have been convinced by the official pronouncement that John of Gaunt's disastrous *chevauchée* in 1373 'did great damage and destruction to the enemy',[15] while the report on the ineffective naval campaign of the same year was equally implausible. It 'bore itself graciously and well against the enemy, as is well known, to the honour, ease, tranquillity and quiet of our lord the king, of the clergy, and of all others of the realm'.[15] The supply of newsletters dried up in Edward III's later years; by far the best propaganda had been the genuine news of the great victories of 1346 and 1356.

The literature of the period reveals the response to the propaganda proclaimed from pulpits and in shire courts. A series of poems by Laurence Minot celebrated in English the victories from Halidon Hill to the capture of the castle of Guines in 1352. Edward III was clearly identified with King Arthur, whose image was that of a bear:

> Men may rede in Romance right
> Of a grete clerk that Merlin hight;
> . . . .
> Merlin said thus with his mowth,
> Out of the north into the sowth
> Suld cum a bare over the se,
> That suld mak many man to fle.[16]

Minot did not revile the French as much as might be expected; they were not hated to the same degree as the Scots. Philip VI was, of course, abused for his cowardice:

> Sir Philip of Fraunce fled for dout,
> And hies him hame with all his rout;
> Coward, God giff him care.[16]

Patriotism has rarely inspired good poetry, but Minot's doggerel probably reflected genuine popular feeling.

A Latin poem, consisting of a dialogue between an Englishman and a Frenchman, shows an attempt to build up chauvinistic attitudes. The Englishman is accused of little worse than gluttony and drunkenness, whereas the Frenchman was effeminate, walking in an affected way; his hair was carefully combed, and he was given to lechery and avarice. Many of the works glorifying Edward III's wars were of a very contrived character, lacking in the spontaneity of some of the invectives against the Scots of Edward I's day. There is an elaborate and very pedestrian poem by Walter of Peterborough on the victory of Nájera, at the close of which the poet complained that his labours were in vain, and his work like a pearl cast before swine.

The wars did not win universal approval. A popular poem written in 1339 condemned the king's advisers who had counselled him to go to the Low Countries, and feared disaster. The author complained bitterly of the multiplicity of financial burdens imposed on the populace, but significantly he did not criticize Edward III himself. In the later years of the reign an elaborate, alliterative *Morte Arthure* simultaneously glorified war and condemned Arthur's pride, ambition and covetousness, plainly reflecting an increasingly ambiguous popular reaction to the French war. The curious prophecies of John Erghome (known as John of Bridlington) reveal something of the same mood, provoked by the failure of the English to win a decisive final success. Through his personal sins, and because of the slaughter of innocent civilians in France and his arbitrary exactions in England, Edward III was not succeeding in his designs. The war as such was not condemned, however, and the final prophecy looked forward to the eventual

triumph when Edward's successor should gain the kingdom of France. More striking, perhaps, than such comments on the war is the attitude of Chaucer, the greatest
English poet of the late fourteenth century. Although much
of his work has war as its background, he avoided specific
mention of the Hundred Years War. Chaucer had taken
part in the 1359–60 campaign, and had the misfortune to be
captured, so the war was not strange to him. Yet in describing his knight, he made no mention of service in France.
Only the squire of the Canterbury Tales had fought in
Flanders, Artois and Picardy. Chaucer was writing at a time
when the war was going badly. His audience lacked the
enthusiasm of earlier generations for it, and his silence
probably reflects a tacit disapproval.

Caution must be exercised in using literary evidence to
make a historical point, particularly when so much of the
popular poetry of the period must have vanished. From
what survives, however, it is possible to see that the war
was only popular as long as it was successful. There was
little enthusiasm in the early stages, when the English were
bogged down in the Low Countries, and in the closing
stages of Edward III's reign there was a mood of ambival-
ence and incomprehension. Minot's militaristic national-
ism, however, probably caught the public attitude during
the years of success. Not surprisingly, the course of the war
itself determined men's attitudes far better than the
government's attempts to disseminate information. News
brought home by returned soldiers was probably more
effective as a means of spreading information than the
proclamations ordered by the crown. The impact of the
king's policies at home was also very important in forming
public opinion, for war necessarily entailed a considerable
domestic burden in the form of taxation and demands for
victuals and manpower. An important element in Edward
III's success, as the next chapter will show, was the way in
which his domestic policies were managed.

There is no simple answer to the question of why the
English armies were so successful in France in the years up
to 1360. In part, an explanation should be sought in the

internal affairs and military organization of the French kingdom, and for that there is no space in this book. For the English, many factors combined. A military revolution had taken place since the accession of Edward I, with the transformation of the scale of the military effort that the country could mount, and the tactical developments that had taken place in the course of the Scottish wars. Edward III was able to send well-organized, highly mobile and very experienced armies to France, under able commanders. They had a striking aptitude for terrorizing the country on their swift *chevauchées*, and in battle held a decisive advantage for many years with their technique of dismounting the men-at-arms to fight, with archers providing supporting fire. The soldiers were inspired by the profit motive and by the military ethos expressed in that easily misinterpreted word – chivalry. For all that, it is still possible to share Jean le Bel's surprise at the way in which the English, so much despised as soldiers at the outset of Edward III's reign, became the most feared military force in Europe within a single generation.

8

Crisis and Stability

The Domestic Policies of
Edward III to 1360

'This king Edward was forsooth of a passing goodness, and full gracious among all the worthy men of the world.' So began the English version of a eulogy of Edward III, which went on to claim that no land had ever been ruled by so noble a king. The praise was, however, not unmitigated: 'Nevertheless, lechery and moving of his flesh haunted him in his old age, wherefore rather, as it was to suppose, for unmeasurable fulfilling of his lust, his life shortened the sooner.'[1] Contemporary opinion of Edward III varied widely. For some, he was a brutal rapist, a fratricide, a man whose lust led him to ignore matters of state. For others, he was a chivalric hero in the Arthurian mould. The views of historians have been ambivalent: many find it hard to give full credit to a man whose greatest achievements lay in aggressive warfare inspired by an opportunistic personal ambition. Edward had not inherited his grandfather's firm determination to maintain his rights, and there have been suspicions that the remarkable co-operation between the king and the political nation was the result of royal weakness rather than of political skill. The king's achievements in his prime are undoubted, but the failures of his last years and the difficulties inherited by his successor cast a shadow over the years of success.

The main problem facing Edward III in his domestic policies was that of war finance. By 1340 the demands made on the country to support the French war in its highly expensive initial phases were such as to provoke political crisis. The events of 1297 seemed in danger of repeating themselves. The crisis of 1340–1 was a watershed and marked the king's final break with the officials he had inherited. The next twenty years were a period of remarkable calm in political terms, despite the continued financial burden. Important problems of law and order, relations with the Church, and of economic policy were apparently resolved without danger of a renewed outbreak of serious political strife. In parliament the commons were able to establish their position in a way that had not been possible previously.

Edward III's personal rule began in 1330, with the execution of Mortimer and the effective exclusion from power of Isabella, the queen mother. Matters were not easy for the young king. He found it hard to rally full support for the Scottish war. There were difficulties in obtaining grants of taxation, and one chronicler refers darkly to plots against the king in 1334. The great offices of state, the chancery and the exchequer, were controlled by men whose loyalties lay in the past, and who were not wholly committed to the new regime. Frequent ministerial changes suggests instability. In the departments of the royal household, the wardrobe and the chamber, Edward was building up a personal following, but his hand was not yet completely sure. The career of the corrupt and greedy chamber knight, John Moleyns, suggests that there was a danger of a return to the ways of the period of Despenser dominance: a former associate of the Despensers, he rigged juries and corrupted justices, and did not stop at murder in order to acquire lands. But the king was steadily strengthening his position, and the appointment of the new earls in 1337 was a clear sign that a new start was being made. By creating a new aristocracy without alienating the old, a firm and secure base for Edward's rule was created.

Unlike Edward I, Edward III was very careful to ensure that he had full support, obtained in parliament, for the war with the French. His strategy, however, was modelled on his grandfather's, and he faced similar problems as a result of the astronomical costs of fighting in alliance with the princes of the Low Countries and Germany. Not only did Edward have to ship his own army overseas, where for a time with misguided generosity he offered double wages, but he also paid massive subsidies to the allies. Early in 1338 royal envoys set their needs at £276,000. The wardrobe accounts from 1338–40 show expenditure totalling almost £200,000. In the autumn of 1339 parliament was told that the king's debts amounted to a staggering £300,000. The total cost of the war up to 1340 was in the region of £500,000. This financial burden provides the background to the complex crisis of 1340–1. In the first phase, a familiar pattern reasserted itself, with demands being put forward for major concessions in return for the financial aid that the king desperately needed. The second part of the crisis resulted from the king's anger with an administration which he felt had failed him. His dismissal of his ministers in the autumn of 1340 led to bitter arguments, which raised wide constitutional issues.

The methods used to raise money between 1337 and 1340 were reminiscent of those used by Edward I during his war with France. Direct taxation of the laity which was willingly granted in 1337 raised about £114,000, while a further £57,000 was due from clerical taxes. The main answer to the financial needs of Edward III appeared to lie on the backs of England's millions of sheep. England had a near monopoly of wool exports to the Low Countries, and the trade could serve as a diplomatic weapon and at the same time provide much-needed revenue.

An ambitious plan was conceived in 1337, whereby leading English merchants were to buy up thirty thousand sacks of wool at specified prices. They would have a monopoly of overseas sales, and agreed to advance £200,000 to the king out of the massive profits they anticipated. They were only able to collect about eleven thousand five hundred sacks, however, and so could only offer 100,000 marks (£66,666) to the royal officials in the Low Countries. This was not acceptable, and the officials bought up the wool on credit, giving the merchants receipts, which were known as the Dordrecht bonds. The trust between the king and the merchants was broken. Without their support,

Edward was unable to collect large quantities of wool in the counties. A parliamentary grant of twenty thousand sacks made early in 1338 yielded under two thousand sacks. Although a further levy in August was more successful, the combined proceeds of sales of wool in the Low Countries and of the high customs duties of the time were quite inadequate. The king had to borrow money. He turned initially to the great Italian banking houses of the Bardi and the Peruzzi: in 1338–9 they advanced over £125,000. As they became increasingly reluctant to lend, Edward approached the English merchant William de la Pole, who raised over £100,000 for him.

By the autumn of 1339 fresh grants of taxation were needed, and with the country already heavily burdened, the demands led to considerable argument. The magnates were sympathetic enough, and offered a tenth of their produce. The commons in contrast asked to be allowed to consult with their local communities before they made a grant, although they recognized the king's need. Early in 1340 they offered the king thirty thousand sacks of wool, on certain conditions. These probably included the election of a council to supervise the king and the administration, and the appointment of a committee to ensure that all revenue was spent on the war. There was a natural reluctance to take up their offer, given the previous failure of grants of wool, and it was only when the king himself returned from Flanders and a new parliament met that it was possible to reach agreement on the form of a grant.

In April 1340 a modification of the earlier proposal of the magnates was adopted, and a tax of a ninth part of agricultural produce conceded. A series of statutes met the points that the commons raised in their petitions. A wide range of legal, administrative and financial matters were covered, and substantial concessions were made by the crown in return for the aid. It appeared that the crisis was over, and the king returned to the war, and won the great naval victory of Sluys.

Unfortunately, the grants made in 1340 failed to produce the expected yields. The intention with the ninth was to collect produce and then sell it off on the king's behalf:

prices were set at too high a level, and receipts in the course of the year amounted to only about £15,000. Before the king sailed for Flanders, he had promised at least £190,000 out of the proceeds of the tax to various creditors. His anger with the administration which he felt was failing him led to the next phase of the crisis.

There were obvious problems in governing the country while the king was abroad. Edward made elaborate arrangements in a set of ordinances issued at Walton on the Naze in 1338. Ultimate control was to be exercised by the king, whose orders would be transmitted in letters under the privy seal. The exchequer was recalled from York, where it had been for the Scottish wars, and attempts were made to ensure efficiency. An auditing committee was set up, and a budget was to be produced. A royal order to cease payment of all fees to royal officials who had other means of support was met by the threat of mass resignation and instructions to cease the payment of debts to the crown by instalments were highly unpopular. The king first showed his dissatisfaction with the government in December 1338, when he dismissed the treasurer, Robert Wodehouse. In the next year, exasperated at the continued failure of the government to provide the funds he needed so badly, Edward gave John Stratford, Archbishop of Canterbury, full authority as the king's chief councillor in England.

Stratford was an obvious choice. He had played a major part in the overthrow of Edward II, and had been an associate of Henry of Lancaster. He had served as chancellor from 1330–4 and from 1335–7, when his brother Robert succeeded him. His task in 1340 was an impossible one, however, and the gulf between the king's entourage in the Low Countries and the administration at home grew. The ambitious keeper of the privy seal, William Kilsby, regarded Stratford as responsible for blocking his promotion to the see of York, and he, with the military captains, influenced the king against Stratford. An unnamed councillor in England wrote secretly to the king, revealing the reality behind Stratford's bland excuses for failing to supply adequate funds. This man suggested that the king should return to England and arrest Stratford and his colleagues. If this was done, 'the king would find enough treasure to complete his war and conquer his enemies.'[2]

This advice fell on fertile soil. The king saw the failure of the government to provide him with money as a deliberate move. Stratford was less than wholehearted in his support of the war, and Edward stated that 'I believe that the archbishop wished me, by lack of money, to be betrayed and killed.'[3] At the end of November Edward sailed up the Thames with a small following and arrived unexpectedly by night at the Tower of London. By the light of a flaring torch he angrily asked for the constable. The news that he was away confirmed the king's fears as to the slack administration of the country. He inspected the Tower, and sent for the mayor of London. He gave him a list of men to be brought before him. Along with officials of the chancery and exchequer, William de la Pole and John Pulteney were summoned before the king; both had been deeply involved in the recent schemes to raise money by manipulating the wool trade. Orders went out to find Nicholas de la Beche, the errant constable of the Tower, and John Moleyns. The treasurer and chancellor were dismissed, and the king set in motion an elaborate inquiry into the misdeeds and oppressions of royal officials, reminiscent of the measures taken by Edward I in 1298.

It might have been expected that the king would gain popularity by the dismissal of unpopular ministers, but his attack on Stratford rebounded. Charges were proclaimed against the archbishop, who withdrew to Canterbury, and a bitter war of words developed between him and the king's advisers. Stratford condemned Edward with a biblical reference to him as a new Rehoboam, who spurned the advice of the old and wise, and turned instead to ignorant young flatterers. He proclaimed himself the champion of the liberties of the clergy, defending their claims to be exempt from the tax of a ninth: he attempted to set himself up as a second Becket. Stratford appealed to Magna Carta, and strongly implied that the king was flouting its provisions. Edward's right to dismiss his officials summarily was questioned, and Stratford demanded the right to trial by peers. In a lengthy letter known as the *libellus famosus*, the king's side replied with a justification of Edward's actions and a savage vilification of the archbishop's character. The argument had moved away from the question of the incompetence of the government that the archbishop had headed.

Parliament met in April 1341, but attempts to exclude Stratford were unsuccessful. The archbishop's case found increasing support from the lay magnates, who saw in his appeal to the principle of trial by peers an opportunity to assert their own privileges. Earl Warenne protested successfully at the presence of Kilsby and various other royal councillors: 'Those who should be the chief here are excluded, and other lowly people are here in parliament who should have no place in such a council, but only the peers of the land, who, my lord king, can aid and maintain you in your great affairs.'[4] Edward wisely appreciated the weakness of his position, and Stratford had no wish to continue the quarrel. The matter of the charges against him was effectively shelved by being referred to a committee.

The general issues that Stratford had raised were taken up by magnates and commons and the continued validity of Magna Carta was conceded by statute. The principle of trial by peers was set out, and it was established that if accusations were made against ministers, they should be punished by judgement of the peers in parliament. The clergy received protection from the actions of royal officials, and were pardoned payment of the ninth. It seemed that the archbishop had completely triumphed. However, Edward calmly revoked the statutes of 1341 later in the same year, and when parliament next met, in 1343, he obtained general agreement to his actions, though not without some opposition from the commons. Stratford had been driven into opposition against his will. He was not in reality a Becket or a Winchelsey, and although his reconciliation with the king was largely superficial, he supported Edward fully over such questions as Anglo-papal relations, and made no attempt to revive the issues of 1340–1.

Historians have made much of the crisis of 1340–1, but the seriousness of what happened should not be overstated.

The real cause lay in the unbridgeable gap between the king's revenues and his massive war expenditure. Stratford's accusations that Edward was acting contrary to the terms of Magna Carta, and that he was flouting the terms of his coronation oath by ignoring the law of the land were exaggerated. Edward was not attempting to introduce a new arbitrary style of government; he was merely dismissing ministers he regarded as unsatisfactory. He had good reason to do this, but his view that Stratford and his colleagues had acted treasonably was unwarranted. The raising of revenue from the sales of the produce yielded by the ninth was mismanaged, but the outcome of the great inquiry set up by the king did not reveal the widespread evidence of criminal incompetence that he clearly expected: there had certainly been much mismanagement and corruption at a local level, but this was endemic in medieval government. Little was proved against the chief victims of the king's anger, with the exception of John Moleyns, and he, to Edward's discredit, did not remain long in disgrace. Chief Justice Willoughby, who was accused of selling the laws of England as if they were cattle, was restored to favour after payment of a substantial fine.

There were fundamental constitutional questions raised in the course of the crisis. The commons in 1340 effectively demonstrated the power that they possessed to obtain concessions in return for taxation, and the principle set out in 1341 of the accountability of ministers to parliament was highly significant. Attempts have been made to see in the opposition to the king a revival of the attitudes of Thomas of Lancaster. Certainly, some of the demands made by the commons and some of Stratford's propaganda echoed the arguments of the past. In 1340 the commons in one of their petitions demanded a resumption of crown lands, which was reminiscent of the Ordinances. Stratford's appeal to judgement by peers perhaps reflected Thomas of Lancaster's emphasis on the role of the peers in parliament. The archbishop had earlier supported Henry of Lancaster, but it would be unwise to categorize the opposition of 1340–1 as Lancastrian. Earl Henry himself was old and blind, and took no part in the events, while his son Henry of

Grosmont was in custody in the Low Countries, acting as a pledge for the king's loans. Earl Warenne could never be accused of Lancastrian sympathies, and the commons, who played a very important part in the crisis, had little place in the so-called Lancastrian tradition. It is a distortion of reality to try to interpret the crisis in terms of a conflict between authoritarian rule based on the royal household, and government through the great offices of state with baronial consent, and it is misleading to apply party labels to any of the protagonists. Although important ideas were developed in the course of the crisis, it was far less serious than that of 1297 had been. Edward III retained the allegiance of the great magnates, and there was never any threat of civil war. Despite the virulence of the arguments, this was not a crisis born out of a fundamental dissatisfaction with the structure of royal government. It was rather the product of short-term financial and administrative problems. With the truce in the Low Countries in September 1340, and the later redirection of the war towards Brittany, stable government could be re-established.

After his experiences with Stratford, Edward III swore that he would never again employ churchmen in high office. He appointed a layman, Robert Parving, as treasurer, but he did not remain in office long, and the post reverted to a cleric, William Cusance, an experienced household administrator. The chancery remained under lay control only until 1345, when John Offord was appointed chancellor. He was an able man, who had a university degree in civil law rather than the usual background of administrative experience. William Edington, Bishop of Winchester, served loyally both as treasurer and chancellor. He was described by one chronicler as a friend of the common people, who by hard work did much to save them from royal extortions, and achieved much for the king and the realm. John Thoresby, another university-educated man, appeared in royal service first in 1330. He served overseas with the king during the campaigns in the Low Countries and became a highly competent keeper of the privy seal, and then chancellor. He paid for the building of the eastern bays of the choir at York Minster, an act which testifies both to the profits of office and to his own piety. Edward III was well served by his officials during the central years of his reign.

The main problem facing the government in the years after the crisis of 1340–1 remained the ever-pressing one of war finance. Edward had perhaps been fortunate in that he had borrowed much of the money he had needed in the Low Countries from foreign bankers. His effective bankruptcy by 1340 did much to cause the collapse of the great Italian banking houses of the Bardi and the Peruzzi: however, their failure meant that there was no need to repay the massive debts that were owed to them. The costs of the war fell from the exorbitant levels of the initial years. War wages in the wardrobe accounts for the three and a half years from April 1344, which included the Crécy campaign and the siege of Calais, amounted to some £150,000. Even with the addition of Henry of Grosmont's costs in Gascony, which approached £40,000, such sums were not totally unmanageable. The total wardrobe expenditure for this period was £242,162, as against £337,104 for twenty-two months from July 1338.

Massive grants were still needed to finance the war, and Edward was highly successful in persuading his subjects of his need for subsidies. Grants were not made unconditionally, however. In 1344 two tenths and fifteenths were offered on condition that all the money was spent on the war, with that raised in the north to go on defence against the Scots. Further, the king was to answer twelve petitions, which set out a range of grievances on such matters as purveyance, the recruitment of troops, trade and coinage. An additional fifteenth was then granted on condition that the king went in person to fight in France. Edward took a consistently reasonable attitude towards the demands of the commons, and as a result found little difficulty in obtaining funds, even in time of truce. Genuine efforts were made to adhere to the terms of the grants.

The question of wool subsidies was more contentious than that of direct taxation. The king sought to make arrangements with English merchants which would replace those that had worked well with the Italians in the past. Attempts to raise money from merchant syndicates, who were granted the customs revenues and near-monopoly rights of export in return for advances of cash, ran into constant difficulties. The merchant syndicates lacked sufficient capital, and the king's incessant demands for money combined with the inevitable wartime disruptions to trade made their position an impossible one. The commons objected to the whole process of separate negotiations with the merchants, and wished to control the grant of subsidies on wool exports themselves. The wool growers feared that they were receiving unduly low prices as a result of the imposition of customs duties over which they had no control.

Renewed crisis at home was threatened by the great military effort of 1346–7. The commons were angered when the magnates agreed that the king should levy a feudal aid on the occasion of the knighting of the Black Prince, for they had already granted a double subsidy, and considered that the king had promised in 1340 to abandon such levies: there was considerable violence offered to the collectors of the tax. The agreement of a great council in 1347 to a forced loan of twenty thousand sacks of wool presaged a return to the expedients which had been so unpopular in the early stages of the war. Large loans had to be raised; one English syndicate advanced about £55,000. One of the ways in which the merchants were rewarded was particularly disliked: they were permitted to pay off royal debts at a huge discount, paying as little as one or two shillings in the pound, while the exchequer later allowed them to set the whole original sum of the debts on the credit side of their account with the crown. Even with such benefits, they did not prosper, and the last main company, that of Walter Chiriton, collapsed early in 1349. The crown also turned to forced loans in 1347. Merchants who did not co-operate were viciously threatened with arrest, and religious houses were subjected to repeated demands for loans.

Further grievances resulted from the crown's recruiting methods. In 1346 a complex scale set out the number of troops which men of different degrees of wealth were obliged to provide for the war: a thirty-pound landholder was to produce a man-at-arms and an archer. There was much hostility to such an innovation in the system of military obligation, and the king had to reassure his subjects by public proclamation that it was not intended to make any precedent of these arrangements. Purveyance was another problem. The huge static army before Calais could not live off the land as the more mobile *chevauchées* did. The quantities of foodstuffs collected from the counties once again approached the levels of Edward 1's reign. The men of Rutland were so appalled at the demands made of them that they successfully petitioned to have them reduced by half. The old complaints that the rich were spared by corrupt purveyors were repeated.

Although the situation was reminiscent of 1297 and 1340–1, discontent did not reach a crisis. There were loud complaints in parliament about the arbitrary nature of royal exactions, and the king prohibited tournaments, perhaps fearing the political consequences of such gatherings. The great magnates, however, were too involved in the war to have any interest in opposing the king. Persuasive arguments in support of the war were put before parliament by Bartholomew Burghersh, who read out the draft French invasion scheme that had been discovered in the sack of Caen. It was above all the news of the king's great victories that defused a potentially dangerous situation.

The king and his ministers learned their lesson from the problems they encountered. The protests raised in parliament in 1348 and in later years led to the abandonment, or at least modification, of unpopular policies and the purchase of old debts at a discount by merchants was drastically curtailed. A statute in 1352 laid down that no one was bound to find soldiers save by common consent in parliament; demands for purveyance were moderated and no further prerogative taxes were requested. A stream of newsletters, proclamations and sermons, encouraged by the king, did much to win the support of the people for the war. Admittedly, when pressed in 1354 as to whether they wanted peace, the commons in parliament shouted 'Yes! Yes!', but they showed little reluctance to support a successful war. The heavy expenditure on the campaign of 1359–60 caused few political problems. The danger of French invasion, which was born out by the attack on Winchelsea, led to the negotiation of a unique tax: a grant of a fifteenth and tenth made in five provincial assemblies, rather than in parliament. This was not, however, an attempt to evade parliamentary control, but an arrangement for the raising of money in the localities to pay for the local defence forces.

The politics of the wool trade were complex in these years. A major shift took place in 1353. Until then, wool had been exported to Bruges under what was termed a staple system. When the crown no longer needed to use wool as a diplomatic weapon in the Low Countries, a system of domestic staples was introduced: foreign merchants would come to specified towns to buy wool for export, and English merchants would be excluded from the export trade. This system was backed by the commons, for it meant an end to the semi-monopolistic companies which had dominated the wool trade since the collapse of the Bardi and Peruzzi. The companies had failed the king, and he showed no mercy in exacting the money they owed him. The exclusion of English merchants from the export trade did not last long, however, and by 1357 a Bruges staple re-emerged. In 1363 it was replaced by one established at Calais, in a move designed to give the English-held town economic viability. This did not, however, mean the revival of the financial system of the 1340s. In 1351 parliament granted the king a subsidy of forty shillings on each sack of wool exported, following a complaint against a similar grant made by the merchants. Thereafter, a continuous series of such subsidies was granted by representative assemblies, and in 1362 the king promised in a statute that he would only negotiate wool subsidies in future with parliament.

These central years of Edward III's reign were of considerable importance for the development of parliament. The need to provide a constant flow of grants to lubricate the machinery of war, and the king's desire to obtain the fullest possible support for his foreign enterprise, led to a considerable change of emphasis. Parliaments became less frequent, and were more dominated by political and financial matters. Whereas in the first decade of the reign there were about twenty parliaments, five of which made grants of taxation, in the next forty years there were some thirty parliaments, only five of which did not grant taxes. Parliament arguably gained more from its willingness to provide the king with funds than it could have done from opposition. In return for aid, the king was prepared to make important concessions. Grants were not made conditional upon redress of grievance; the normal procedure, as in 1352 and 1355, was for the commons' petition for redress to be presented at the same time that they answered the royal request for taxation. Collaboration with the king was rewarded by the abandonment of attempts to raise funds without parliamentary consent. The attempts to negotiate subsidies on wool with merchant assemblies foundered as the merchant syndicates were bankrupted and splintered. Edward tried to use great councils as tax-granting bodies. These were normally magnate assemblies, but might include representatives; unlike parliament, a great council had no judicial authority. In 1353 one such gathering consisting of magnates with one knight from each shire and a small number of urban representatives, granted a wool subsidy, but the experiment was not repeated. The local negotiations of 1360 were highly exceptional; by that year, parliamentary control over taxation was largely assured. Similarly, the superiority of parliament in legislative matters was established. In 1351 it was necessary to embody in a parliamentary statute the labour regulations which were ordained by a council in 1349.

In these central years of the fourteenth century the bulk of parliamentary records was no longer made up of the many petitions presented by private individuals. Other means were being developed by which people could obtain redress of their private grievances. On the other hand, common petitions put forward by the representatives in parliament became far more important. These were not dealt with by the receivers and triers of petitions like the individual ones. Rather, they were sent directly to the king and his council for decision, which might be expressed in a statute. The importance of the representatives obviously increased as a result.

Despite these indications of the growing importance of the commons in parliament, their part should not be exaggerated. They made their grants of taxation jointly with the lords; it was highly exceptional that they made a separate offer of a subsidy in 1340. The advice of the lords was obtained through joint committees, and there is no means of knowing who had the upper hand in the discussions. It was the knights of the shire who dominated the commons rather than the burgesses, who considerably outnumbered them. There was a growing identity of spirit between the king, lords and knights, all of whom were committed to the enterprise in France. Their willingness to grant taxes can easily be explained in the bitter words of a poet, who wrote probably in 1339: 'Those who make grants pay nothing to the king, only the needy pay.'[5] With the abandonment of individual assessment of taxation from 1334, and the adoption of a standard sum due for parliamentary subsidies from each locality, the burden of payment had shifted down the social scale. The co-operation of the lords and commons with the crown in the years leading up to the treaty of Brétigny should not be taken as a sign of weakness: rather, parliament was acquiring a wider range of competence and a new authority, as the final years of the reign were to demonstrate.

Under Edward I the constant pressure of war in the later years of the reign had caused the flow of legislative activity to dry up. The Hundred Years War did not have a similar effect; the early 1350s in particular saw some notable measures promulgated. In contrast to the great statutes of Edward I's day, these were not for the most part inspired by the crown, nor did they result from inquiries instituted by the government. Rather, they germinated in the fertile soil of popular grievance.

Two statutes concerned relations with the papacy, that of Provisors of 1351, and that of *Praemunire* issued two years later. With a French Pope in residence in Avignon, it is not surprising that anti-papal feeling should have been rife in England. The chronicler Knighton reported gleefully a saying current after the battle of Poitiers: 'The Pope has become a Frenchman, and Jesus an Englishman. Now we'll see who does best, the Pope or Jesus.'[6] Another author directed scurrilous propaganda against the admittedly corrupt Clement VI. Every evening the Pope held an audience for ladies, and each time one less came out than had gone in. When admonished, Clement declared that he was acting on medical advice, and produced a little black book, in which were written the names of all previous popes who had indulged in the sins of the flesh. He pointed out, so the story continued, that these men had ruled the Church far better than those popes who had been chaste.

Edward himself had certain anti-clerical instincts; he resented the claims of churchmen to be exempt from lay jurisdiction. It was this which had caused him to turn to lay ministers in 1341. In 1355 he took the part of Blanche Wake, Henry of Grosmont's sister, in her feud with the Bishop of Ely. When Thoresby and Edington were remiss in seizing the bishop's temporalities, Edward wrote angrily to them: 'We are of the opinion that had the matter concerned a great peer of the land other than a bishop, you would have acted differently.'[7] On the face of it, popular demands coincided with the king's prejudices to produce anti-papal legislation. The reality,. however, was more complex.

The statute of Provisors dealt with the system of papal appointment to vacant church livings. In certain circumstances, such as the death of the previous holder at or near the papal court, or his promotion by the Pope to higher office, the papacy claimed the right to override the traditional rights of patrons. This was particularly disliked when the papal candidate was a foreigner, as it was suspected that the proceeds of the living would be exported, so diminishing the wealth of the nation. The system had come under heavy fire as early as the Carlisle Parliament of 1307, and although some realized that it often led to the appointment of well-trained men to high Church office, opinion against it was hardening in Edward III's time. There were strong petitions presented in parliament in 1343 and 1344, and a further demand for action in 1351.

The statute enacted in 1351 was clear-cut. Bishops were to be freely elected, patrons were to exercise their rights of appointment to vacancies, and if they did not do so, the right fell to the king. Severe penalties were set out against those appointed by the pope. Two years later the statute of *Praemunire* forbade the practice of appeal to Rome in cases where the crown claimed jurisdiction. In these measures some have seen the seeds of the English Church's later independence from Rome.

The formal language of the statutes fails to reveal the realities of the situation. Such measures could only be effective if the crown chose to enforce them, and the evidence suggests that in fact they were little more than window-dressing which did not substantially alter royal policy. The crown already possessed in the common law an ample armoury that could be employed against papal provisions. Legal doctrines evolved in the 1340s enabled Edward III to maintain a much more effective control over the English Church than that exercised by either of his two predecessors on the throne. However, in the years immediately following the capture of Calais in 1347 Edward's attitude had softened, since for diplomatic reasons he did not wish to antagonize the papacy. The statute of Provisors of 1351 was not put into effect by the king for the same reason, although he did use it as a weapon in negotiations with the papacy. The statute of *Praemunire* did not establish any new principle, but merely created a more efficient legal machinery for summoning those who were unwise enough to appeal outside the realm. Edward III had to tread a delicate balance between the extreme demands of his subjects and the need to maintain good relations with the papacy. In conceding the statutes of 1351 and 1353 he did much to assuage the feelings of the former, while his attitude towards the enforcement of the new legislation ensured that in practice the status quo was little changed.

The statute of Treason of 1352 is another legislative act which can easily be misinterpreted. It set out a limited number of treasonable offences, headed by plotting the death of the king or queen. Levying war against the king; raping the king's eldest daughter; killing royal justices while they performed their duties; and importing forged coins, were the other main crimes in a list which could only be added to with the consent of parliament. The statute appears to mark the final renunciation by the crown of the methods used to obtain many of the convictions which led to the judicial executions of Edward II's reign and its immediate aftermath. It was, coincidentally, in 1351 that John Maltravers, a survivor of those methods, received his pardon. He had been convicted of treason for his part in persuading the Earl of Kent to rebel in 1328, but escaped to France. Through good service abroad, he won his way back into favour. However, although the statute of 1341 had plainly looked back to the violent politics of Edward II's day, with its specific reference to the way in which magnates had been 'put to death without the judgement of their peers', the origins of the statute of 1352 lay in a different direction. It was primarily the result of objections to one of the techniques employed by the king's justices to deal with the problem of law and order.

Medieval England was a lawless country, where a quarrel over a badly cooked herring could end in violent death, as happened at Lincoln in 1353. Edward III inherited a particularly difficult situation: most alarming were the activities of gangs led by men of knightly status. Two have been analysed in detail, those of the Coterels and the Folvilles. Both began their operations in the late 1320s, the former by accepting a commission from the canons of Lichfield to drive the vicar of Bakewell from his living, the latter by murdering a baron of the exchequer. In 1332 the two gangs combined to kidnap a royal justice. The Gresleys of Staffordshire were another family prominent on the criminal scene. Joan de Gresley, a widow with six sons, was raped and forced to remarry in a typical act of gang warfare; however, in 1323 she with her four younger sons successfully carried through the murder of her new husband. She was charged with at least one other murder, and until the early 1330s the annals of the family are a continual tale of homicide, robbery, riot and mutilation. One son was himself murdered. The most notorious – Robert – escaped conviction by claiming to be a cleric, and obtained a pardon as a result of his good service in the Scottish campaign of 1333. The remainder of his career saw his destructive talents safely diverted to the French war.

This was the sordid reality behind the romanticized picture of the Robin Hood tales. The law was in disrepute, with at least one criminal leader, the picturesquely styled Lionel, 'king of the rout of raveners',[8] issuing letters in deliberate parody of the royal style from his 'castle of the four winds'.[8] The Archbishop of Canterbury claimed that the criminals were worse enemies of the realm in the 1330s than the Scots. One of the problems facing the crown was that the very class of men who should have been maintaining law and order were themselves eager participants in acts of violence. A strong argument has linked the fictional sheriff of Nottingham in the Robin Hood stories with the real holder of that office in the 1330s, John of Oxford. He was guilty of a long catalogue of acts of arbitrary imprisonment, extortion, fraud and other offences.

Various solutions were tried in the first decade of Edward III's reign. The legal establishment headed by chief justice Scrope, a remarkable political survivor, favoured an extension of the jurisdiction of the court of king's bench, associating it with trailbaston inquiries in a way strongly reminiscent of the measures of Edward I's final years. The magnates wanted to take over responsibility themselves for maintaining order, while in the first parliament of the reign the commons asked for good and loyal men to be appointed in each county to keep the peace, with powers to determine cases. This amounted to a demand for local gentry to act as justices of the peace. There was no easy solution to the problem, but by 1338 the commons had the better of the argument. Locally appointed keepers of the peace were given powers to hear cases of felony and trespass.

The administration of justice was still ineffective in the 1340s, as such incidents as the siege of Colchester by an armed gang in 1343 testify. In the next year a man was murdered at Ipswich because he took the side of the royal justices: his murderers were given lavish presents by the townspeople, and a mock trial of the justices was held. There was a crime wave of massive proportions in 1346 and 1347; a result of the crown's preoccupation with the war, and of the activities of those returning from France. One notable outrage was the abduction and rape of Margery, widow of John de la Beche, from the manor of Beams. The king's son Lionel was staying there at the time, and members of the royal household were at least indirectly involved in the affair. The response of the judges to the evident breakdown of law and order was to extend the use of the extremely serious charge of treason. In some cases it was used where the offence consisted of little more than highway robbery. A man found guilty of treason would be hanged, drawn and quartered, and in addition his lands and goods would be forfeited to the crown, rather than to his feudal overlord. Another charge, that of accroaching the royal power, also entailed forfeiture to the king. It was used in cases as diverse as the plundering of ships about to take grain to Gascony, and the breaking up of judicial sessions.

In 1348 the commons petitioned against the activities of the justices, which they claimed impoverished the people and did little to promote order. The way in which lords were deprived of forfeitures was a further grievance. In return for a grant of taxation the judicial commissions were abandoned, and in 1352 the crown gave way over the question of treason in the statute of that year. The new rigid definition of treason meant that the attempt to terrorize the criminals of the land by threatening them with the direst of penalties had to be abandoned. The statute demonstrates the king's willingness to compromise and to make concessions, rather than his far-sighted statesmanship.

The government had to change its tactics after 1352; the statute of Treason could not be ignored like that of Provisors. Hopes were not abandoned of simultaneously promoting domestic peace and increasing royal revenue from the profits of justice. An attempt was made at the request of the commons to make the process less painful by using the fines raised by the justices to reduce the burden of the lay subsidies. The benefit to taxpayers, however, totalled no more than six per cent at most, and did not prevent the activities of chief justice Shareshull and his colleagues from being highly unpopular in the 1350s. In 1357 the crown abandoned its claims to a large part of the profits of justice in return for a grant of taxation. When as a result special commissions and eyres of the King's Bench no longer proved profitable, the crown was prepared to concede the view held by the commons that justice in the shires should be left to local men to enforce. Shareshull left office in 1361, and in the same year the powers of the justices of the peace were confirmed by statute.

The final area of royal policy that remains to be examined is that of economic measures, notably those affecting trade and currency. Here, Edward III's reputation has undergone striking changes among historians. At one time the king was thought to have aimed systematically to encourage trade, the manufacture of cloth, and even the solid Victorian virtue of thrift. A contrary view saw the steps that were taken as the product of pressure put on the crown by various interest groups and of the ever-present financial needs, rather than resulting from the consistent application of a deliberate policy.

It is wrong to assume that medieval governments were incapable of evolving policies designed to promote economic well-being. In Flanders, for example, the domestic cloth industry was protected from English competition by a strict embargo on the sale of English cloth. In England in 1326 steps were taken to promote the cloth industry: the wearing of foreign cloth was prohibited, and at the instigation of the Londoners the export of teasels and other cloth-making materials was forbidden. It is clear from the petitions of the commons in Edward III's reign that contemporaries were very well aware of the economic implications of such matters as the imposition of heavy customs duties and of currency manipulation.

In the early years of his reign, Edward III permitted Flemish weavers to settle in England, and in 1337 he issued what amounted to a general invitation to foreign cloth workers. An important element of his war finance was the heavy export duties on raw wool. Cloth exports, in contrast, were lightly taxed, and became as a result extremely competitive in the markets of the Low Countries. Yet it is unlikely that the king was deliberately fostering the domestic cloth industry. His moves in 1337 were a part of his diplomatic offensive in the Low Countries, and were intended to put pressure on the Flemings to force them into the English camp. In taxing the country's most valuable export trade very heavily, Edward was simply following precedents set by his grandfather. Cloth exports were not sufficiently important for it to be worth charging them heavily. There is no evidence that the economic consequences of these decisions were taken into account.

Some measures concerning trade were intended to improve the economy, but they were taken as a result of petitions from the commons, rather then reflecting the king's own policies. There was a striking liberalization of trade in the early 1350s, with foreigners being allowed to buy and sell where they chose with almost total freedom. The aim was to exclude English middlemen from trade, as it was thought that they pushed prices up unjustifiably. English merchants were even excluded from the wool export trade for a time. Similarly, in 1368 English traders were briefly forbidden to import wine from Gascony, as it was thought that they were being forced to pay too high a purchase price there. Such measures, like the constant interference with the wine trade, were neither logical nor consistent, but they do show that policies were not solely formulated in order to try to fill the crown's bottomless coffers with silver. In the case of the decisions taken with regard to the currency, it was hoped to increase the wealth of both the country and the crown.

Contemporaries tended to judge prosperity by the simple criterion of how much money there was in the land. Of course, the real wealth of England lay in its agriculture, manufacture and trade, rather than in the volume of bullion in circulation. Yet in an economy with few forms of credit, where the value of money was directly related to the quantity of precious metal each coin contained, the question of the scale of the currency was important. The chronicler Adam Murimuth correctly observed that in 1339 prices were low, 'not because of an abundance of corn, but because of a scarcity of money',[9] and a poem of the same period complained that the lack of coin reduced the number of commercial transactions that could take place.

Royal policy could affect the currency substantially. Interference with the wool trade could influence the balance of trade. Prohibitions on the export of bullion might slow the drain of coins overseas. If royal mints offered a good price for silver, bullion could be attracted into the country. If, however, English mints were not competitive with those in the Low Countries and France, the country might be swamped by imports of low-quality foreign coins. There had been a real danger of this happening in the last years of the thirteenth century. Alongside such considerations, governments always faced the temptation of debasement. Reducing the weight or purity of the coinage provided an easy way of raising large sums of money without resorting to taxation, though the economic consequences of such a measure were clearly undesirable.

The early years of Edward III's reign saw no new measures taken. The English currency was in a poor state, with many badly-worn coins in circulation. No reform had taken place since the initial years of the fourteenth century, when the low-quality foreign coins that had been imported earlier were reminted into good sterling. Analysis of the mint accounts and of surviving coin hoards has shown that the amount of money in circulation fell rapidly from the second decade of the fourteenth century. By the early 1340s the level was only about £500,000; half that of forty years before. The heavy costs of the early stages of the Hundred Years War had aggravated an already serious situation. The shortage of money was an important element in the crisis in the country in 1340–1, making it far harder for the government to raise the funds required by the king. The unique expedient of the ninth raised in produce rather than cash was an unsuccessful attempt to find a way round the problem of the scarcity of cash.

Various solutions were put forward. In 1339 the commons proposed that merchants should bring back forty shillings of silver for every sack of wool they exported. The measure was adopted, but cannot have been very effective: it flew in the face of economic realities, and placed an intolerable extra burden on the wool trade. Another suggestion was that the king should permit the free circulation in England of gold coins. Gold had been steadily infiltrating the economies of north-western Europe since the first western gold coinage was minted in Italy in 1252; by the 1320s and 1330s French écus and Florentine florins were being used illegally in England. The king was not prepared to give official recognition to coins whose quality he did not control and which did not bear his image, so late in 1343 it was decided to produce an English gold coinage. The new money, based on the florin, was intended to serve as an international currency. It could be freely exported from the realm, unlike the silver coinage, and the hope was that in exchange merchants would import much needed silver. The concept was logical, but unfortunately the new coinage was issued shortly after a dramatic fall had taken place in the price of gold. The new English florins were considerably overvalued, and it was not until several experiments with different weights and values had taken place that the English gold coinage became really successful in the 1350s. Even then, gold was not exported in exchange for silver; it took its place alongside silver as part of the domestic currency, helping to swell the money supply.

The silver coinage could not be left in the deplorable state it had reached by the late 1330s. In 1344 the crown began a process of debasement, which culminated in the decree made in 1351 that three hundred pennies should be produced from every pound of silver, in contrast to the old standard of 243. On the continent, debasement was widely used as a means of raising revenue, notably by the Valois kings, and a desire to make a profit was certainly one of Edward III's motives. His debasement was very mild in contrast to French measures, however, and was in part intended to set a price for silver which would prove attractive to merchants. The new coinage was most successful. The menace of poor quality imitation sterlings, known as lushbournes – after Luxembourg where many of them originated – was countered, and the mints began to turn out new coins at a rate not seen since the early fourteenth-century boom. In the 1350s as part of the measures to liberalize trade the crown even permitted the free export of gold and silver from England in an attempt to encourage foreign merchants to come to the country. Royal revenues benefited from the higher customs duties they paid, and from the profits made by the mints. The situation could not last, however, given the inevitably cyclical nature of mint activity. In 1364 harsh prohibitions on bullion exports were once again imposed. A new mint was set up at Calais, so that foreign buyers of English wool would exchange their own coin for English money there, and this measure had some success.

The monetary policies of Edward III's reign worked surprisingly well. It is to the king's credit that he avoided the temptation of entering into an unending series of debasements and recoinages solely for his own profit. Somewhat accidentally, the new gold coinage helped to compensate for the shortage of silver, while the debasement that took place resulted in a real increase in the number of coins in circulation. The situation was considerably eased from the mid 1340s by the substantial flow of French ransom money into England. No accurate figure can be placed on this, but one indication of the ample supply of French money is that when a sum totalling ten thousand marks was received at Plymouth by the Prince of Wales's treasurer in 1355 for transmission to Gascony, all save 252 gold nobles and three silver pennies was in the form of French écus. It is impossible to determine Edward III's own part in formulating monetary policy, and it would be wholly wrong to see him as a proto-Cobden, advocating free trade in the 1350s. The decisions that were taken, however, stand as an important achievement from which the country benefited considerably.

An examination of Edward III's rule of England in the years up to 1360 suggests that he was a man of more complex character than the simple heroic warrior of the Hundred Years War. The accounts of the royal household unfortunately provide less informative detail than those of his father's and grandfather's reigns. Edward appears as a keen gambler, on one occasion losing as much as £61 at dice in a single sitting. He was an enthusiastic patron of minstrels, and an attractive picture is conjured up by an entry recording a payment of twenty marks to one of the Earl of Northampton's musicians who played before the king and queen at the request of their four-year-old son Lionel. This aspect of life at court is illustrated by accounts for Christmas 1348, when the performers in theatrical presentations used masks of men's heads surmounted by lions, elephants and bats' wings, while there were also masks for wild men and virgins. The king was prone to personal extravagance; on one occasion he paid £162 for a horse. At one tournament he wore a velvet tunic 'powdered with small Saracens of gold and silver, each having a jewel with the king's motto, and embroidered with trees and birds, and with effigies of the Saracens, both holding a shield of the king's arms'.[10] The comradeship he enjoyed with his companions is suggested by a purchase of red and black cloth in 1335 to make tunics for the king and his knights; they presumably all dressed in the same style. Edward was prepared to discard the majesty of his position; at one tournament he appeared wearing Thomas Breadstone's coat of arms, and in 1348 he fought incognito at Calais under the command of Walter Mauny.

Edward was well-educated; the hesitantly formed words *pater sancte* in the celebrated letter to the Pope of 1330 are the first known piece of royal handwriting in England. The king counted among his tutors the celebrated bibliophile Richard de Bury, on whose instructions a service book was bought in 1335 for the royal use at matins. In the same year Edward bought a romance from a nun at Amesbury, and at the time of his death he owned twenty books, thirteen of them romances reflecting his chivalric tastes. He showed a concern for intellectual matters by financing the scholars of the King's Hall in Cambridge. He was a conventionally pious man: in 1335 he spent a month on pilgrimage, and gave lavish alms at the shrine of Thomas Becket in Canterbury.

The king's interests were far from exclusively military.

His building programme stands in marked contrast to that of Edward I. He was responsible for only one military fortress, in the Isle of Sheppey, which could compare with the chain of revolutionary castles in North Wales built by his grandfather. He was, however, a great patron of architecture and painting. Windsor was converted at vast expense in the 1360s into a most sumptuous establishment, with the new collegiate church of St George, and lavish chambers, lodgings, hall and chapel added to the old structure; the earliest-known mechanical clock in England was set up there. The king also built extensively at Gravesend, Eltham, King's Langley, Sheen and Rotherhithe. These were comfortable houses, not castles, and featured such luxuries as bath-houses and fine gardens. Heavy expenditure on hunting-lodges indicated the pleasure that the king obtained from the chase. Edward employed some of the most noted painters of the day, men such as Hugh of St Albans and Gilbert Prince. He even took two painters with him on his expedition to France in 1359.

The fourteenth century was a great age of architectural achievement in England, and in employing such men as William Wynford and William Herland to work at Windsor the king did much to make this possible. It is significant that William of Wykeham, the royal minister who played an important part in the later years of the reign, first came to the king's attention when he was helping to organize the building works at Windsor. The elegance of fine tracery and vaulting, the ingenuity of complex wooden roofs, the extravagance of rich tapestries all represent an important facet of the character of the victor of Crécy.

The chroniclers provide few revealing anecdotes about Edward III. Froissart has a famous passage which describes the king aboard ship before the battle with the Castilian fleet in 1350. He wore a black velvet jacket and a small beaver hat, which suited him well. He asked his minstrels to play a German tune, recently introduced to court by John Chandos, and amused himself by asking Chandos to join in the singing. When the enemy were sighted, drinks of wine were ordered, and the mood changed from one of levity to determination. Edward ordered the master of his ship to lay alongside a great Spanish vessel, and the battle began. The story indicates something of the king's spirit and sense of fun. Edward, one of whose favourite mottoes was 'Hay, hay, the White Swan, by God's soul, I am thy man', possessed a gift of conviviality lacking in both his father and grandfather.

The king's reputation was not beyond reproach, but although there is no doubt of his attachment to his mistress Alice Perrers in the closing years of his life, there is nothing to support the other accusations made against him by the chroniclers. The most detailed story is that of his rape of the Countess of Salisbury. According to Jean le Bel, when the king came to her castle on the Scottish border in 1342, he was so overcome with her beauty that he could hardly eat his dinner. All his declarations of love were in vain, and eventually in anger and desperation he raped the countess in a most brutal manner. As it was told, the story was obviously derived from the classical tale of the rape of Lucretia, and in many details it does not tally with the known facts. It bears all the marks of French propaganda. Equally, there is no evidence to support the charge made in a curious mixture of history and prophecy, that the king's attentions were diverted from the siege of Calais as a result of his amorous inclinations. This may have been intended as a covert attack on Alice Perrers. Edward seems, in fact, to have been remarkably faithful to his queen, Philippa of Hainault, at least until the last years of her life.

The Scottish chroniclers accused Edward of murdering his own brother, John of Eltham, in a bitter quarrel at Perth in 1336. Again, this looks like propaganda. The English *Scalacronica* merely states that John died 'a fine death'[11], and only one English writer, a Westminster author, even hints at anything mysterious. John's death was certainly sudden, but it is not even clear that the king was present in Perth at the time. A remarkable entry in a royal wardrobe book dated two days before John's death which records thirty-two shillings sent by the king from Berwick to Perth for the expense of covering the corpse is more probably an indication of the occasional inaccuracy of the records, than of a premeditated plot.

Edward could be hot-tempered, as was shown by his dismissal of his ministers in 1340. He was not a man to bear grudges, however, and there were few who were not able to win back a degree of favour following disgrace. John Moleyns and chief justice Willoughby are two cases in point; a third is that of chief justice Thorp. In 1346 an ordinance forbade the acceptance of retaining fees and bribes by royal justices. Thorp was personally warned as to his future conduct. Yet when he was tried for taking bribes, his disgrace was short lived. Edward pardoned him, and continued to employ him on judicial commissions.

In parliament in 1377 the chancellor in his opening sermon declared: 'Behold, lords, if any Christian king, or any other ruler in the world, has had so noble and gracious a lady as wife.'[12] Queen Philippa of Hainault was probably an important moderating influence on the king, but the almost universal praise she received from the chroniclers makes it hard to capture a real personality. A later writer was unkind enough to attribute her selection as queen to the good child-bearing quality of her hips. She was a prolific producer of children, with at least a dozen to her credit, though no more so than Eleanor of Castile had been. She was also extravagant; an exchequer entry for 1335 records a bed made for her confinement, 'of green velvet embroidered in gold with sea sirens, bearing a shield with the arms of England and Hainault'[13], while she also had 'a white robe worked with pearls, and a robe of velvet cloth embroidered with gold of divers workmanship'[13] for the same occasion: the bill approached £700. The story that the queen addressed the troops before the battle of Neville's Cross is probably apochryphal, but there may well be truth in the tale of her intercession on behalf of the burghers of Calais whom the king wished to execute. The royal family was characterized by a degree of mutual affection unusual in this period, and for this the chief credit must go to Philippa. Nor did she bring with her a host of relatives and compatriots, eager and greedy for advancement, like the Savoyards who came with Eleanor of Provence under Henry III. Edward did, however, gain much in diplomatic terms from his connection with Hainault, and recruited some devoted followers there, notably Walter Mauny. The importance of the queen can best be seen, perhaps, from the undoubted deterioration in the king's character in his last years, after her death in 1369.

A study of Edward III's policies at home reveals him to have been a politician rather than a far-sighted statesman. He did not initiate many changes in the law or the administration. In the one major crisis of the period covered in this chapter, that of 1340–1, he displayed his intention to be an effective master of his kingdom, but he also showed a readiness to compromise when faced with the harsh realities of his position. Concessions were lightly granted, and then casually revoked. The chivalric virtues were important to Edward, but honour was an attribute better displayed on the battlefield than in the council chamber. The statutes of the period were not all that they seemed: that dealing with treason was not an act of consummate statesmanship by a king determined to prevent future injustice, but was part of a long story of compromise and confusion over the question of law and order. The trenchant statutes governing relations with the papacy were scarcely enforced.

It was the king's need for money which largely conditioned his policies. Concessions were granted to the commons in recognition of their power to grant subsidies. Commercial measures, notably with regard to the wool trade, were the result of a combination of financial and diplomatic circumstances; the benefit that accrued to the English cloth industry was almost an accidental by-product.

Edward was a man who learned from his mistakes. The intolerable financial burden of the first four years of war with France was not repeated, and the criticisms voiced in the later 1340s were soon met. The machinery of public proclamation and political sermon was used with great effect to obtain wide support for the king's endeavours. Despite the many arguments over matters of detail, notably over commercial policy, there were no major challenges to the king between the conclusion of his quarrel with Archbishop Stratford and the truce with the French agreed in

1360. Much of the king's success must be attributed to his good relations with the nobility. A skilful use of patronage, combined with a few judicious concessions, forms part of the explanation for this. Above all, the successful war ensured that domestic matters were of no major concern; the nobility were as keen as the king to see that adequate supplies of funds were forthcoming for the campaigns. The wealthier magnates even advanced money to the crown, as in 1359 for the financing of the great expedition to France.

The achievement of the government at home during the years of triumph abroad was considerable, if not spectacular. An expensive war was financed, an unruly countryside brought under a degree of control, and difficult problems of the organization of trade and the state of the currency were resolved. An examination of Edward III's rule at home shows how much the political framework had changed since Edward I's day. The king himself was not cast in the same mould as his grandfather, and did not have a similar overall vision of reform and redirection. Edward I had tried to impose his will on the country from above; in contrast, many of the measures taken in Edward III's reign were not the result of royal initiative, but emerged in the course of the bargaining process over the king's financial demands. The success of Edward III's rule provides a sufficient justification for his approach to the government of the realm. In the pragmatic measures that were taken the achievement of a nation that had acquired a new equilibrium and maturity after the stormy days of the crisis of 1340–1 can be seen. Despite the various arguments that took place, the fundamental collaboration between king, nobility and people was striking: Edward III was far more than a mere military adventurer; he was a skilful ruler as well as a chivalric hero.

9

Plague, Famine and War

The Fourteenth-Century Economy

When the Hainaulter Jean le Bel came to England in 1327, he was pleasantly surprised by the wealth of the land. He stayed at York for six weeks, and wrote: 'We never ceased to marvel at how so great an abundance could come there.'[1] It is tempting to assume that the military successes of the English, notably under Edward I and Edward III, were achieved because the country was prosperous with many resources of money, manpower and supplies which could be mobilized for war. English writers, however, painted a dismal picture of the economic fortunes of the country. The St Albans chronicler, William Rishanger, described a great storm in 1289, and stated that for some forty years after that there was a scarcity of grain, with consequent high prices. Edward II's biographer commented on the famine years 1315–16: 'Alas, poor England! You who once helped other lands from your abundance, now poor and needy are forced to beg.'[2] Official records from the early 1340s give a picture of infertile lands and poverty stricken villagers, incapable of paying their taxes. Then in 1348 came the first visitation of the Black Death – bubonic plague. The chronicler Henry Knighton wrote that 'After the pestilence many buildings both great and small in all cities, towns and boroughs fell into total ruin for lack of inhabitants; similarly many small villages and hamlets became desolate, and no houses were left in them, for all those who had dwelt in them were dead.'[3] Was it then the case that war offered a means of escape from economic hardship, rather than being the product of a booming economy?

245

By about 1300 England was a densely populated country. There is no secure evidence from which figures can be calculated, but a level of up to five or six million seems probable. This is of course very low by modern standards, but only a small proportion lived in towns, and the system of agriculture was, in today's terms, appallingly inefficient. It was very satisfactory if wheat yielded four times the quantity of grain sown. In order to feed the population more land was probably under the plough than was the case in any later period, and some of it was only of marginal fertility. This was not a purely peasant economy of a primitive type, however, dominated by subsistence farmers working meagre inherited holdings; many villagers were bound to the land and obliged to perform labour services to their lord, but there were opportunities to buy and sell land. Even unfree tenants could, by the exercise of skill and with good fortune, prosper at the expense of their fellows. The multiplying number of local markets meant that profits could be made by putting surplus produce on sale. Wage labour was common, with many landless men available for hire.

In the late twelfth and early thirteenth centuries great landlords had responded to the problems presented by inflation and a rising population by adopting a system of management known as high farming. This meant that they exploited their estates directly, rather than leasing them out for a fixed rent. They profited from rising prices by selling much of the produce of their manors, and benefited from the ample supply of labour which ensured that wages were low. Indeed, by 1310 at Battle Abbey the cost of providing free meals for those performing labour services was higher than the wage-rate for the job. Most manors were run by means of a mixture of customary labour services and wage labour, but the convenience and low cost of the latter by the end of the thirteenth century meant that in some cases the traditional services were being commuted, or exchanged for a money payment. There are signs that by then some landlords were turning back towards a system in which rents predominated, rather than continuing to rely on the riskier technique of direct management. The accounts of the wealthy Earl of Cornwall, dating from 1296–7, show that he relied for the most part on rents. With a high population, demand for land was acute, and it was therefore possible to increase rents and other charges on the tenants.

Edward I's reign saw difficulties, but no economic catastrophes. There were some murrains – or animal plagues – and occasional bad harvests. It was unfortunate for the king that the years of greatest political difficulty, 1294–7, coincided with the high grain prices that are indicative of poor harvests. In the later years of the reign grain yields were good, but as bullion was pouring into the country as a result of a boom in wool exports, prices remained high, and went on rising in the early years of Edward II's reign. This situation caused some alarm. It was wrongly suspected that the king had been meddling with the coinage, and early in 1315 the magnates requested legislation to set maximum prices on certain foodstuffs. The measure was doomed to failure, for later in the year disaster struck in the form of famine.

The great famine of 1315–16 was caused by that most English of meteorological phenomena, too much rain. The autumn of 1314 was wet, and in 1315 it poured incessantly all summer. Even if the seed managed to germinate, the grain rotted on the stalk. Only in the West Country was there any relief from the downpours. Conditions became even worse in the next year. Seedcorn was in short supply, and further torrential rain brought another dreadful harvest. On the Winchester estates the wheat yield in 1315 was about sixty per cent of the average, falling to fifty-five per cent in the following year. On the estates of Bolton Priory in the north, wheat yields on some manors fell to a fifth of their normal level. Other crops were badly affected, and there was even a shortage of salt, as the coastal salt pans could not evaporate. The crisis was one which affected northern Europe as a whole, and although some supplies of grain were imported from the south, the quantities were too inadequate to bring much relief. Prices inevitably shot up. Manorial accounts suggest a rise from a normal level of between five or six shillings a quarter for wheat to 26s 8d by the summer of 1316, but townspeople had to pay far more –

one London chronicler noted a price of forty shillings. With grain in such short supply, demand for other foodstuffs rose, and price levels duly responded.

The chroniclers produced horror stories about the effects of the famine. Reports of cannibalism were probably an exaggeration, but the pleas of the garrison of Berwick strike an authentic note: as the horses died, their carcases were boiled by the cavalrymen, who ate all the meat and left the bones for the footsoldiers. The latter were led by desperation to attempt a raid against the Scots contrary to orders, which ended in inevitable disaster. Although one poet wrote; 'A man's heart might bleed to hear the cry of poor men lamenting "Alas, I am dying of hunger"'[4], the upper classes did not respond to the situation by trying to alleviate suffering; instead, they cut down the amount they gave to the poor in alms, and reduced the size of their households as an economy measure. Not surprisingly, statistics show a marked increase in crime – notably theft – during the famine years, but there was no real threat to the social order. There is little evidence of hunger riots, although one Genoese ship, laden with wheat, was seized by a mob at Sandwich.

Disease stalked in the wake of famine. Weakened by malnutrition, many succumbed. The precise nature of the epidemic is not clear; typhus, which is often associated with famine, was unknown in medieval Europe. Mortality was particularly heavy among the lower classes according to the chroniclers, but did not spare the wealthy, even though they are unlikely to have had to go hungry. The death rate was probably about ten per cent. Disease was not confined to humans: sheep were highly vulnerable to liver rot and other diseases in wet weather, and flocks were decimated. Wool exports slumped in 1315–16, and on the royal estate of Clipstone in Nottinghamshire about half the sheep died. Improvement in the weather did not end the problems faced by farmers, for a severe cattle epidemic, probably of rinderpest, then occurred. At Clipstone twenty per cent of the herd was lost in 1318–19, and almost forty per cent in the next year. On the Winchester estates the numbers of cattle fell by over half in two years, despite efforts to replace losses by purchase. The fall in animal stocks had serious consequences. Not only were supplies of meat, milk and cheese affected, but also grain production, for oxen were the chief draught animals at this period. Some well-off landlords were able to buy horses for ploughing, but lesser men would not have had the resources to do this. The country was not free of the wave of animal pestilence until the late 1320s. To make matters worse, the harvest of 1321 was again disastrous, and prices rose close to the levels of 1316. The sheriff of Nottingham, purveying food for the royal expedition to Scotland in 1322, was unable to buy wheat for less than eighteen shillings a quarter, and the victualling bill for the army totalled almost £15,000; an unprecedented sum.

In the 1320s the economy began to suffer from a problem of a different order, which became acute by the end of the next decade. Coin, which had been plentiful at the start of Edward II's reign, became increasingly scarce. Existing stocks of silver were depleted by natural wastage, hoarding and export, and because no change had taken place in minting policy since Edward I's reign, English mints lost the competitive edge they had enjoyed over their continental rivals. Little silver was brought in for recoining and the shortage of coin forced prices down. Records of grain yield suggest that the harvest of 1339 was almost as poor as those of 1315 and 1316, following a winter of floods and frost, and a summer of drought. Prices, however, rose to little more than an average of seven shillings a quarter for wheat. The inflationary tendencies of the thirteenth century had been abruptly halted.

There is a great deal of evidence of the economic difficulties that England faced in the late 1330s and early 1340s. An inquiry into the lands held by the knights of the Hospital showed that in 1338 rents at Greenham in Berkshire had fallen 'because of the poverty of the community and the tenants, and the lack of money',[5] while the voluntary aid collected by the knights, which used to be worth about £18, now raised £10 with difficulty. At Bothemscombe in Devon only 160 acres out of a total of 240 were under cultivation, because of the infertility of the soil. At Godsfield in

Hampshire rents stood at two-thirds of their normal level. The national inquiry into the tax of a ninth granted in 1340 revealed a similar picture, with impoverished tenants unable to farm the land, much of which lay waste because it was of such poor quality. In Buckinghamshire at least 5,539 acres were recorded as having gone out of cultivation since 1291. Some Oxfordshire manorial accounts showed renewed problems caused by cattle epidemics; at Waterperry where two ploughs were needed, seven oxen died in 1336, leaving only nine – a full plough team consisted of eight oxen. Records of crops at Bourchier Hall in Essex suggest that over-intensive cultivation may have caused a real degree of soil exhaustion.

The picture in the second quarter of the fourteenth century was not, however, one of unremitting gloom. Some landlords found ways of meeting the challenge of the times. While exhausted lands were going out of cultivation, some new fields were put under the plough for the first time. In the 1320s John Stonor created new manors in Buckinghamshire by buying up many small tenements. He relied on rents and the sale of produce from a large demesne worked by wage labourers to obtain his profits. Lionel de Bradenham in Essex raised his rent income substantially, and in the 1340s he expanded the acreage under cultivation at Langenhoe by sowing a large crop of oats. The general trend, however, was one of retrenchment and contraction, though not all landlords and communities responded in the same way to the problems of the age.

One explanation for the difficulties of the first half of the fourteenth century is that the population had simply outgrown its resources. This is the classic theory, set out by the political economist Malthus at the end of the eighteenth century, of a fast-growing population laying itself open to be checked by famine, disease or war. Landlords were putting very little of their profits back into improvement of their estates. There were no new crops or novel farming techniques available, as there were to be in the eighteenth century, to transform the productivity of the land. The evidence of the grain yields on the Winchester estates shows a marked deterioration in the last quarter of the thirteenth century, which suggests that the agrarian economy had reached the furthest possible limits of expansion. Yet the decline of yields did not continue at the same pace in the first half of the fourteenth century, and in some cases there was a recovery. Archaeological evidence of peasant housing suggests that at the least some of the richer members of village communities were increasing in prosperity; there was not the universal distress to be expected if the whole society had been perched precariously on a marginal level of subsistence. At the same time, documentary evidence shows that the average size of peasant holdings had shrunk considerably since the early thirteenth century, and the degree of correlation that existed between death rates and years when grain prices were high shows that there was no ample reserve of resources available to provide a cushion against shocks.

An alternative to the strict Malthusian explanation is that the difficulties of the early fourteenth century were less the result of increasing internal strains than of unprecedented external factors. It may be that there was an overall deterioration in the weather. Vines were going out of cultivation in southern England and the freezing over of the Thames at London in the winter of 1309 could be an indication of the coming of what is known as the Little Ice Age, which lasted until about 1700. The evidence of grain yields, however, does not suggest that average temperatures were becoming much colder, so shortening the growing season. Rather, it seems that the weather became far more variable. Against the wet years 1315–16 could be set the hot summer of 1326, when lakes dried up and the Thames at London was permanently salty. Conditions in 1315–16 may be compared with those in 1816–17, when wet and cold conditions caused world-wide crop failures. The cause on that occasion was not a long-term change in weather patterns, but a remarkable increase in volcanic activity, notably the eruption of Tomboro in Indonesia in 1815. The resultant dust cloud produced a catastrophic temporary transformation of the weather. There were eruptions in Iceland in the early fourteenth century, but there is insufficient evidence to demonstrate that the rains of 1315–16 were caused in the same way as those five hundred years later. It may well be, however, that there was a link between the major eruption of Öraefajökull in Iceland in 1362 and the below-average harvest of that year. Like the highly changeable weather, the animal pestilences of the fourteenth century were extraneous factors working on the economy. Over-population may have rendered the country more vulnerable to the effects of bad harvests and diseases, but no pre-industrial society could have weathered such difficulties unscathed. The fact that the death-rate rose in years of famine should not be taken as a sure sign of imminent Malthusian crisis, but as an inevitable concomitant of a primarily agrarian economy.

In 1348 a setback of unprecedented proportions took place. In the early summer of that year two ships hailing from Gascony sailed into harbour at Melcombe Regis in Dorset, bringing with them the Black Death. This traditional account of the origin of bubonic plague in England is probably correct, although Bristol and Southampton have also been suggested as candidates for the initial outbreak. The disease had been unknown in western Europe since the Dark Ages. It had spread with horrific speed from southern Russia, devastating populations which had no resistance to it. Contemporaries had few ideas of what caused the plague, which only acquired the name Black Death in the sixteenth century. Corruption of the air was one possibility, and there was an awareness of the contagious nature of the disease. St Bridget of Sweden appears to have considered that the plague was a divine response to earthly vanity, and believed that abolition of extravagance in dress was one means of dealing with it, along with alms-giving and regular masses. Even as late as the nineteenth century there was still total ignorance of the real nature of bubonic plague. The nineteenth-century economic historian Thorold Rogers considered that it was caused by the projection into the atmosphere of 'foreign substances of a deleterious nature',[6] which were the result of earthquakes in 1347, and he looked forward to the day when chemical analysis would be able to discover the nature of these materials. So horrific was the disease that it attracts eccentric theories to this day; the eminent astronomer Fred Hoyle has postulated that the plague bacillus is of extra-terrestrial origin.

Although there are still some unresolved problems, the nature of bubonic plague has been established with reasonable certainty. It is a complex disease. The bacillus, *yersinia pestis*, is normally endemic among rodents. It is spread by fleas, which catch the infection from their hosts. The rapidly-breeding bacillus can block the insect's gullet completely, and when this happens it becomes voraciously hungry, and attacks any available victim, notably man. It is also possible for the bacillus to be spread directly from man to man should the disease take a pneumonic form, for it can then be transmitted simply by coughing or sneezing. Plague has been extremely well studied, notably during the epidemics which took place in India and Manchuria in the late nineteenth and early twentieth centuries. Medical authorities are agreed that the black rat and its flea parasite *xenopsylla cheopis* were primarily responsible for the spread of these outbreaks. This flea thrives in warm, damp conditions. Temperatures outside the range fifty-six to seventy-five degrees Fahrenheit are not conducive to bubonic plague, so in a temperate climate the disease should only be prevalent in the summer months. In the winter, however, it could spread in its more virulent pneumonic form.

There are obvious dangers in assuming that the plague of 1348 took the same form as recent epidemics in hot regions. For one thing, the disease was not already present among the rat population in England. There has been no modern study of a major plague epidemic taking place in a country which had no previous experience of the disease and where there were no residual pools of infection in the rodent population. The fact that in recent times plague has not occurred on a large scale in regions with a temperate climate suggests that it may have changed its character since the medieval period. There is no reason to doubt the importance of rats in spreading the disease in the fourteenth century, although rabbits may have also played a role. *Xenopsylla cheopis*, however, is an unlikely villain as far as north-western Europe is concerned. The common rat flea, *nosopsyllus fasciatus*, is more likely to have been responsible. It is common upon mice as well as on all varieties of rat, and thrives at a lower temperature than its tropical relative. In the only English outbreak of plague to be scientifically investigated, a very small one in 1909–10, it is interesting to note that some cases of the bubonic form of the disease occurred in the winter months of December and January, and *nosopsyllus fasciatus* was the only flea to be found on the rats of the locality. Although this flea has not caused any major epidemics in recent times, scientific evidence shows that it can serve as a highly efficient carrier of the plague bacillus. A further possibility is that the human flea, *pulex irritans*, may well have helped in the spread of the Black Death.

Not only may the flea responsible for the 1348 plague have been different from that involved in recent epidemics, but the bacillus itself may have altered. Diseases undoubtedly do mutate, and it has been suggested that the strain which caused the Black Death may have been one which had developed a capacity to survive the cold winters of the Russian steppe as its hosts, probably marmots, hibernated. It may be that plague disappeared from north-western Europe in the late seventeenth century because of a further mutation, although with a disease which depends on complex environmental factors for epidemics to take place, no certainty is possible. There is certainly no reason to follow one medical authority on the history of plague, J. F. Shrewsbury, who assumes that because of the 'immutable nature' of plague, only a twentieth of the population could have died in the 1348 outbreak.

To this day, the word 'plague' conjures up greater overtones of horror than are associated with almost any other disease. Bubonic plague is revolting. The symptoms are distinctive and repellent. The disease strikes fast. Within two or three days the characteristic buboes appear. These are large swellings in the groin, neck or armpit, which might suppurate, giving off a vile smell. Black gangrenous carbuncles are another feature of the disease, which rarely takes more than a week to kill. The pneumonic version acts still faster, causing a high fever which brings death within two days.

The English chroniclers do not provide any really vivid accounts of plague symptoms, although they are clearly described by Geoffrey le Baker, who noted that recovery was more likely if the victim developed buboes than if carbuncles appeared all over his body. A Welsh poet wrote in terms which suggest that he had actually had the disease, as he described the bubo:

It is seething, terrible, wherever it may come, a head that gives pain and causes a loud cry, a burden carried under the arms, a painful angry knob, a white lump. It is of the form of an apple, like the head of an onion, a small boil that spares no one. Great is its seething, like a burning cinder, a grievous thing of an ashy colour.[7]

It is worth quoting the account of one of the survivors from the 1909–10 outbreak in Suffolk, a girl of eighteen:

On Sunday December 19th my mother had a headache when she awoke. She got up about 10 o'clock and was sick. She had sickness and diarrhoea and got worse and on Wednesday 22nd. she went to bed about 4.30 p.m. . . . at about 5 p.m. I went up again and found she was dead . . . My mother had a knot in her neck when she was ill . . . I was ill in the same way as the others and had spots on my legs and also a knot inside my thigh and my face and arms were swollen.[8]

The simple factual style does not disguise the stark horror of the situation.

In 1909–10 the progress of the disease was contained. In 1348, however, it spread with virulent rapidity. The date of the initial outbreak is given as just before 24 June by the best chronicle evidence, but records show that the sheriff of Devon failed to appear at the exchequer on 16 June because of illness. None of his staff could take his place, as they had all died of plague. Initially the epidemic was confined to the West Country, but efforts such as those of the men of Gloucester to bar entry to anyone from the afflicted town of Bristol were in vain. In January 1349 the king postponed parliament on the grounds that plague had suddenly broken out in London, and in the early months of the year the disease was spreading inexorably on all fronts. By the autumn it had reached all parts of the kingdom, but in 1350 it died down, its initial force spent. It did not, however, vanish from the land. In 1361 England was visited by 'the second pestilence', and bubonic plague reappeared in 1368–9. It was to recur with distressing regularity until the seventeenth century.

The way in which the plague spread is far from clear. The black rat, almost certainly the only species of rat present in fourteenth-century England, is a relatively timid beast, which does not travel far from the nests it makes in house roofs and similar places. It does not seem likely that the human plague was preceded by a spread of the infection throughout the rat population; in all probability, the epidemic moved with equal speed through human and animal populations alike. It may be that the active trade in wheat and other grains was the chief medium for the transmission of the fatal bacillus. This is the most likely explanation for the way in which this scourge could have reached remote rural communities and great cities with equally deadly effect. The cramped and insanitary living conditions of the day undoubtedly facilitated the spread of the plague.

How many people died of plague? This question has caused much controversy among historians, for there are no true censuses to give a reliable answer. The evidence of bishops' registers gives the level of death rates among the beneficed clergy, and suggests an average mortality of over forty per cent. A sample composed solely of adult males, such as the clergy, does not give a proper cross-section of the population, and not all vacancies were caused by plague. Manorial records give figures of the deaths of those who held land in the villages. Again, these are not fully representative samples but some very high figures emerge. At Bishop's Waltham in Hampshire sixty-five per cent of the tenants died, while on the Glastonbury estates mortality ranged from roughly one-third to two-thirds. The considerable local variation in the incidence of the plague makes it hard to give an overall figure. This type of evidence does not extend to the towns, where in all probability the death-toll was higher than in the countryside. The chroniclers suggest that the situation in London was particularly appalling. The Bishop of London and Walter Mauny, the famous warrior, bought land to make new cemeteries for the plague victims, since there was no room in the old churchyards. It seems safe to assume a nationwide death-toll of at least one-third of the population.

The only evidence which points to a lower level of mortality is that relating to the upper classes. The death-rate of royal tenants-in-chief was only about twenty-seven per cent, while of those summoned to the House of Lords a mere four and a half per cent died in 1348, and thirteen per cent in the following year. There is an obvious explanation for this low aristocratic mortality. Better housing and living conditions would make exposure to the rat fleas far less likely; this is surely why only one member of the royal family, the king's daughter Joan, died of plague, and only two of the bishops succumbed to the disease. This English experience was not unique. It has been observed that in northern France the upper classes similarly escaped the 1348–9 plague relatively unscathed.

What is extremely puzzling is that the partial immunity of the upper classes to plague did not extend to the second outbreak, that of 1361. In this epidemic, the overall death-rate was lower than in 1348–9. At Bishop's Waltham only fifty-three tenants died, as against 264 in the first outbreak. Fourteen per cent of the beneficed clergy in Yorkshire died. Yet over twenty-two per cent of tenants-in-chief died, and almost twenty-four per cent of the parliamentary peerage. The chronicler Knighton commented on the way in which the great men were affected as well as the poor this time, while other writers noted that more men than women died. The author of the *Brut* complained that the widows who were left, 'forgetting their own worship and birth, coupled and married themselves with them that were of low degree and little reputation'.[9] Children were said to be badly hit.

As the incidence of the 1361 epidemic was so different from that of 1348–9, it is tempting to think that it must have been a different disease. An influenza virus has even been suggested. Yet contemporaries called the epidemic 'the second pestilence'; it is unlikely that they would have given this name to a wholly different disease. The coincidence of two deadly, different epidemics sweeping Europe within little more than a decade seems highly unlikely. It is, however, improbable that one of the most eminent victims claimed for bubonic plague in 1361 died of that disease. Henry Duke of Lancaster was ill as early as February, and died only on 23 March – too long an illness for plague. The high death-toll among children can be explained, on the other hand, by a second visitation of plague having a greater incidence among that part of the population which had not gained any immunity from the first occurrence of the disease.

The effect of the continued visitations of plague, combined with other diseases such as that reported in the *Brut* for 1366 from which 'many men, anon as they were go to bed whole and in good point, suddenly they died',[10] was to prevent any recovery of the population. Indeed, examination of replacement rates – the rate at which children survive their parents – suggests a continued decline of the population from 1348 until well into the fifteenth century.

Such a devastating visitation as the Black Death must have affected society in many ways, both in the short and long term. The English sources are disappointingly muted on the contemporary reaction to the plague. English medical men did not write treatises on the pestilence as many of their continental counterparts did; they concentrated on more straightforward matters, like John of Arderne who expatiated at great length on the bowels. They did not suggest such remarkable methods of avoiding infection as that adopted by Pope Clement vi, who on the advice of his physician withdrew into isolation in his chamber where two huge fires blazed all summer, precautions which proved effective. On the continent pogroms of Jews were a common occurrence in the aftermath of plague, as were processions of flagellants – bands who chanted as they lashed each other until the blood ran. There were of course no Jews in England, and when a group of flagellants crossed from the Low Countries their repulsive rites were observed with curiosity. No Englishmen could be persuaded to follow their example. The bishops certainly ordered the performance of penitential psalms, with barefoot processions, as it appeared that the plague was a form of divine retribution for sin. Although it was claimed that the epidemic was halted in Hereford as a result of a procession bearing the shrine of St Thomas Cantilupe, such ceremonies appear to have been neither widespread nor effective. The response of the government was more practical. The crown complained about the foul and insanitary condition of the London streets, which was seen as contributing to the spread of disease. After both the first and second outbreaks of plague the number of commissions of sewers appointed increased; improvements in land drainage would reduce the number of stagnant ditches and drains, thought to be a source of infection.

There is no parallel from England to the famous passage in which the Florentine chronicler Villani described the way in which the survivors of the plague abandoned themselves to gluttony, adultery and all forms of vice. The great epidemic of 1348–9 was regarded quite clearly, however, as a watershed. The poet Langland considered that the evils he castigated in the society of the later fourteenth century dated from the period of the plague. John Trevisa dated the adoption of English rather than French as the main language in schools similarly. One implausible story was that all children born after 1348 had two fewer milk teeth than in the past, while another effect was said to be that women who survived the epidemic were barren for a time. Undoubtedly the Black Death must have had a sharp psychological effect on the populace, but this is hard to document. A considerable wave of violence preceded, rather than followed, the Black Death in England; it was probably the work of soldiers returning from the wars. English art does not demonstrate clearly that sense of sombre pessimism which has been sent to engulf Siennese painting in the later fourteenth century. Nevertheless, the impact of the plague must have been immense. The chronicle of the *Brut* gives some impression of the disorientation that the great epidemic must have brought with it: 'In these days was death without sorrow, wedding without friendship, wilful penance, and dearth without scarcity, and fleeing without refuge or succour.'[11]

Contemporary opinion was remarkably unanimous as to the economic effects of the plague. Knighton described the abandonment of houses and villages, and remarked on the acute scarcity of labour and the low price of goods. In parliament in 1351 it was said that the common people had been greatly diminished by the plague, and that cities, towns and hamlets were impoverished and in some cases uninhabited. As a result of the shortage of labour the Ordinance of Labourers was enacted in 1349 to try to keep wages down to pre-plague levels, and a statute to the same effect was made two years later. In contrast to the low prices for foodstuffs, a rise in price was noted for manufactured articles. It was claimed in parliament that iron had risen from 3d to 1s a pound. These are exactly the sort of changes that would be expected to follow a sharp fall in the size of the population. Demand for food would fall, bringing prices down, but the scarcity of labour would push wages up, and with them the cost of manufactured goods would rise.

Historians, however, are rarely satisfied with simple answers. Some have argued that although the evidence for a heavy mortality in the short term is undeniable, the evidence of permanent change of the type noted by contemporaries is far less conclusive. On the estates of Winchester and St Albans new tenants for the many vacant holdings were found with remarkable speed. At Cuxham in Oxfordshire it took six years to fill the tenements of the plague victims, but filled they were. Study of deserted villages has not shown any prompt abandonment in 1348–9, and such examples as that of the hamlet of Tusmore in Oxfordshire, reported in 1357 to be 'void of inhabitants since their deaths in the pestilence',[12] appear to be exceptional. Nor is the evidence of prices as clear-cut as contemporaries suggested. Although grain prices were low in 1349 and 1350, they soon rose, and stood at relatively high levels for the next quarter century. The average price for the decade 1341–50 was 4s 9d a quarter, while in the next ten years it stood at 7s, rising to 8s in the years 1361 70. After a poor harvest in 1369 the average on the Winchester estates was 13s 1d, with levels approaching those of 1315–16 being reached. Thereafter prices began to fall, and a long epoch of low grain prices began.

The evidence of wages is far from clear-cut. On the manors of Westminster Abbey they moved just as the chronicles indicate; those of the decade following the Black Death were almost double those of the previous ten years. The Winchester evidence indicates a far more gradual rise, though the calculations are not wholly reliable. In 1349 in London some of the bakers' workmen were accused of conspiring among themselves to obtain wages double or even treble those that had prevailed before the plague, but it is most unlikely that many men were able to better themselves to such an extent. If real wages are considered – that is wages expressed in terms of the quantities that could be bought with pay – it becomes clear that no dramatic improvement took place in the wake of the Black Death. It was not until the last quarter of the fourteenth century that a rise in money wages and a fall in food prices transformed the lot of the working man.

An examination of changes in the way in which landlords ran their estates provides some instances where the plague obviously had a dramatic impact, but against these can be set examples where the records show few alterations to long-established routines. At Cuxham in Oxfordshire virtually no labour services were performed after the Black Death, and the amount spent on hired labour, which had rarely exceeded £3 in the past, rose in 1349–50 to over £12. In 1359 the manor was leased out by its owners, Merton College in Oxford. On the Canterbury estates, however, the change from direct exploitation to leasing only began in the 1380s. The immediate consequences of the plague there were a reinforcement of the traditional obligations to perform labour services, and a reluctance to permit the unfree to acquire free status. In general, the late fourteenth century did see a tendency to abandon direct farming of the

demesnes, and to commute labour services for cash payments, but the chronology of change cannot be directly
linked to the heavy mortality of 1348–9 save for a few
examples. In the long term, however, the decline of the
population, accentuated as it was by later outbreaks of
plague, inevitably caused a transformation of many aspects
of the economy.

Why were the immediate consequences of the Black
Death less striking than the chroniclers indicated, with the
statistics in many cases only revealing fundamental
changes by the last quarter of the fourteenth century? One
suggestion is that pre-plague England was suffering from
such a degree of over-population that the loss of many men
made little difference to the workings of the economy. The
way in which so many vacant holdings were quickly taken
up suggests that there was indeed a large reserve of manpower to replace those who died. There is also some evidence to suggest that the survivors of the plague worked
harder and more productively. At the Battle Abbey manor
of Marley it has been shown that output per man rose
significantly. Women came forward to do much of the work
previously performed by men; it is significant that their
wages rose proportionately more than men's.

There are good reasons why prices should not have fallen
in the twenty years following the plague, despite the fact
that the lower population meant a reduced demand for
foodstuffs. Harvests were poor. On the Winchester estates
the average yield in the second quarter of the century had
been 3.96 bushels for every bushel of wheat sown; from
1349–80 the figure was 3.66. At the same time, the success
of the crown's monetary policy meant that there was a
relative abundance of coin in England which had an
inflationary effect. Interestingly, one chronicler even linked
the high wages of the period with the debasement of 1351,
rather than with the mortality two years earlier. In the later
fourteenth century mint output declined. Scarcity of coin
combined with good harvests helps to explain the low
prices of the last quarter of the century. As far as wages
were concerned, there is no doubt that the legislation of
1349 and 1351 had some effect in keeping levels down.

Accordingly, the effects of the plague were disguised, emerging in some cases only after a considerable period.

The argument for an essential continuity of economic life despite the plague, and for a rapid recovery from its immediate effects, should not be overstated. There is more to be said for the contemporary analysis of the situation than many historians have allowed. At Cuxham the manor had recorded profits of some £40 a year up to 1348, but for the one post-plague year for which they are recorded they stood at a mere £10 13s: the manor was eventually leased for £20 a year. Spene in Berkshire was said by a local inquest to have halved in value as a result of the plague. The rent income from the free tenants at Bradford in Shropshire fell from 26s to 15s and the value of land fell by a third. The plague caused an immediate relaxation of the demands made on the tenants on the estates of the Bishop of Coventry and Lichfield, and even so, the bishop failed to find new men to take up vacant holdings, particularly in Staffordshire. The bishops of Worcester were more successful in reorganizing their methods of management to deal with the changing situation, but the signs of real improvement after the initial catastrophic fall in revenue in 1349 only came in the mid-1360s. Even if new tenants were found to fill vacancies, difficulties might occur, as a letter concerning the Black Prince's manor of Berkhampstead written in 1356 shows:

As a result of the frequent changes of tenants during the pestilence and afterwards, and the manifold divisions and dismemberments that have occurred in the tenements which are held of the Prince there, the bailiffs and ministers cannot be fully informed of who are the Prince's real tenants, nor can they get at the Prince's rents, which are embezzled and made away with in many different ways.[13]

In 1360 there was still some land at Berkhampstead that had not been sown since the dark days of 1348–9. At Ramsey, a fall in expenditure of thirty-four per cent after 1361–2 reflects the drastic economies necessitated by the second outbreak of plague. The cumulative effects of successive epidemics were drastic, making a full recovery impossible. Although it has been estimated that the incomes of great landlords were in many cases no more than ten per cent lower in the 1370s than in the 1340s, the crude figures often disguise considerable changes. The lords of the Welsh Marches, for instance, pushed up the proportion of their income which did not derive directly from agriculture, such as the profits of justice and other concomitants of lordship. Conflicts such as the revolt of some of the villein tenants of the Abbey of Meaux in the 1350s demonstrate the difficulties facing landlords who failed to respond to the changing economic circumstances, and presaged the great explosion of the Peasants' Revolt of 1381.

It has rightly been suggested by one historian, A. R. Bridbury, that the Black Death was perhaps more purgative than toxic in its economic effects. Even if the pre-plague situation was not one of imminent Malthusian crisis, the drastic reduction in the number of mouths to be fed did restore a more healthy balance to the economy. It was possible to adjust the proportion of arable as against pasture land. On the Winchester estates the number of animals on the demesnes after 1348 rose, despite the murrains of the period. Where there was more livestock, grain yields improved as more manure was available. At Bourchier Hall in Essex the plague marked a clear watershed in the way in which the manor was farmed: the traditional crop rotation was abandoned, animal husbandry became more important, and land left fallow began to recover its fertility. Elsewhere it took longer for the full effects of *yersinia pestis*'s activities to be felt; overnight changes are not to be expected in agricultural techniques. The Black Death did not halt a booming economy in its tracks; in many ways its effects had been presaged by the famine and its accompanying mortality in Edward II's reign, so that it confirmed and accentuated existing trends, rather than reversed them. However, the fundamental importance of the advent of plague in 1348 cannot be denied, for all the resilience that the country displayed. The loss of over a third of the population is a fact which cannot be ignored.

Famine and plague were elements beyond human control which influenced the economy; war fits into a different category. Its effects are relatively easily discerned in regions like the north where campaigning took place, but the impact of war was far wider than the actual areas that were fought over. The whole country was affected by war taxation, the purveyance of foodstuffs, the recruitment of soldiers, the impressment of ships and the manipulation of trade. The gains made in France have to be offset against the disturbance caused to the domestic economy.

It is not difficult to see the importance of war at an individual level. Many examples can be cited of men who lost out, and of men who gained from warfare. In 1297 the Earl of Arundel explained why he could not fight overseas. The cost of campaigning in Wales, Scotland and Gascony had been high, and he had been forced to demise lands worth £500. Now he was unable to find anyone to advance him funds on security of lands worth £100, and he could not afford to join the king's expedition. In Edward II's reign there were many who lost lands and wealth as a result of the unsuccessful wars against the Scots. Even during the triumphant years of Edward III's war against the French there were men who lost all or part of their livelihood. Thomas de Thorleton of Great Yarmouth had possessed two ships and goods worth £100 early in the reign. Because of losses caused by the impressment of ships for war he was reduced to total poverty, and had to leave the town. John Taillart was captured by the French in Brittany in the 1350s and not only did he have to pay for his ransom, but he also lost his lands to his brother who acquired them by means of forged charters during his imprisonment abroad.

On the other side of the coin there were many, both magnates and commoners, who prospered through war. John Colier, an Englishman, settled in Harlech while Edward I's castle was being built there. He did well through supplying building materials and victuals to the workmen and soldiers, and founded one of the town's dominant families. It was, however, service in France under Edward III that brought the really striking gains. Thomas Breadstone was a retainer of the Berkeley family, who had redeemed his life and lands after the 1322 rising with 100 marks. He obtained a position as a valet in Edward III's household, was knighted in 1331, and received grants of lands to support him in his new dignity. A steady flow of gifts followed, including one of a ship, the *Christmas*, taken from the French. In 1339 he was made a banneret and granted 500 marks a year. Four years later he achieved baronial rank. He fought in all the major expeditions of the war, including those of Crécy and Poitiers, and died shortly after his return from the 1359–60 campaign. Royal patronage and the profits of war raised Breadstone from the ranks of the Gloucestershire squirearchy into the elite of the English nobility. Many of the more famous captains, such as James Audley, Robert Knollys and Hugh Calvely gained fame and fortune by a similar route. The most striking example of a man rising in society is that of Robert Salle, a bondman recruited for the wars in the 1330s who rose to knighthood, served in the royal household, and by the 1370s achieved command of the castle of Marck, near Calais. His lowly origins were not forgotten, however, by the peasants who killed him in the course of their revolt in 1381. Along with the successful soldiers were the profiteers. Among the names of the merchants that of William de la Pole is pre-eminent. In 1339 this wealthy wool-exporter was rewarded with the rank of banneret when he came to the king's rescue as the supply of Italian loans began to dry up. A less fortunate man was John of Denton, a Newcastle merchant, whose unscrupulous methods were said to extend to trafficking with the Scots. He gained a fortune, and with it the jealousy of his fellow-citizens, who put him to death.

An accumulation of individual examples helps to demonstrate the importance of war as an instrument of social change, but cannot indicate the overall impact of war on the economy. There is little agreement to be found among historians as to what this was. For some, the French war has been seen as bringing the country profits from gains such as ransoms and plunder; for others, success was won at a heavy cost to the economy in coin and manpower. It has been argued that the heavy war finance of the years from 1294 onwards saw an almost intolerable strain imposed on the English peasantry as a result of war taxation and purveyance, with the situation becoming particularly acute in the late 1330s. On the other hand, it has been suggested that the wealth of the economy was such that it could easily afford the wars of the three Edwards, and that perhaps 'the fuss made when things went wrong was utterly disproportionate to the damage done or the costs incurred'.[14]

Nearly all taxation during this period was justified in terms of military necessity, and most of the money raised was indeed spent on war. 'Ever the fourth penny must go to the king',[15] bewailed the husbandman in a poem of Edward I's day, and a song of 1339 complained that the common people were forced to sell cows, crockery and clothes to meet the demands of the tax-collectors. In 1334 twenty-four of 134 tenants at Ottery St Mary abandoned their holdings because of an unprecedented rise in their tax assessment. In the inquiry into the low yield of the ninth of 1340, heavy taxation was one frequent explanation for the poverty of the populace. In 1347 the men of Chirchull in Warwickshire complained that they would have to leave the place *en masse* as a result of the combination of a wool levy with a tax bill of almost £10, and at the same date the townspeople of Derby were said to be leaving for Nottingham as a result of an unreasonable assessment.

It may seem surprising that medieval levels of taxation were high enough to cause such distress. For the great lay landlords the burden was certainly not insupportable; it has been calculated that only about four and a half per cent of the Earl of Norfolk's revenue went on taxation between 1294 and 1297. Ecclesiastical institutions might be more affected. In 1294–5 a quarter of Bolton Priory's cash expenditure went in taxation, though the level fell later. The hospital of God's House, Southampton, had to pay £25 as one instalment of the 1294 tax, and when it failed to do so, eighteen oxen were seized from its lands. At Ramsey the taxes of the early fourteenth century had to be paid out of borrowed money, as income was inadequate: the common people were harder hit than the landlords. A poem of Edward II's time explained

> A man with goods worth forty pounds has to pay twelve round pence,
> And another, brought to the ground by poverty, has to pay as much,
> And he has a heap of children, all girls, sitting about his floor.
> They must have God's curse on them, but it is well established
> That the poor are robbed like this, and the rich excused.[16]

In fact, the poorest classes were exempt from taxation until after 1334, though that did not prevent landlords passing some of their burden on to them. From 1334 each locality paid a fixed sum, and this meant an end to individual valuations. Exemptions were abandoned, and the number of taxpayers rose as the burden was shifted lower down the social scale. When heavy taxation coincided with poor harvests, as in 1315–16, or 1339, life must indeed have been hard, while the corrupt practices of many tax-collectors increased a bitter sense of grievance.

It is impossible to know what the effect of taxation was on the budget of a medieval villager, but the poorest are unlikely to have had to pay more than the equivalent of a few days' wages. It is hard to see how this could have forced men to leave their villages. It is, however, likely that a tax removed from a locality much of its coin, so dislocating markets. It was because of royal taxation that the husbandman in the poem of Edward 1's day could not buy his seedcorn. The amount raised in taxation was a considerable proportion of the total monetary wealth of the country; between 1294 and 1298 lay taxation alone raised approximately £200,000, at a time when the currency probably totalled about £1,000,000. By the late 1330s the position was much graver. A single fifteenth and tenth yielded about £38,000, and there was probably only about £500,000 in circulation. Of course, some of the money raised in taxation must have returned fairly quickly into local economy, but that did not ease the short term crises, such as that in 1339–40. In the long term, of course, it was not direct taxation, but the balance of trade, mint policy and the loss of silver through wear and hoarding which controlled the scale of the currency.

Recruiting was another burden placed on the economy

by war. It is improbable that this ever caused a real shortage of labour: the campaigns of Edward I's reign have been likened to 'an outing for the unemployed'. The cost of equipping soldiers and paying their expenses until they were enrolled in royal service was a matter for much complaint. In 1295 the array of 187 men in the hundred of Launditch in Norfolk cost £52, as against a tax assessment in the previous year of £242. With the attempts in Edward II's reign to provide heavily armed infantry, costs rose sharply. In 1322 the county community of Lincolnshire complained, no doubt with a degree of exaggeration, that the charge for recruiting four thousand troops amounted to £8,000. In 1344 the commons protested that every archer recruited for the war cost at least a mark or a pound, with the total coming to £1,000 for each county. The heavy calls for troops in 1346 provoked bitter complaints. The scheme by which men of different degrees of wealth were assessed to provide varied numbers of troops was said to cause 'piteous' impoverishment. Although a statute in 1352 limited the power of the crown to demand military service save by common consent in parliament, the counties were still often charged with the expenses and payment of troops until the royal muster took place. They sometimes paid them until they reached the port of embarkation.

The compulsory purchase of foodstuffs was perhaps the most hated of the ways in which the crown mobilized the resources of the country for war. Under Edward I huge quantities of grain were collected by royal purveyors: in 1304, for example, over seventeen thousand quarters were sent north to Scotland and it has been calculated that in 1296–7 the king took the produce of about four thousand nine hundred acres in Kent. The seizure of such quantities might well affect local grain prices, and individuals were certainly badly hit on occasion. One Norfolk parson complained that as he had had seven quarters of wheat and two of barley taken he could not sow his land for six weeks, and lacked fodder for his beasts. The situation was aggravated by the dilatory and often inadequate payment for the goods, and by the inevitable corruption. It is not surprising that in 1337 the county of Lincolnshire paid 2,000 marks rather than submit to the activities of royal purveyors. Abuses of the system were rife in the early years of the Hundred Years War, though subsequently the adoption of a means of supplying armies by making contracts with merchants eased the situation. Even so, purveyance for the royal household was still a major grievance, and in 1362 the commons complained of the 'outrages and grievances committed by the purveyors of victuals', and suggested among more important reforms a cosmetic improvement, that henceforth 'the heinous name of purveyor should be changed, and called buyer'.[17]

Manorial accounts reveal some of the reasons for the unpopularity of the purveyors. The Cuxham records for the 1340s reveal that the manor staff made many journeys, often in vain, to try to obtain payment for the goods that had been taken. At Gamlingay in Cambridgeshire in 1350 the purveyors were bribed not to take five quarters of corn worth 3s 4d and a quart of wine. Legal records provide many cases. In 1297 one man claimed that the purveyors had driven off thirty of his sheep because he would not hand over five quarters of wheat to them. The measures that were taken to avoid purveyance ranged from excommunication of those responsible to armed assault. Of course, seizures of grain did not diminish the productive capacity of the country, but a small farmer could well be badly affected by the loss of part of his carefully husbanded reserves of grain. When draught beasts were taken, ploughing and other tasks might be made impossible. The degree of disturbance to the local economy should not be underestimated, even if the quantities of food taken were hardly such as to reduce men to starvation.

The way in which Edward III managed the wool trade in order to provide himself with badly needed funds has already been described. Although it is clear that a considerable part of the burden of the heavy additional customs duties was borne by the purchasers of wool in the Low Countries who had to pay higher prices, and although the large-scale decline of the export trade in raw wool did not begin until the late fourteenth century there is no doubt that English wool exports were severely hampered by the war.

Even in the 1350s, when restrictions were relaxed and large quantities of wool were exported, prices were lower than might have been expected, as a result of the high customs duties. Landlords, therefore, were not obtaining the profits that they should have had from their flocks. The wine trade, too, was hard hit, even though it was not as heavily taxed as that in wool. War in Gascony affected production, and the need to introduce an expensive convoy system for the wine fleets raised transport costs for the merchants.

The crown needed large numbers of ships in order to fight the French. Transports were required for the expeditions abroad, and fleets had to be maintained for the task of coastal defence. The crown possessed few ships of its own, and the impressment of ships for naval service involved the English ports in heavy expenses. In addition, trade was affected by the withdrawal of ships from their normal commercial activity. Only the Cinque Ports were obliged to provide vessels for the fleet at their own expense, but royal officials had the power to requisition ships elsewhere. In 1296 the ports between Harwich and King's Lynn alone provided a total of ninety-four for coastal defence. It has been estimated that in the 1340s and 1350s some one thousand arrests of ships were made to make up the massive fleets needed to take English armies to France. For the transport of the army for the siege of Calais in 1346, seven hundred ships were needed.

In Edward I's reign seaports had to obtain royal assistance to compel the men of the surrounding countryside to contribute towards the cost of providing ships. In 1304 the men of Dunwich petitioned for £1,000 compensation for the loss of ten ships in the wars. The situation became more serious in Edward III's reign. A Yarmouth jury in 1347 stated that there had been ninety great ships in the port in Edward II's day, and that the number had since dwindled to a mere twenty-four. In the next year the little port of Buddleigh Salterton was struck a hard blow when the French captured three ships and twelve boats, with the additional loss to the town of 141 sailors and merchants. Few owners were as fortunate as those of the *Bertelmeu* of Fowey who received £120 compensation for their losses in

war. A petition in parliament in 1347 complained that ship-
owners were receiving no such payments. The sailors were
of course paid wages by the crown, masters receiving 6d a
day, and ordinary seamen 3d. These were hardly adequate
to make up for the loss of revenue from trade. Wage-rates
remained static throughout Edward III's reign, like those
paid to soldiers. The general rise in levels of payment that
followed the Black Death did not extend to the military
sphere. Ships were often held in port for long periods
awaiting the arrival of troops while they could have been
engaged in trade; it is not surprising that desertion was a
common problem. The king's demands on the country's
naval resources were extremely damaging. In 1371 the
commons complained in parliament that the English navy
was 'nearly destroyed' as a result of royal policy. The constant impressment of ships and failure to provide adequate
compensation was undoubtedly more damaging than the
Earl of Pembroke's defeat off La Rochelle in 1372. It was
with bitter irony that the commons commented that a mere
twenty years earlier Edward III had been acclaimed as the
king of the sea.

In addition to the burdens imposed on the populace in
order to support the offensive war in France, the north of
England was, as has already been shown, badly affected by
the Scottish wars over a long period. French raids on
English seaports also had their effect, although like the
Zeppelin raids of the First World War, their psychological
impact was greater than the physical damage they caused.
There is no doubting the seriousness of the attack on
Southampton in 1338, however, and in 1340 it was reported
that lands in Sussex were not being cultivated for fear of
French attack; the raid on Winchelsea in 1360 caused widespread panic. The threat of invasion, often exaggerated by
the crown for propaganda purposes, led to the introduction
of expensive and time-consuming arrangements for home
defence.

The costs of war were heavy, but what of the benefits?
Many of those who fought were motivated as much by
hopes of material gain as by anticipation of winning

chivalric fame. In strictly financial terms, Edward III's French war brought gains which may be set against the heavy expenditure incurred. It is not possible to put an accurate figure on the profits made from ransoms, but the castles built by the English nobility during the reign stand as tangible evidence that investment in overseas war brought some good returns. The yield of the great ransom of the French King John was certainly over £200,000, and may have been over £250,000. Although Edward III regarded this money as his own, and not part of the national revenue, England was spared many years of taxation because of it. The recovery of English mint production in the 1350s is surely to be explained in part by the fact that much bullion was coming into the country in the form of the profits of war. Even in the later stages of the reign, the English were able to make some gains, if not so honourably as in the years of triumph. The French were prepared to buy castles and territory from their opponents, and paid 53,000 francs for the surrender of St Sauveur.

War offered landlords a means of making up the loss of income caused by declining profits from agriculture, and at lower levels of society there must have been many who gained from the needs of armies for equipment and arms. In 1346 and 1356 royal officials were scouring the country for bows and arrows: fletchers and armourers must have done well. War may also have expanded the domestic cloth market, as magnates bought robes for their retainers and uniforms for their soldiers. In Edward I's reign masons had found ready employment working on the Welsh castles, and in the later fourteenth century a building entrepreneur, John Lewyn, found many customers in the north of England who wanted their castles repaired and new fortifications built.

There is a certain artificiality in attempting to assess the economic implications of war in a period when it was endemic. If Edward III had not fought in France, it is unlikely that his martial enthusiasms would have been stilled; even in times of peace, magnates would have spent money on castles and retinues. In this period, there was no extended peaceful phase with which wartime conditions might be compared. Faced with such a problem, historians of more recent ages have sometimes constructed statistical models of alternative scenarios, but fortunately there is insufficient data for the application of such techniques of counter-factual history to the Middle Ages. The fact that it is not possible to draw up an accurate balance sheet of the gains and losses that may be attributed to war does not lessen its importance. The effects of war were certainly far from uniform. Many captains and soldiers profited greatly from it; many of the common folk blamed war-taxation for their ills. Some merchants were bankrupted through involvement in the government's wool schemes and loss of ships in war, while others made their fortunes. At some periods, notably 1294–7 and 1337–40, the costs of war were so great as to bring the country to the brink of disaster, with political crisis exacerbated by economic troubles. The last year of Edward III's reign again witnessed considerable difficulties as a result of war. At other times success in France brought visible prosperity at home, as the English ladies who flaunted the fine clothes and furs brought home as booty in 1346 must have felt.

Famine, plague and war were the dominant facts in the transformation of the English economy in the century ruled by the three Edwards. At the beginning of the period the population was rising towards its medieval maximum, prices were going up, and landlords were profiting from cheap labour and a system of direct exploitation of their estates: by the end of Edward III's reign, villages were being deserted and lands were lying uncultivated. The population had fallen dramatically, and showed no signs of recovery; prices were falling, and wages were rising, in complete contradiction to the position a hundred years before. Landlords were turning to a *rentier* system of estate management.

The changes were not the result of a simple Malthusian crisis, in which a growth of population was reversed as it exceeded the development of resources, so forcing many below subsistence level. Certainly the size of the population by the early fourteenth century was a strain on the country's agricultural capacity, but the natural disasters of the famine in Edward II's reign and more particularly the Black Death under Edward III were not a consequence of over-population. They contributed much to the reversal of economic trends, but at the same time war added greatly to the difficulties of the period. Heavy taxation increased poverty in the countryside and in the towns, particularly at times when coin was scarce, and purveyance of foodstuffs by royal officials was another element of dislocation. Trade was affected both by royal taxation and by seizures of ships for naval service.

At the same time, as the tide of success in the Hundred Years War ran in Edward III's favour, so war brought some benefits. Ransoms and plunder brought wealth into the country. The drain of bullion, which began in the 1320s with a natural wastage of the currency and which was then accentuated as a result of the heavy war expenditure of the late 1330s, was reversed in the 1350s. The pattern of change was complex and even contradictory, but the combination of many elements meant that by the end of Edward III's reign the late medieval pattern of the English economy had been firmly established.

10

The Years of Decline, 1360–77

The later years of Edward III's reign were a sad anti-climax after the period of his triumphs in war. In place of a thirst for glory the king displayed an appetite for luxury. Indolence replaced activity, and the politician failed to mature into an elder statesman. Yet even in decline, Edward's abilities should not be underrated. Despite the dismal record of military failure in the 1370s, which led to political crisis in 1376, the power of the crown was restored unimpaired at the close of the reign. Edward had a large family, and in his later years the activities of his sons became increasingly important. As the history of Henry II's reign showed only too clearly, sons could pose difficult problems for a medieval monarch. Not only was there the probable impatience of the eldest to gain the throne, but there was also the difficulty of providing adequately for the younger sons without weakening the crown in the process. No less than five of Edward's sons survived to adulthood, and the king's management of them was remarkably successful.

The most noted of Edward's children was of course his eldest son Edward, the Black Prince, a sobriquet given to him in the sixteenth century, possibly because he was thought to have worn black armour. The prince's courage at Crécy, his generalship at Poitiers and Nájera and his romantic marriage to Joan of Kent all combine to form a compelling picture. Yet there were cracks beneath the splendid, haughty façade. The prince's sense of chivalry was not sufficiently tempered by a pragmatic realism. He did not possess his father's political sense, and it is hard to see his premature death as a major disaster.

There was no great difficulty in providing the king's eldest son with an adequate estate. From his birth the earldom of Chester was intended for him, and he was formally given the title before his third birthday in 1333. The convenient death of his uncle John of Eltham made the earldom of Cornwall available for him in 1337, and in 1343 he was made Prince of Wales. He was one of the greatest of English magnates, with an income in the last years of his life of some £8,600 a year. Edward III was prepared to add responsibility to wealth, and in 1362 the heir to the throne received his greatest honour when he was given the novel title of Prince of Aquitaine. Edward III retained ultimate sovereignty over the former duchy, but gave his son far greater authority than any previous royal lieutenant had exercised. In allowing the prince to be virtually an independent ruler, Edward III diverted his energies away from any possible political ambitions in England. At the same time, the Black Prince accepted his position, and did not try to take undue advantage of it.

Much is known about the administration of the prince's estates in England and Wales, which was characterized by an understandable desire to maximize revenue. A great deal was done by his officials to create an efficient centralized administration at Westminster; this was more a result of the prince's lack of interest in his lands than of a desire to see them run more efficiently. He never visited Wales, following the example of Walter Mauny who never saw Merioneth, of which he was life sheriff. In the mid-1340s there was great alarm: the prince's general attorney in North Wales was murdered, and the English inhabitants declared that they had never been in such a perilous plight since Edward I's conquest. It was not only the Welsh who were aggrieved by the harsh nature of the prince's administration. The Marcher lords were alienated by threats to their traditional liberties, notably in 1347, just when the king was most anxious not to irritate the magnates. In a high-handed letter, the prince threatened the

Earl of Hereford that if he continued with his plans to hold a judicial eyre, 'to the diminution of his lordship of Wales, and against the dignity of his coronet', he would 'need to take other means for the salvation of the rights of his lordship and of the dignity of his coronet'.[1]

Cheshire also caused the prince's officials frequent problems. While suggestions that an actual rising took place there in 1353 are an exaggeration, there was considerable disorder in the county. A general eyre might have settled matters, but the prince, in need of money for the wars, accepted 5,000 marks in lieu from the local communities. Forest fines were threatened later, and again fines were paid in order to avoid the visitations of the justices. The prince's exactions can in part be justified by the fact that Cheshire was exempt from the ordinary parliamentary taxation, but their arbitrary nature was much resented. This was recognized by the prince himself on his death-bed, when he asked that the Wirral be no longer subject to forest law since its inhabitants had suffered so much from his officials. That act of kindness came too late, and earlier individual acts of generosity, such as an order to pay 4s 8d to a man whose oats had been trodden down by the prince's horse, or even the pardon of a substantial £90 fine, hardly compensate for the consistently overbearing character of the administration.

In marrying Joan of Kent the prince made a remarkable match. She was the daughter of the unfortunate Edmund Earl of Kent who was executed in 1330. She went through a form of marriage secretly with Thomas Holland when she was only twelve, but when he was on crusade in Prussia she was given in marriage to William Montague, son of the Earl of Salisbury. An extraordinary love triangle was created, with Thomas Holland being appointed steward of William and Joan's household. In 1347 Holland decided to plead before the papal court for the annulment of Joan's marriage to William, and in the next year the two rivals fought on opposite sides in a tournament. In 1349 the Pope decided in favour of Holland, and it was on his death in 1361 that the beautiful Joan, aged thirty-two, married the Black Prince in what was undoubtedly another love-match.

It was clearly her physical attractions that made Joan such an envied prize; even the king is thought to have cast a lascivious eye in her direction. She was not a notably wealthy woman: her selection as the prince's bride says more for his romantic inclinations than for his statesmanship. Edward III must have hoped to use his son's marriage as a diplomatic weapon; Joan made this impossible.

An assessment of the Black Prince's statesmanship must largely depend on his record in Gascony. Here he has received a bad press. According to the *Anonimalle Chronicle*, he was so haughty and of such grand demeanour that he would keep local lords waiting four or five days to see him, and made them kneel for quarter of an hour in his presence. His court was extravagant, and the chronicler saw the heavy taxation, known as *fouage*, as the cause of the collapse of his authority in 1369. The Spanish adventure may have added chivalric lustre to an already shining reputation, but it was ill-advised. It placed an excessive financial burden on the Gascons, and the prince's demands on Pedro displayed a disastrous failure to appreciate the importance to England of the Castilian alliance.

It can be argued, however, that the taxation levied by the prince was properly granted by the estates, and that it represented a realistic attempt to establish a secure basis for an administration newly divorced from the control of Westminster. England and France both bore heavy burdens of taxation; why should Gascony be exempt? The prince was making a genuine attempt to modernize an archaic administration, and until 1369 there were few signs of trouble in Gascony. It may be right, as the contemporary life of the prince suggests, that the collapse came when his enemies realized that they could easily take advantage of his declining state of health. Although the prince had antagonized some of the most influential Gascon nobles, the crisis of 1369 owed much to the machinations of Charles v of France, and was not solely due to the misgovernment of the duchy.

The prince's last campaigns lacked the panache and drive of his earlier exploits; his strength was severely sapped by disease probably contracted in Spain, and thought by contemporaries to have been dropsy. The brutal sack of Limoges in 1370, in fulfilment of a vow made after the local bishop had deserted him, was the act of an embittered and exhausted man, who had to be carried on a litter to the scene. Although the prince's conduct was entirely defensible in terms of the contemporary laws of war, it achieved little in military or political terms. In the next year the prince returned to England, where he resigned Aquitaine to his father. He died in 1376, his body swollen and distorted by disease, at the age of forty-six.

Contemporaries regarded the Black Prince in his prime as an exceptionally gifted man, highly intelligent, brave and personally impressive. His extravagance and lack of concern over the financial impositions necessitated by his military enterprises boded ill, however, and he plainly did not have his father's gift for dealing with the magnates. One contemporary, John Erghome, thought that the prince would have a successful reign as king. There would be a severe plague, hampering the wars in France and Scotland, but in the end he would succeed to his rightful inheritance and gain the Scottish throne. This guess is as good as any, but in view of the prince's known career, it is perhaps over optimistic. What was disastrous about the Black Prince's early death was not that he did not become king as a result, but that he left as heir to the throne a mere boy of nine, Richard of Bordeaux.

Edward III could not afford to endow the rest of his family as generously as he had done the Black Prince. Lands granted to younger sons might ultimately be lost to the crown for good, and the best way of providing for them was to arrange good marriages. Lionel of Antwerp, the second son to survive to adult age, was married at the remarkably early age of four to Elizabeth de Burgh, heiress to both the earldom of Ulster and to much of the old Clare inheritance of the earls of Gloucester. The marriage was consummated when he was fourteen. When Edward III made a major settlement of his family affairs in 1362, he made Lionel Duke of Clarence – a wholly new title. He became the king's lieutenant in Ireland, and like so many Englishmen failed miserably to control or even comprehend that violent country. His wife died in 1363, and three years later he left Ireland. In 1368 he married Violante, daughter of Galeazzo Visconti of Milan. He died in somewhat mysterious circumstances shortly after the lavish ceremonies, at the age of twenty-nine.

After the Black Prince, John of Gaunt is the most famous of Edward III's sons. Born in 1340, he was granted the earldom of Richmond two years later. He was not married young like Lionel; presumably his father hoped to use him as a diplomatic pawn. In fact he married wealth and beauty in the form of Blanche, daughter of Henry of Grosmont. Through her he gained his father-in-law's title of Duke of Lancaster in 1362, although it was not until 1377 that he acquired the full palatinate powers that Duke Henry had enjoyed. Gaunt went with the Black Prince to Spain, and when the latter's health failed, took over as his lieutenant in Gascony. The appointment was only of limited duration, however; Gaunt's ambitions lay in Spain, rather than south-west France. Blanche, probably the inspiration for Chaucer's *Book of the Duchess*, had died in 1368:

> I have of sorwe so gret won
> That joye gete I never non,
> Now that I see my lady bryght,
> Which I have loved with al my myght,
> Is fro me ded and ys agoon.[2]

Two years later Gaunt married Constance, daughter of Pedro I of Castile, while she was in exile in Bayonne. The marriage gave Gaunt a powerful claim to the Castilian throne, held by the usurper Henry of Trastamara. He was as a result the only one of Edward III's children to bear a royal title, and his policies in England have to be seen against the background of his Spanish ambitions.

John of Gaunt was unfortunate that his rise to real eminence came in the 1370s, when affairs were going so badly for the English. To one contemporary, the author of the *Chronicon Anglie* (a work often attributed, questionably, to Thomas Walsingham), he was the villain *par excellence* of

Edward III's last years: a changeling who was in reality the son of a Flemish butcher; a coward; a traitor; a wicked uncle determined to oust his nephew Richard from his royal inheritance; an adulterer – there was scarcely an imaginable charge which this writer did not bring against the duke. Only the last cannot be denied. Gaunt's liaison with Katherine Swynford was well known, and in time she was to become his third wife. The rest of the lurid indictment has little warrant in fact, but expresses a view strongly held in the early years of Richard II's reign, particularly in London. Gaunt shared the taciturn haughtiness of the Black Prince, but lacked his charismatic appeal. He was inevitably, if not fairly, blamed for much that went wrong in the decade of failure, the 1370s.

Edward III's younger sons did not play a notable part in his reign. Edmund of Langley, born in 1342, was made Earl of Cambridge in 1362. He had been granted Earl Warenne's northern estates, but was not a wealthy man: marriage at Gaunt's instigation to another of Pedro of Castile's daughters brought him neither a title nor money. Thomas of Woodstock, born in 1355 when his mother was in her forties, was not endowed as might have been expected of a royal prince until the very end of the reign, after parliament criticized the inadequate grants he and his brother Edmund had received.

Edward III did not succeed in using his daughters as pieces in the diplomatic chess-game in the way that Edward I had done. The eldest, Isabella, was suggested as a bride for Pedro of Spain, the son of the Duke of Brabant, the Count of Flanders, and Charles IV of Bohemia, before definite arrangements were made for her to marry the eldest son of the great Gascon noble, the Sire d'Albret. However, the nineteen-year-old princess, who had plainly inherited all her father's headstrong qualities, refused at the last minute to sail for Gascony, and remained unmarried until the age of thirty-three. Surprisingly, Edward does not appear to have been angry at his daughter's behaviour; rather, he spoiled her with ample grants of lands and money, accommodating her extravagant tastes. Her eventual husband was Enguerrand de Coucy, a French noble who had come to England as one of the hostages given as guarantees for the payment of King John's ransom. Isabella's sister Mary made an obviously diplomatic marriage to the Duke of Brittany in 1361, while Margaret married John Hastings, who was to be Earl of Pembroke, in 1359. She died two years later, probably of plague. The rest of Edward III's large family died in childhood, the fate of so many born at that time.

Edward III managed his children with surprising success. In the long term, of course, the fact that he had so large a surviving issue was to cause great dynastic problems, but as far as his own reign was concerned the picture was one of remarkable amity. The king might well have made more diplomatic use of his children's marriages; the fact that he did not prevent the Black Prince's match with Joan of Kent, and that he permitted Isabella to remain so long unmarried, perhaps bears witness to his genuine affection for his children. Margaret's marriage to John Hastings was apparently another love-match, which succeeded after the failure of a plan to wed her to the son of the Duke of Austria. Edward made adequate provision for his children without alienating royal estates, and so weakening the crown. There was every reason to suppose that the links he established through his children's marriages into the English aristocracy would benefit the monarchy in the future. Above all, there was never a breath of revolt by his sons against him, in striking contrast to the bulk of his predecessors on the throne. If Edward III experienced the sadness of losing his eldest son on the verge of his own death, at least he never suffered as Edward I must have done, from the knowledge of the inadequacy and unsuitability of the heir to the throne.

The years from 1360 until the renewal of war in 1369 should have been glorious and constructive. Edward III, however, was a better wartime leader than peacetime statesman. The end of war did not mark an end to financial difficulties: indeed, in a sense it made matters worse, for it was no longer possible to plead military necessity as a justification for taxation. The king himself was rich as a result of the

French and Scottish ransoms; he used the money to finance the military ambitions of the Black Prince and others, and above all to carry through his great building programme at Windsor and elsewhere. Estimates of income and expenditure prepared by the exchequer, however, showed potentially disastrous deficits of over £50,000. Wool subsidies were granted, though no direct taxes could be obtained, and the government had to concede full parliamentary control over the future negotiation of customs duties.

The dominant figure in the administration at this time was William of Wykeham, a Hampshire man possibly of servile origin. His administrative expertise was initially demonstrated in the organization of building works, but he was promoted rapidly after 1360, becoming keeper of the privy seal in 1363. Four years later the king persuaded the Pope to elevate him to the bishopric of Winchester, in spite of the latter's misgivings over Wykeham's lack of learning. In the same year he was appointed chancellor. It was said that the king would do nothing without his advice. The treasurer, John Barnet, co-operated admirably with Wykeham. Despite this harmony, there were scandals which reflected badly on the government. In 1365 a dispute between the chamberlains of the exchequer, with accusations of fraud on both sides, resulted in the dismissal of both men. The chief baron of the exchequer and the chief justice of king's bench also lost their offices. Two years later the steward of the royal household, John atte Lee, was dismissed and imprisoned after being accused of a range of offences in parliament, most notably the unwarranted extension of the jurisdiction of the household.

Edward I would probably have used such a period of peace to investigate the workings of royal government throughout the country, but Edward III did little to attend to the alarming state of affairs that existed in some areas. In the north the murder of John of Coupland, captor of David II, showed that peace abroad did not mean peace at home. In Suffolk the constables of two hundreds kept the sheriff completely in the dark about the widespread corruption and subversion of justice that was taking place. One of them, William Rous, described as 'the greatest maintainer and procurer of all manner of inquisitions in the county',[3] achieved a lawyer's dream by representing each side in the same dispute, profiting from both.

The renewal of war in 1369 met with general approval. The king optimistically promised his subjects that they could retain any lands taken from the French, save for possessions of the crown and the Church. In fact, no gains were achieved, and by the time of the truce of Bruges in 1375 the war had probably cost almost £650,000. In 1369 a large subsidy on wool exports was conceded in parliament, while the clergy agreed to pay a tenth for the same period. This was hardly sufficient, and in 1370 the government asked for loans totalling 100,000 marks; it received about half that sum. In the next year the king asked for subsidies of £100,000. The laity in parliament demanded the removal of churchmen from high office in government, for the same reason that the king himself had objected to them in 1341 – that they could not easily be brought to justice. The king aquiesced. Wykeham was dismissed, along with the treasurer and the keeper of the privy seal. In return, a novel subsidy of £50,000 assessed on parishes was granted, and after pressure the clergy promised a similar sum. In 1341 it had been the king himself who had reacted angrily to the failure of clerical ministers to provide adequate war finance. Now it seems that the lead was taken by the lay nobility acting with the commons; the young Earl of Pembroke was singled out by some chroniclers as particularly responsible. Edward III may well have been sympathetic to the opposition, but Wykeham was not wholly disgraced, and continued to witness royal charters after his removal from office.

In these last years of the reign, particularly after Philippa's death in 1369, Edward III took a steadily less active part in government. Many of the associates of his prime were dead; Henry of Grosmont had died in 1361, Northampton in 1360, Warwick in 1369: the king was surrounded by a new generation of men, with whom he did not have the same rapport. The knights of the royal household who had been so dominant in war and administration in earlier years disappeared from court. Guy Brian had been in receipt of royal fees and wages since the 1330s, and although he addressed parliament on Edward's behalf as late as 1372, he ceased to witness charters in the following year. Roger Beauchamp was another who became conspicuously less active in court circles. The king himself withdrew increasingly from the full royal household, which remained for long periods at Windsor while he stayed at such favourite manors as Sheen and Havering with a small chamber staff.

The man who came to dominate the small court circle was William Latimer, who became chamberlain in 1371. An experienced soldier, he bore a considerable responsibility for the conduct of the war since 1369, particularly in Brittany. A man of considerable wealth, he was not above using his position for self-advancement. John Neville, who became his son-in-law, was steward of the household from 1371, and was also deeply involved in Breton affairs and royal finances. Another powerful influence on the king was his flamboyant mistress, Alice Perrers. She was the subject of much malicious gossip. She was said to be in league with a magician, whose potions and herbs placed the king in a state of unseemly sexual excitement; it is worth noting that she bore him a son. An ambitious woman, she meddled in lawsuits and other matters which should not have concerned her. In 1375 she flaunted her relationship with the king when she rode through the streets of London to attend a tournament dressed as the Lady of the Sun, possibly even wearing some of the queen's jewels which the king had given her two years before. For the poet Langland, she was the prototype of Lady Meed, who used bribery and corruption to attack Conscience.

In the early years of the reign one of the reasons for Edward III's success had been the skilful way in which he built up support by means of patronage; the creation of the new earldoms of 1337 is the most striking example of his technique. The last period of the reign saw no such measures, and the scarcity of entries on the charter rolls shows that the well of patronage was drying up fast. The king was compelled by diplomatic necessity in 1372 to transfer the earldom of Richmond from John of Gaunt to the Duke of Brittany, for which Gaunt received ample compensation. Otherwise, no new earls were created. The inheritance of Juliana de Leyburne, Countess of Huntingdon, might have been used to endow some new recruit to the higher nobility, but her lands were allocated for the implementation of the pious benefactions detailed in the king's will. Latimer, of course, used his position to obtain grants for himself. He was made constable of Dover Castle and warden of the Cinque Ports, and bought from the crown the wardships of the heirs of the Mowbray, Courtenay and Beaumont families. Neville received surprisingly little, and very few grants save for leases on commercial terms were made to men outside the immediate royal circle. Such a situation invited criticism.

Finance presented increasing problems as the war went on. Edward could no longer turn to Italian or other foreign lenders to meet the shortfall from taxation, as he had done in the early phases of the Hundred Years War. The wealthy Earl of Arundel made some large short-term loans, possibly taking interest of one-third on some of them. Funds were also borrowed from London merchants, among whom Richard Lyons was pre-eminent. The payment of interest was formally prohibited at this period, but ingenious ways round this were devised. The favourite was for the loan to take the form of two-thirds cash, and one-third repayment of royal debts. These could be paid off by the lender at a very heavy discount, which would not be revealed to the exchequer; the lender would be repaid their full value. This discounting of debts could give rise to considerable grievances. Richard Lyons paid Joan de Coupland 540 marks for tallies, or wooden receipts, made out to her by the exchequer to a value of 1,140 marks. She lacked the influence to obtain payment in full for them, but Lyons received their full face value. Latimer also was suspected of taking money from the king's chamber, and then lending it to the exchequer, taking the profit himself. It is more likely that Walter Bardi, representative of a new company formed out of the ashes of the one bankrupted in the 1340s, advanced money to Lyons in the hope of obtaining payment of at least part of the debts due to the original firm. In addition, some wealthy Londoners contributed to the loans.

The policies as well as the techniques of government in the mid-1370s were unpopular. The unsuccessful war was followed by an unpopular truce, negotiated by John of Gaunt in 1375. In the same year, the popular policy of resistance to papal demands was abandoned. An agreement was reached with the papacy, by which the Pope made various concessions with regard to the practice of provision to English benefices. In return, he was allowed to collect an unpopular subsidy from the clergy. Gregory XI also co-operated with the ruling clique in England in various nominations to vacant bishoprics.

In parliament in 1376 the government came under fierce attack. In what became known as the Good Parliament the commons for the first time took the lead in precipitating a political crisis. Fortunately the *Anonimalle Chronicle* preserves an eye-witness account of what took place during the deliberations in the chapter house at Westminster. A southern knight spoke first in the discussion on the inevitable demand for fresh subsidies. He argued that the king should finance the war from his own resources, without impoverishing his people, and made veiled hints of corruption. Later speakers began to name names. The discussions were summed up in a masterly manner by Peter de la Mare, who was selected as the commons' spokesman. He asked for a committee of magnates to assist in the deliberations, and eventually specific charges were brought forward against Latimer, Lyons, Alice Perrers, John Neville and some of their associates.

According to the extremely biased account of the *Chronicon Anglie*, Gaunt, who was presiding in parliament since both his father and elder brother were too ill, was astonished at the temerity of the commons: 'Do they think they are kings or princes of the land? ... I shall appear before them in such splendour tomorrow, and so impress them with my power, and so terrify them with such severity that neither they nor any like them will dare to damage my majesty.'[4] In reply, one of his retainers pointed out that the knights of the shire had considerable support, both from the Londoners and, implausibly, from the Black Prince. Their demands were not to be resisted.

The first of the accused was Latimer. Like the rest of the defendants he was impeached, with the commons acting as prosecutors and the lords hearing the case. The charges relating to the war were the most difficult to uphold. Latimer was accused of taking improper profits in Brittany, and of responsibility for the fall of the fortresses of St Sauveur and Bécherel: the latter had been commanded by one of his subordinates, but although the constable of St Sauveur was one of his retainers, Latimer was not directly involved in its fall. The chief of the financial charges related to a loan of 20,000 marks arranged by Latimer and Lyons, on which the commons claimed that interest of 10,000 marks had been paid. They pointed out that two London merchants had been prepared to advance 15,000 marks without interest. This offer, however, had been conditional upon a strict adherence to the Calais wool staple, and Latimer and Lyons had been involved in the profitable business of selling licences to export to other ports. The way in which they had bought up royal debts at a heavy discount was also raised. Further charges related to extortions by Adam de Bury, a former mayor of Calais, and to the corrupt practices of William Ellis, a customs farmer at Yarmouth. John Pecché had, it was said, abused his monopoly of the sale of sweet wines in London, causing an intolerable rise in price, 'to the great damage and oppression of the people'.[5]

It has to be admitted that the range and gravity of the charges were perhaps less than might have been expected from the opening speeches in the commons' debates: nevertheless, they shook the government to its foundations. Gaunt was placed in a most unenviable position, but for all the calumnies of the *Chronicon Anglie*, seems to have acquitted himself well. He did not try to prevent Richard Scrope, treasurer from 1371 to 1375, and one of his retainers, from providing some of the evidence against John Neville. Wisely, Gaunt waited until after the parliament was over to re-establish the authority of the government.

The opposition in the Good Parliament did not aim to make fundamental constitutional changes. They asked for the appointment of nine additional councillors; an important though hardly revolutionary step. Significantly, these included the old royalists Guy Brian and Roger Beauchamp. The many petitions presented by the commons covered familiar ground, starting with a request for the terms of Magna Carta to be adhered to, and going on to such questions as salmon fishing in the Thames. Perhaps the most important achievements of the parliament lay in the procedural sphere. Peter de la Mare was probably the first real Speaker of the commons; although William Trussel acted as their spokesman in 1343, he was probably not one of their number.

In the process of impeachment, the commons acquired a new and significant weapon. It appears to have developed almost by accident in the course of the session. Normal procedure called for individual accusers, but when challenged by Latimer, de la Mare insisted that he was acting for the commons as a whole, and that they were prosecuting on behalf of the king. There has been much debate over the origins of impeachment. This was in fact a well-recognized procedure, though it had never been used in parliament before. In 1368 the Abbot of Abingdon had been impeached, with the local community prosecuting on behalf of the crown. A very early example dates from 1318, when the king sent a writ to the council asking them to delay hearing a case in which his butler Stephen Abingdon was impeached 'at our suit and by the merchant vintners of England and Guyenne'.[6] All the later principles of impeachment were there, with a communal accusation on behalf of the crown against a royal minister: what was new and important in 1376 was the fact that the impeachments took place in parliament. De la Mare had not, however, aimed at impeachment. He had hoped for a more summary form of hearing, but once the accused were permitted to answer, the cases fitted naturally into the established legal framework of impeachment.

Although the events of the Good Parliament are remarkably well documented, some problems remain. The degree to which the commons were acting on their own initiative has been questioned. It is most unlikely that the Black Prince was behind their actions, even though it was popularly believed that he supported them, and that he had refused a bribe from Latimer; he died in the middle of the session, and was in no state to take political initiatives. De la Mare was the steward of the Earl of March, who had his own grievances over the conduct of the war, and over Irish affairs. The Speaker probably had the support of his lord, but it does not seem likely that responsibility for the attack on the court clique lay with March. De la Mare, after all, did not begin the debate in the chapter house; he merely concluded it. The commons may have had the backing of the king's two youngest sons, aggrieved that they had not received the grants of lands and offices that their birth entitled them to, but they were not likely to have led the opposition to their father's ministers. William of Wykeham showed his sympathy for the commons in the course of the hearing against Latimer, and he was treated as a scapegoat after the parliament was over. It is hard, however, to accept an interpretation of the Good Parliament which sees it as Wykeham's retaliation for his dismissal in 1371. The commons evidently had the support of many influential Londoners; the strongly financial character of many of the charges reveals this. There is, however, no reason to doubt the view of the chroniclers, that the initiative for the attack on Latimer, Lyons, Neville, Alice Perrers and the others came primarily from the knights of the shire.

Dramatic as the events of the Good Parliament were, and significant as the session was in terms of future precedent, the immediate achievements of Peter de la Mare and his colleagues were not great. It is not clear how far John of Gaunt had been responsible for the conduct of events before 1376: his primary concerns had been with foreign policy, and his long absences from court suggest that domestic matters had not greatly concerned him. After the Good Parliament, however, he strove to establish himself in a position of clear authority. He followed up the demands for a full-blooded anti-papal policy, using his ally John Wyclif to give it intellectual backbone. For the rest, the

work of the parliament was soon undone. The new councillors did not last long, and within six months the disgraced
favourites were back at court. Peter de la Mare was imprisoned, and early in 1377 Wykeham was brought to trial. A
largely compliant parliament, said to have been rigged by
Gaunt, demanded the reversal of the judgements against
those impeached in the Good Parliament. A new financial
expedient was introduced in the form of a poll tax, levied at
the rate of 4d from every lay person over fourteen years old.
This was at the suggestion of the knights of the shire, and
marked a further shift of the burden of taxation down the
social scale. A similar, but heavier, tax was to precipitate the
Peasants' Revolt in 1381. The fact that such a direct tax
could be negotiated in time of truce was a measure of the
government's strength. Gaunt's own power is indicated by
the fact that he was able to secure payment of about £6,000
arrears of wages due to him.

It was towards London that Gaunt overplayed his hand.
Late in 1376 Henry Percy became marshal in place of the
Earl of March, and he began to threaten the independent
jurisdiction of the City. The term of office of the aldermen
was restricted, and according to the *Chronicon Anglie* Gaunt
proposed the replacement of the mayor by a captain nominated by the crown. The citizens reacted angrily. Gaunt's
protégé Wyclif was summoned by the Bishop of London to
answer for his heretical teachings. Gaunt ordered Percy to
arrest anyone who opposed Wyclif, and threatened to drag
the bishop from his chair by his hair. The London mob
assembled, and an ugly scene ensued. Gaunt's palace of
the Savoy was attacked, and his coat of arms was hung
upside down in full public view; the sign of a traitor. It was
at this time that the story gained currency that Queen
Philippa's own baby had been smothered at birth, and that
for fear of the king's anger a butcher's son had been substi-
tuted for it. Crisis was averted, however, by the timely
mediation of the Princess Joan, widow of the Black Prince.
Wykeham received his pardon on 18 June; it is said that he
bribed Alice Perrers to obtain it. A precarious political
balance had been achieved in anticipation of the new reign
and the imminent renewal of war.

Edward III had been little more than a passive onlooker of these events. He had never shown his ministers the loyalty that Edward I had accorded to Burnell and Langton, and he was clearly content to let the commons do their worst in 1376. He had learnt from the crisis of 1340–1 that concessions could easily be revoked later. It was said, however, that it was his anger at violent attacks by the villeins and tenants of the Earl of Warwick on the property of Evesham Abbey that led him to dismiss the councillors imposed on him in the Good Parliament and turn to John of Gaunt; the same author said that in the final years of his life the king had no more discernment than a boy of eight. In the autumn it was Edward himself who handed Latimer's petition for pardon to the chancellor, and ordered him to implement it.

The king was taken seriously ill in September, but with the aid of a diet of broth and bread dipped in goat's milk he made a recovery. Early in 1377 he left Havering, travelling by boat to Sheen. In April he was at Windsor for his last celebration of St George's day; he knighted both the future Richard II and his supplanter, Henry Bolingbroke, Gaunt's son. On 21 June the old king died at Sheen, probably of the stroke whose effects can be seen in the effigy made from his death mask. In the highly coloured account of the *Chronicon Anglie*, Alice Perrers stripped the rings from the dying man's fingers, and left him deserted by all save one priest who gave him a crucifix to hold. Edward gave signs of repentance, and expired.

The body was taken from Sheen in solemn procession to Westminster Abbey for burial. The journey took three days, and the coffin was accompanied by poor men clad in black, bearing torches. In all, one thousand seven hundred torches were used, along with three hundred large ones placed round the tomb, and fifteen large candles. Edward was buried with proper pomp and dignity; the expenses of his household, shortly to be disbanded, rose to £566 for the day of the funeral. His tomb was constructed ten years later; the effigy is not that of a warrior, like that on the tomb of the Black Prince, but of a dignified elderly figure, with patriarchal flowing locks and beard. Delicately carved small effigies of his children are set round the monument.

England was transformed in many ways during the century of the three Edwards, and this book has attempted to set out some of the most important. The nature of politics had changed with the development of parliament; the events of the Good Parliament would have been inconceivable in Edward I's day. In administrative terms, the growth in the importance of the royal household, striking in Edward I's day, had been halted, with the exchequer gaining a new predominance in financial matters under Edward III. What amounted to a military revolution took place in the course of the three reigns, as the large armies of Edward I's day were transformed into the fighting machine that proved so effective against the French in the Hundred Years War. There were many social changes. The stratification of society was more apparent by the late fourteenth century, with the higher nobility enjoying an increased sense of exclusiveness. The fortunes of the knightly class fluctuated during the period, but by the close of Edward III's reign it was becoming clear that the attempts of the monarchy to maintain and even increase the number of knights in the country were doomed to failure. At the bottom of the social order the economic changes of the fourteenth century, especially those resulting from the decline in the population, made a great difference to the position of the poorest classes. They benefited from the rise in wage rates, as landlords abandoned their earlier practice of direct management of their estates in favour of a system of leases.

It is no longer fashionable to place kings in the centre of the historical canvas, even though in recent years a biographical approach has been replacing the concentration on institutional development which dominated historical writing earlier in this century. Yet it is evident that the personalities of the three Edwards had a powerful influence on the changes which took place in the England they governed. The stark contrast between the highly successful reigns of Edward I and Edward III and the depths of degradation to which the monarchy fell under Edward II cannot be explained by impersonal historical forces.

It is hard to recapture personalities through the conventional accounts of the chroniclers and the frequently arid entries on the rolls. Edward I was formidable, ambitious and autocratic, yet he was far from lacking in human qualities. His devotion to his first queen, Eleanor of Castile, was striking, while on the other side of the coin there is ample evidence of his violent temper – his brief utterances, well larded with oaths, were frequently memorable. He was capable of deviousness, and the great legislator could take a surprisingly cavalier attitude towards the law. There is no doubt that he was, as contemporaries appreciated, a great king. His son Edward II, on the other hand, was one of the most incompetent men to sit on the throne of England. The fact that he did not lack ambition for the monarchy made him all the more disastrous as a monarch. To have lost the throne within five years of the great royalist triumph of Boroughbridge demonstrated a degree of incapacity far exceeding that of a Louis XVI or a Czar Nicholas II. His tastes and habits were most unsuitable for one of his station, and the weakness he displayed towards his favourites was fatal. In contrast, Edward III was almost all that could be wished of a king. He was brave and chivalrous, as his dramatic ride to rescue the Countess of Atholl at Lochindorb indicated. He was capable of impressive extravagance, but could discard the dignity of his position in favour of a cameraderie which endeared him to his followers. Edward I had exploited the Arthurian cult, but it was Edward III who made the most of the chivalric culture of the day, with the Order of the Garter and the elaborate tournaments and court masques he so enjoyed. There was not the iron in his character that there had been in Edward I's, and the last years of his life were a sad anti-climax, as the great king lapsed into indolence and self-indulgence.

Many influences went to shape the England of the late thirteenth and fourteenth centuries; some, like the dreadful weather of 1315–16, or the arrival of bubonic plague in 1348, were beyond human control. One dominant theme was provided by war. The careers of the three monarchs emphasize that one key to political success was triumph in war. Edward III admired his grandfather not for his legislative achievements, but because 'there was no one more illustrious or braver in feats of arms, or wise in the management of armies'.[7] These two kings were cast in very different moulds, for all their outward resemblances. Edward I fought his wars out of a real sense that his cause was just, and cannot be accused, like Edward III, of being a mere military adventurer prepared to abandon his claims in return for substantial territorial or financial gain. The flavour of victory in the two reigns was very different. Edward I decorated London with the heads of his defeated foes, and distributed portions of their bodies to all quarters of his kingdom. John Balliol was stripped of his regal dignity without respect. In contrast, David II enjoyed a comfortable captivity under Edward III, and even acquired an English mistress. When the Black Prince brought the captive French king John to London, maidens showered the procession with gold and silver leaves and John led a distinctly luxurious life in England. For the English, Edward III's successes were far sweeter than Edward I's conquests in Wales and campaigns in Scotland, for they brought substantial profits in the form of booty and plunder.

Edward II's reign saw the other face of war. Military ineptitude went hand-in-hand with political failure at home. With the wars going badly, Edward could not reward his followers out of conquests as his father had been able to do. Defeat was seen as an expression of divine disapprobation, and the natural ambition of the magnates to enrich themselves was turned in upon themselves, resulting in local feuds and ultimately civil war, rather than in expansionist campaigns in Wales, Scotland or France. Ironically, however, these were perhaps the most formative years for English armies. It was then that the experiments took place which led to the abandonment of the huge, relatively disorganized armies of Edward I's time, and the evolution of new tactics in which men-at-arms fought on foot with archers in support. Once the archers were mounted, in the early years of Edward III's reign, armies became highly mobile, and the scene was set for the *chevauchées* of the Hundred Years War, and the great English victories.

War affected the country in many ways. It made and broke individual fortunes, and influenced every aspect of economic life. It was very costly, and much recent research has emphasized the importance of finance in this period. The significance of the efforts made to raise the funds needed to fight was very great. The whole structure of the wool export trade, for example, was in large part determined by royal financial policy. It is striking, however, that both of the successful kings were at one time effectively bankrupt. In contrast, Edward II amassed a substantial treasure, from which he gained little advantage. Political crisis in 1297 and in 1340–1 had a financial background, but the far more serious events of 1321–2 and 1326–7 were not the result of the impoverishment of the crown.

The political techniques of the three kings were very different. Edward I, mindful of the precedents of Henry III's reign, was most reluctant to make any concessions; those of 1297 were only agreed in his absence from the realm. His reluctance to create new earls shows that he maintained a tight control over royal patronage; he relied on a few loyal officials, notably Robert Burnell and Walter Langton, and on the support of a small number of close associates among the aristocracy, among whom the Earl of Lincoln was notable, along with such men as the Cliffords, John Botetourt or Otto de Grandson. He was also capable of turning against men who had served him with devotion, like Anthony Bek, Bishop of Durham, for little apparent cause.

Edward II was as unwilling as his father to concede the demands of his opponents, but he was incapable of inspiring respect from his subjects. His unseemly devotion to his favourites, demonstrated by his lavish grants to them, as well as in other ways, was unacceptable. He was fortunate for a time in that his leading opponent, his cousin Thomas of Lancaster, was almost as unsuited as he was to play a leading political role, but the manner of his government in the last years of his reign led inexorably to his downfall. The base manipulation of the processes of the law and the cynical management of patronage in the interests of the Despensers amounted to tyranny. The institution of the monarchy, however, was strong enough to survive the events of 1327 without diminution of its theoretical powers. The constitutional programme set out in the Ordinances of 1311 had failed, but the personal attack on the king succeeded with remarkable ease.

Edward III spread his generosity more widely than his predecessors on the throne. He built up a loyal following among the lay aristocracy, and it is striking that through all the political troubles of the reign, there was no serious personal opposition to him from the baronage. In part Edward III succeeded by making concessions that Edward I would have regarded as quite unacceptable. He gave the highest possible jurisdictional authority to Henry of Grosmont with the palatinate of Lancaster; his grandfather had wanted to confine the higher forms of franchises to members of the royal family. The creation of new duchies and earldoms assisted in the formation of a new atmosphere of co-operation between king and nobility. Edward was not perfect; he was capable of irresponsibility, and not only in the days of his unfortunate senility. His attack on his ministers in 1340 was ill-judged, and the way in which he permitted disgraced ministers to recover a degree of royal favour did him little credit. Yet his reign saw the establishment of a political stability almost unparalleled in the Middle Ages in England, which was made the more remarkable by the fact that it coincided with the social and economic upheavals caused by the loss of at least a third of the population in the Black Death.

The policies of the three kings and the pressures of war, helped to mould the development of the English parliament. Edward I did much to create parliament. It served the king's judicial and financial ends, while at the same time it provided his subjects with a convenient means of obtaining redress of their individual grievances. Under Edward II the aristocracy gained increasing influence, as the reiterated demand for consent by the baronage in parliament over a whole range of matters in the Ordinances of 1311 shows. The parliamentary peerage was evolving rapidly, with the lists used to summon magnates to fight also being used to request their presence to provide counsel and consent. Continual demands for taxation, which could only be granted with the consent of the representatives, led to the increasingly regular attendance of what became the House of Commons. By Edward III's reign the financial importance of the commons gave them a new degree of political authority. The majority of statutes were a royal response to their petitions, rather than a product of direct royal initiative. The Good Parliament, with its attack on the unpopular ministers launched by the commons, was a suitable climax to fifty years of the development of the latter's authority. It was above all the king's need to finance his wars that had led the English parliament to develop in this direction, rather than evolving into a purely judicial tribunal.

For all his fame on the continent, Edward III was a far more national king than Edward I had been. The great castles of North Wales had been built at Edward I's command under Savoyard direction, with such details as the latrine shutes and the windows betraying the influence of Master James of St George and his men. A major place in Edward I's financial system was occupied by the bankers of Lucca and Florence and the famous Bolognese lawyer Francesco Accursi was in his employ. At the end of his reign Scotland was entrusted not to an English nobleman, but to John of Brittany: there was a strongly international flavour to Edward's achievements.

Despite the favour granted to his Gascon favourite Piers Gaveston, and the importance of his French queen Isabella, Edward II's rule was not strongly characterized by foreign influence. Indeed, some contemporaries blamed the English national character for what went wrong in the course of the reign: 'The English race excel all other nations in three qualities, in pride, in craft, and in perjury.'[8] Although Edward III attracted many foreign adventurers to his service, such as Walter Mauny and Eustace d'Aubrichecourt, his achievements were substantially those of the English nation. It was an English merchant, William de la Pole, who came to his assistance when the Italians began to doubt the king's creditworthiness, and it was an English mason who was responsible for the remarkable fortress of Queenborough. The French war, like that against the Scots earlier, helped to promote a fierce national pride and the English language became socially acceptable among the aristocracy and at court; with Chaucer, it came to rival French as a literary tongue, and in 1362 it became the official language of the law.

The age of the three Edwards was one of many varied achievements, of triumphs and disasters. Against Falkirk, Crécy and Poitiers there must be set the black two days of Bannockburn. The ineffectiveness of the baronial opposition to Edward I, and the stability of the central years of Edward III's reign, stand strongly contrasted to the nadir of political life reached under Edward II. It is almost a convention among historians to claim that theirs is an age of transition, but along with the many changes which took place in this period, the strength and resilience of English society also stand out. England did not suffer similar problems to those created by popular rebellion in Flanders in the 1320s, or the social anarchy that the *Jacquerie* brought to France: it was only in 1381 that the Peasants' Revolt took place. Although the response to the problems of government, war and natural disaster was far from consistent throughout the three reigns, the difficulties of the period, like the successes, ultimately served to unite rather than divide the nation.

Appendices

I. THE HOUSE OF PLANTAGANET AND ITS BRANCHES

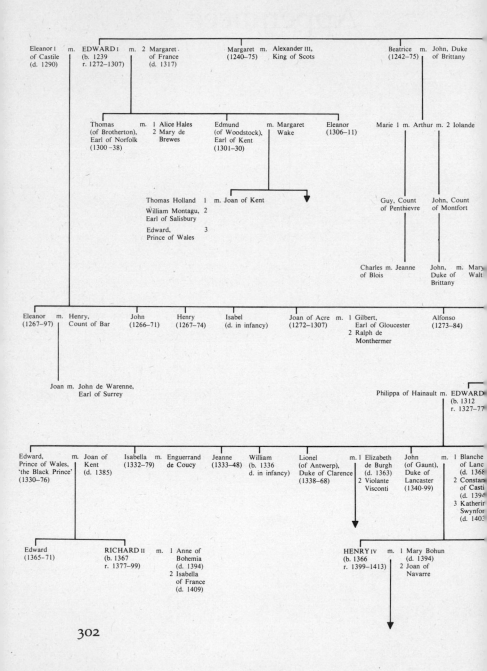

Eleanor I of Castile (d. 1290) m. EDWARD I (b. 1239 r. 1272–1307) m. 2 Margaret of France (d. 1317) — Margaret (1240–75) m. Alexander III, King of Scots — Beatrice (1242–75) m. John, Duke of Brittany

Thomas (of Brotherton), Earl of Norfolk (1300–38) m. 1 Alice Hales 2 Mary de Brewes — Edmund (of Woodstock), Earl of Kent (1301–30) m. Margaret Wake — Eleanor (1306–11) — Marie 1 m. Arthur m. 2 Iolande

Thomas Holland 1 m. Joan of Kent
William Montagu, 2 Earl of Salisbury
Edward, 3 Prince of Wales

Guy, Count of Penthievre — John, Count of Montfort

Charles m. Jeanne of Blois — John, Duke of Brittany m. Mary Walt

Eleanor (1267–97) m. Henry, Count of Bar — John (1266–71) — Henry (1267–74) — Isabel (d. in infancy) — Joan of Acre (1272–1307) m. 1 Gilbert, Earl of Gloucester 2 Ralph de Monthermer — Alfonso (1273–84)

Joan m. John de Warenne, Earl of Surrey

Philippa of Hainault m. EDWARD (b. 1312 r. 1327–77)

Edward, Prince of Wales, 'the Black Prince' (1330–76) m. Joan of Kent (d. 1385) — Isabella (1332–79) m. Enguerrand de Coucy — Jeanne (1333–48) — William (b. 1336 d. in infancy) — Lionel (of Antwerp), Duke of Clarence (1338–68) m. 1 Elizabeth de Burgh (d. 1363) 2 Violante Visconti — John (of Gaunt), Duke of Lancaster (1340-99) m. 1 Blanche of Lanc (d. 1368 2 Constan of Casti (d. 1394 3 Katherin Swynfor (d. 1403

Edward (1365–71) — RICHARD II (b. 1367 r. 1377–99) m. 1 Anne of Bohemia (d. 1394) 2 Isabella of France (d. 1409)

HENRY IV (b. 1366 r. 1399–1413) m. 1 Mary Bohun (d. 1394) 2 Joan of Navarre

APPENDIX I

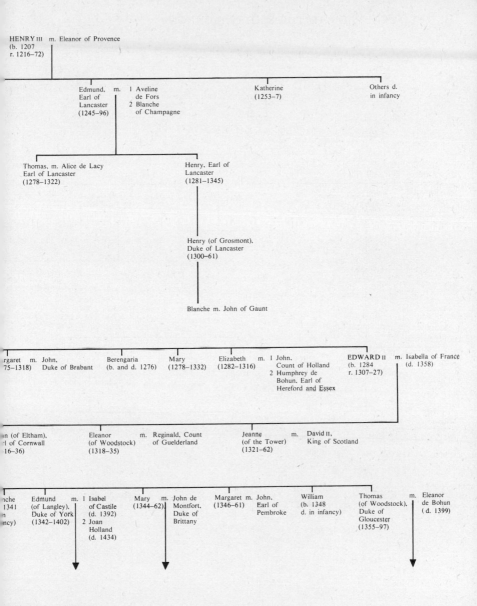

HENRY III   m. Eleanor of Provence
(b. 1207
r. 1216–72)

Edmund,   m.   1 Aveline
Earl of   de Fors
Lancaster   2 Blanche
(1245–96)   of Champagne

Katherine
(1253–7)

Others d.
in infancy

Thomas, m. Alice de Lacy
Earl of Lancaster
(1278–1322)

Henry, Earl of
Lancaster
(1281–1345)

Henry (of Grosmont),
Duke of Lancaster
(1300–61)

Blanche m. John of Gaunt

rgaret   m.   John,
75–1318)   Duke of Brabant

Berengaria
(b. and d. 1276)

Mary
(1278–1332)

Elizabeth   m.   1 John,
(1282–1316)   Count of Holland
                            2 Humphrey de
                               Bohun, Earl of
                               Hereford and Essex

EDWARD II   m. Isabella of France
(b. 1284   (d. 1358)
r. 1307–27)

n (of Eltham),
l of Cornwall
16–36)

Eleanor   m.   Reginald, Count
(of Woodstock)   of Guelderland
(1318–35)

Jeanne   m.   David II,
(of the Tower)   King of Scotland
(1321–62)

nche
1341
n
ncy)

Edmund   m.   1 Isabel
(of Langley),   of Castile
Duke of York   (d. 1392)
(1342–1402)   2 Joan
                          Holland
                          (d. 1434)

Mary   m.   John de
(1344–62)   Montfort,
                   Duke of
                   Brittany

Margaret m.   John,
(1346–61)   Earl of
                      Pembroke

William
(b. 1348
d. in infancy)

Thomas   m.   Eleanor
(of Woodstock),   de Bohun
Duke of   (d. 1399)
Gloucester
(1355–97)

II. THE SUCCESSION TO THE SCOTTISH THRONE

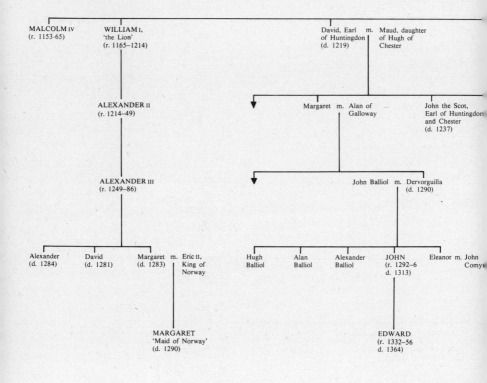

MALCOLM IV
(r. 1153-65)

WILLIAM I,
'the Lion'
(r. 1165–1214)

David, Earl   m.   Maud, daughter
of Huntingdon   of Hugh of
(d. 1219)   Chester

ALEXANDER II
(r. 1214–49)

Margaret   m.   Alan of
Galloway

John the Scot,
Earl of Huntingdon
and Chester
(d. 1237)

ALEXANDER III
(r. 1249–86)

John Balliol   m.   Dervorguilla
(d. 1290)

Alexander
(d. 1284)

David
(d. 1281)

Margaret   m.   Eric II,
(d. 1283)   King of
Norway

Hugh
Balliol

Alan
Balliol

Alexander
Balliol

JOHN
(r. 1292–6
d. 1313)

Eleanor m. John
Comyn

MARGARET
'Maid of Norway'
(d. 1290)

EDWARD
(r. 1332–56
d. 1364)

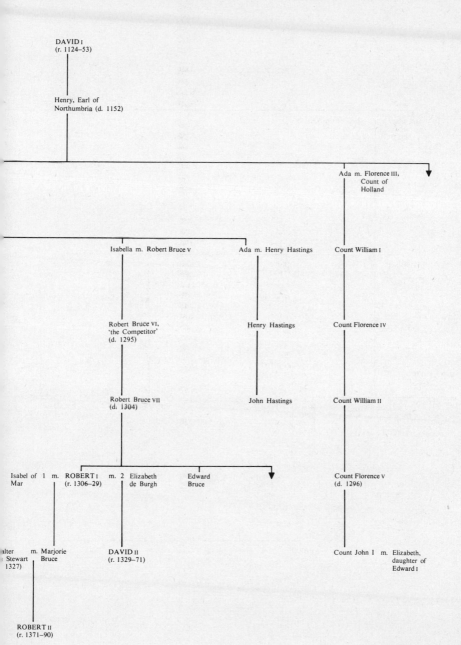

DAVID I
(r. 1124–53)

Henry, Earl of
Northumbria (d. 1152)

Ada m. Florence III,
Count of
Holland

Isabella m. Robert Bruce V   Ada m. Henry Hastings   Count William I

Robert Bruce VI,
'the Competitor'
(d. 1295)

Henry Hastings   Count Florence IV

Robert Bruce VII
(d. 1304)

John Hastings   Count William II

Isabel of 1 m. ROBERT I m. 2 Elizabeth   Edward   Count Florence V
Mar   (r. 1306–29)   de Burgh   Bruce   (d. 1296)

alter   m. Marjorie   DAVID II   Count John I m. Elizabeth,
Stewart   Bruce   (r. 1329–71)   daughter of
1327)   Edward I

ROBERT II
(r. 1371–90)

III. THE HOUSE OF VALOIS

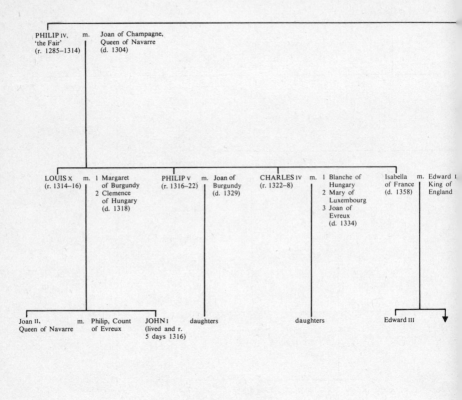

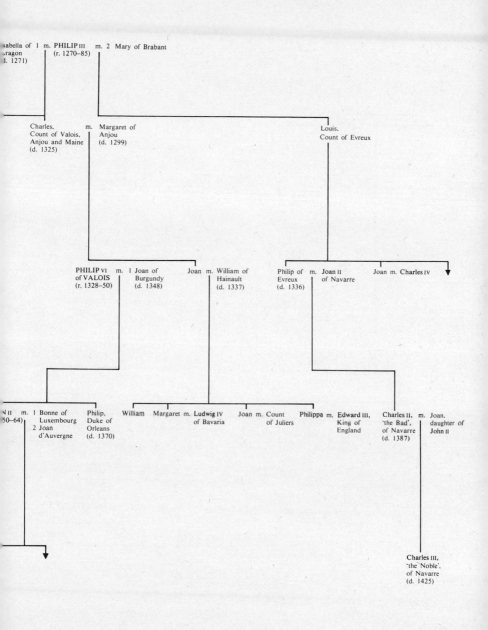

References to Quotations

Abbreviations

EHR   English Historical Review
TRHS Transactions of the Royal Historical Society
BIHR Bulletin of the Institute of Historical Research
RS   Rolls Series
EcHR Economic History Review

All manuscripts cited, unless otherwise indicated, are in the Public Record Office.

Chapter One

1 *The Political Songs of England* ed. T. Wright (London, Camden Society, 1839), p. 93
2 SC 1/22, 26
3 *Liber de Antiquis Legibus seu chronica maiorum et vicecomitum Londoniarum* ed. T. Stapleton (Camden Society, 1846), p. 173
4 R. R. Davies, 'Colonial Wales', *Past and Present* 65 (1974), p. 18
5 M. C. Prestwich, 'A New Account of the Welsh Campaign of 1294–5', *Welsh History Review* vi (1972), p. 94
6 *The History of the King's Works* ed. R. A. Brown, H. M. Colvin, A. J. Taylor (London, 1963), vol i, p. 399
7 *Statutes of the Realm* (London, 1810), vol i, p. 26
8 T. F. T. Plucknett *Legislation of Edward I* (Oxford, 1949), p. 73
9 *Year Books, 3 Edward II, 1309–10* ed. F. W. Maitland (Selden Society, xx, 1905), pp. 196–7

10 *Historical Manuscripts Commission; Report on Manuscripts in Various Collections* (London, 1901), vol i, p. 256
11 *Willelmi Rishanger, Chronica et Annales* ed. H. T. Riley (London, RS, 1865), p. 121
12 SC 1/16, 157
13 *The Chronicle of Walter of Guisborough* ed. H. Rothwell (Camden Society, 1957), p. 290
14 *Flores Historiarum* vol iii, ed. H. R. Luard (RS, 1890), p. 102
15 *Political Songs of England*, p. 232
16 P. Chaplais, 'Some Private Letters of Edward I' *EHR* lxxvii (1962), p. 85
17 *The History of the King's Works* vol i, p. 252
18 E 101/371/21, 14
19 E 101/368/18

Chapter Two

1 *Willelmi Rishanger, Chronica et Annales*, p. 373
2 *Scalacronica by Sir Thomas Grey of Heton Knight* ed. J. Stevenson (Edinburgh, Maitland Club, 1836), p. 123
3 E. L. G. Stones and G. G. Simpson *Edward I and the Throne of Scotland, 1290–96* (Oxford, 1979), vol ii, p. 292
4 *Documents illustrative of the History of Scotland* ed. J. Stevenson (Edinburgh, 1870) vol ii, p. 198
5 *Willelmi Rishanger, Chronica et Annales*, p. 187
6 *The Chronicle of Pierre de Langtoft* ed. T. Wright (RS, 1868) vol ii, p. 326
7 E 159/75, m. 8
8 *Political Songs of England*, p. 214
9 *Anglo-Scottish Relations, 1174–1328: Some Selected Documents* ed. E. L. G. Stones (London, 1965), p. 125
10 *The Chronicle of Lanercost* trans. H. E. Maxwell (Glasgow, 1913), p. 240
11 *Rotuli Parliamentorum* (London, 1783–1832), vol ii, p. 63
12 *The Roll of Carlaverock* ed. T. Wright (London, 1864), p. 1
13 *Chronicon Galfridi le Baker* ed. E. M. Thompson (Oxford, 1889), p. 51
14 *Political Songs of England*, p. 337
15 SC 1/28, 107
16 *Calendar of Documents Relating to Scotland* ed. J. Bain (Edinburgh, 1881–8), vol iii, no. 625
17 *Vita Edwardi Secundi* ed. N. Denholm-Young (London, 1957), p. 103

18 *Political Songs of England*, p. 179
19 *The Chronicle of Pierre de Langtoft* vol ii, pp. 248–9
20 A. A. M. Duncan *The Nation of Scots and the Declaration of Arbroath* (Historical Association, 1970), p. 36

Chapter Three

1 *Chronicles of the Reigns of Edward I and Edward II* ed. W. Stubbs (RS, 1882), vol i, p. 262
2 British Library, Cottonian MS. Nero C. VIII, f. 57
3 *The Brut* ed. F. W. D. Brie (Early English Text Society, 1906, 1908), vol i, p. 208
4 J. R. S. Phillips *Aymer de Valence, Earl of Pembroke* (Oxford, 1972), p. 316
5 *Select Documents of English Constitutional History, 1307–1485* ed. S. B. Chrimes and A. L. Brown (London, 1961), pp. 4–5
6 *The Brut* vol i, p. 207
7 *Vita Edwardi Secundi*, p. 30
8 Ibid., p. 33
9 Ibid., p. 139
10 R. R. Davies *Lordship and Society in the March of Wales* (Oxford, 1978), p. 279
11 *Vita Edwardi Secundi*, pp. 108–9
12 *The Brut* vol ii, p. 223
13 Ibid., vol ii, p. 232
14 Ibid., vol i, p. 220
15 *Political Songs of England*, p. 335
16 *Vita Edwardi Secundi*, p. 74
17 Ibid., p. 104
18 Ibid., p. 89
19 *Chronicles of the Reigns of Edward I and II* ed. W. Stubbs (RS, 1882), vol i, p. 199
20 *Calendar of Close Rolls, 1318–23*, p. 260
21 *Calendar of Fine Rolls, 1319–27*, p. 78
22 *Political Songs of England*, p. 336
23 *Chronicon Galfridi le Baker*, p. 46

Chapter Four

1 J. G. Edwards '"Justice" in Early English Parliaments', in *Historical Studies of the English Parliament* ed. E. B. Fryde and E. Miller (Cambridge, 1970), vol i, p. 284

2 *Rotuli Parliamentorum* vol i, p. 188
3 *Select Charters* ed. W. Stubbs (9th ed. Oxford, 1921), p. 473
4 Ibid., p. 482
5 Ibid., p. 477
6 Ibid., p. 480
7 P. Spufford *Origins of the English Parliament* (London, 1967), p. 128
8 *Rotuli Parliamentorum* vol ii, p. 104
9 Ibid., p. 148
10 *Documents Illustrating the Crisis of 1297–8 in England* ed. M. C. Prestwich (Camden Society, 1980), p. 122
11 *Fleta* ed. H. G. Richardson and G. O. Sayles (Selden Society, 1955), vol ii, p. 109
12 *Rotuli Parliamentorum* vol i, p. 77
13 Ibid., vol i, p. 282
14 *Chronicles of the Reigns of Edward I and II* vol i, p. 282
15 *Select Cases in the Court of King's Bench* ed. G. O. Sayles (Selden Society, 1955), vol iv, p. 64
16 *The Mirror of Justices* ed. W. J. Whittaker and F. W. Maitland (Selden Society, 1893), p. 155
17 *Select Charters* ed. Stubbs, p. 442
18 *Statutes of the Realm* vol i, p. 189
19 *Rotuli Parliamentorum* vol i, p. 295
20 Ibid., vol i, p. 308
21 Ibid., vol i, p. 281
22 *Mum and the Sothsegger* quoted in H. M. Cam *Liberties and Communities in Medieval England* (Cambridge, 1944), p. 234
23 *Vita Edwardi Secundi*, p. 32
24 *The Works of Geoffrey Chaucer* ed. F. W. Robinson (Oxford, 1957) (*The Canterbury Tales*) The Prologue, ll. 355–360
   Anlaas: dagger. gipser: purse. contour: auditor. vavasour: vassal
25 *Parliamentary Writs* ed. F. Palgrave (London, 1827–34) vol ii, p. 272
26 *Liberties and Communities in Medieval England*, p. 234
27 M. W. Beresford *New Towns of the Middle Ages* (London, 1967), p. 3

Chapter Five

1 J. E. Powell and K. Wallis *The House of Lords in the Middle Ages* (London, 1968), p. 356
2 *The Roll of Carlaverock*, p. 11

3 *Political Songs of England*, p. 153
4 *Political Songs of England*, p. 237
5 *The House of Lords in the Middle Ages*, p. 326
6 *The Chronicle of Walter of Guisborough*, p. 216
7 V. H. Galbraith 'A New Life of Richard II', *History* xxvi
   (1941–2), p. 227
8 SC 1/47, 192
9 *The Brut* vol i, p. 249.
10 *Testamenta Vetusta* ed. N. H. Nicolas (London, 1826) vol i, p.
   74
11 Ibid., vol i, p. 80
12 Ibid., vol i, p. 67
13 *Chronique de Jean le Bel* ed. J. Viard and E. Déprez (Paris,
   1904) vol i, p. 43
14 *Testamenta Vetusta* vol i, p. 77

Chapter Six

1 Quoted in N. H. Nicolas *The History of the Royal Navy* (1847)
   vol i, pp. 387–8
2 *Scalacronica*, p. 168
3 *Chronique de Jean le Bel* vol i, p. 302
4 .. *Robertus de Avesbury, De Gestis Mirabilibus Regis Edwardi
   Tertii* ed. E. M. Thompson (RS, 1889), p. 374
5 *Chronique de Jean le Bel* vol ii, p. 338
6 *Adae Murimuth, Continuatio Chronicarum* ... ed. E. M.
   Thompson (RS, 1889), p. 200
7 .. *Robertus de Avesbury*, p. 359
8 *Adae Murimuth*, p. 203
9 *Oeuvres de Froissart* ed. K. de Lettenhove (Brussels,
   1867–1876) vol v, pp. 62–3
10 SC 1/37, 170
11 *Foedera* ed. T. Rymer vol III, i, p. 129
12 *Robertus de Avesbury*, p. 442
13 *The Life of the Black Prince by the Herald of Sir John Chandos* ed.
   M. K. Pope and E. C. Lodge (Oxford, 1910), p. 41

Chapter Seven

1 .. *Robertus de Avesbury*, p. 382
2 G. Wrottesley 'Crécy and Calais' *Historical Collections,
   Staffordshire, William Salt Society* xviii (1897), p. 261
3 C 47/2/29

4 *The Alliterative Morte Arthure* ed. V. Krishna (New York, 1976), p. 60. The passage may be translated as follows:
Bring horses on board and strong helmets;
Securely load caparisoned steeds
Cabins, sacks of clothing and noble coffers,
Horses and hackneys and chargers;
Thus they stow in the stuff of very bold knights.
5 *Chronicon Galfridi le Baker*, p. 65; translated in *English Historical Documents 1189–1327* ed. H. Rothwell (London, 1977) vol iii, p. 65
6 J. Quicherat in *Bibliothèque de l'école des chartes*, 4th series vol iii, pp. 359–60
7 *Thomae Walsingham, Historia Anglicana* ed. H. T. Riley (RS, 1863) vol i, p. 272
8 *Oeuvres de Froissart* vol vi, pp. 153–4
9 *Chronique de Jean le Bel* vol ii, p. 119
10 *The Canterbury Tales* (the Squire's Tale) ll. 67–71
sewes: dishes. Heronsewes: young herons
11 *The Canterbury Tales* (the Prologue) l. 49
12 *The Life of the Black Prince*, p. 2
13 *Adae Murimuth*, p. 210
14 Ibid., p. 211
15 *Rotuli Parliamentorum* vol ii, p. 316
16 *Political Poems and Songs* ed. T. Wright (RS, 1859) vol i, pp. 69, 75

Chapter Eight

1 *The Brut* vol ii, page 333; see also *Walsingham, Historia Anglicana*, p. 329
2 *Chroniques de London* ed. G. J. Aungier (Camden Society, 1844), p. 83
3 *Calendar of Papal Letters* vol ii, p. 585
4 *Chroniques de London*, p. 90
5 *Political Songs of England*, p. 184
6 *Chronicon Henrici Knighton* ed. J. R. Lumby (RS, 1895) vol ii, p. 94
7 B. Wilkinson 'A Letter of Edward iii to his Chancellor and Treasurer', EHR xlii (1927), p. 249
8 *Select Cases in the Court of King's Bench* vol v, p. 93
9 *Adae Murimuth*, p. 89
10 N. H. Nicolas *History of the Orders of Knighthood of the British Empire* (London, 1842) vol ii, p. xvi

11 *Scalacronica*, p. 166
12 *Rotuli Parliamentorum* vol ii, p. 361
13 *Issues of the Exchequer, Henry III–Henry VI* ed. F. Devon
    (London, 1847) pp. 144–5

Chapter Nine

1 *Chronique de Jean le Bel* vol i, p. 47
2 *Vita Edwardi Secundi*, p. 70
3 *Chronicon Henrici Knighton* vol ii, p. 64; translated in *English
    Historical Documents* vol iii, p. 91
4 *Political Songs of England*, p. 341
5 *The Knights Hospitallers in England* ed. L. B. Larking
    (Camden Society, 1857), p. 1
6 J. E. Thorold Rogers *A History of Agriculture and Prices in
    England* vol i, p. 293
7 quoted in P. Ziegler *The Black Death*, p. 190
8 D. Van Zwanenberg 'The Last Epidemic of Plague in
    England? Suffolk, 1906–1918', *Medical History* xiv (1970),
    p. 67
9 *The Brut* vol ii, p. 314
10 Ibid., vol ii, p. 316
11 Ibid., vol ii, p. 303
12 *Calendar of Inquisitions Miscellaneous* vol iii, p. 258
13 *The Register of the Black Prince, 1346–1365* (London, 1930–33)
    vol iv, p. 194
14 A. R. Bridbury 'Before the Black Death', *EcHR* 2nd series
    xxx (1977), p. 401
15 *Political Songs of England*, p. 149
16 *Political Songs of England*, p. 337
17 *Rotuli Parliamentorum* vol ii, p. 269

Chapter Ten

1 *Calendar of Ancient Correspondence concerning Wales* ed. J. G.
    Edwards (Cardiff, 1935), pp. 225–6
2 *The Works of Geoffrey Chaucer (The Book of the Duchess)*, ll.
    475–9
3 *Calendar of Inquisitions Miscellaneous* vol iii, p. 699

4 *Chronicon Anglie* ed. E. M. Thompson (RS, 1874), p. 74
5 *Rotuli Parliamentorum* vol ii, p. 328
6 J. Conway Davies, *Baronial Opposition to Edward II*, p. 555
7 *Chronica Johannis de Reading et Anonymi Cantuariensis,
    1346–1367* ed. J. Tait (Manchester, 1914), p. 133
8 *Vita Edwardi Secundi*, p. 63

Select Bibliography

This is not intended to be a comprehensive bibliography; it concentrates on the more recent publications, and does not aim to give full references to the manuscripts consulted. Many of the works cited below contain full lists of sources and secondary works, while *The High Middle Ages in England, 1154–1377*, compiled by B. Wilkinson (Cambridge, 1978) is a useful listing of over two thousand titles.

General

Valuable selections of translated chronicle and record evidence are to be found in *English Historical Documents* vol. iii, *1189–1327*, ed. H. Rothwell (London, 1977); and vol. iv, *1327–1485*, ed. A. R. Myers (London, 1969). The voluminous official records have been published in part in various forms; of especial note are the *Calendars* of chancery rolls, in particular the *Calendars of Patent Rolls* and the *Calendars of Close Rolls* (London, various dates). *Foedera* ed. T. Rymer (London, 1816–30), contains a wide range of diplomatic and other material given *in extenso*. Relatively few exchequer records have been published; *Issues of the Exchequer, Henry III – Henry VI* ed. F. Devon (London, 1847), gives the flavour of some of them.

There are many general works covering all or part of this period. The Oxford Histories are F. M. Powicke *The Thirteenth Century, 1216–1307* 2nd ed. (Oxford, 1962); and M. McKisack *The Fourteenth Century, 1307–1399* (Oxford, 1959). M. H. Keen *England in the Later Middle Ages* (London, 1973) is an excellent recent survey. For the economy, E. Miller and J. Hatcher *Medieval England: Rural Society and Economic Change, 1086–1348* (London, 1978). T. F. Tout *Chapters in Mediaeval Administrative History* 6 vols

(Manchester, 1923–35) is far more wide-ranging than the title suggests. B. Wilkinson *Constitutional History of Medieval England* 3 vols (London, 1948–58), concentrates on the main political crises. Works of a specialized nature which range over the whole period of this book include G. L. Harriss *King, Parliament and Public Finance to 1369* (Oxford, 1975); M. R. Powicke *Military Obligation in Medieval England* (Oxford, 1962); R. R. Davies *Lordship and Society in the March of Wales* (Oxford, 1978); T. H. Lloyd *The English Wool Trade in the Middle Ages* (Cambridge, 1977).

Chapter One

The reign of Edward I is covered by many chronicles, none of great distinction. The main ones are *The Chronicle of Walter of Guisborough* ed. H. Rothwell (London Camden Society, 1957); *Willelmi Rishanger, Chronica et Annales* ed. H. T. Riley (London, RS, 1865); *Bartholomaei de Cotton, Historia Anglicana* ed. H. R. Luard (RS, 1859); *The Chronicle of Pierre de Langtoft* vol. ii, ed. T. Wright (RS, 1890). There is important material in *Annales Monastici* vols iii and iv, ed. H. R. Luard (London, RS, 1866, 1869); and *Chronicles of the Reigns of Edward I and II* vol. i, ed. W. Stubbs (London, RS, 1882). The manuscript Hagnaby Chronicle, British Library Cotton Vespasian B xi, has some material not contained elsewhere.

The records of the household are extremely important for this reign. Four wardrobe accounts have been published: *Records of the Wardrobe and Household, 1285–1286* ed. B. F. Byerly and C. R. Byerly (London, 1977); *The Book of Prests of the King's Wardrobe for 1294–5* ed. E. B. Fryde (Oxford, 1962); *Liber Quotidianus Contrarotulatoris Garderobae, 1299–1300* ed. J. Topham (London, Society of Antiquaries, 1787); *The Court and Household of Eleanor of Castile in 1290* ed. J. C. Parsons (Toronto, 1977). An invaluable guide to the voluminous household records still unprinted was compiled by P. M. Barnes *List of Documents relating to the Household and Wardrobe, John to Edward I* (London, 1964); there are also important wardrobe books in the British Library.

There is, surprisingly, no recent full biography of Edward I. L. F. Salzman *Edward I* (London, 1968) languished undeservedly for some forty years in manuscript before being published. E. L. G. Stones *Edward I* (Oxford, 1968) is a good short account. For the king's early career, see F. M. Powicke *Henry III and the Lord Edward* (Oxford, 1947). On the legal reforms, see T. F. T. Plucknett *Legislation of Edward I* (Oxford, 1949); D. W. Sutherland *Quo*

Warranto Proceedings in the reign of Edward I (Oxford, 1963); and both for this reign and those of Edward II and Edward III *Select Cases in the Court of King's Bench* ed. G. O. Sayles (London, Selden Society, 1936–65). The pioneering study of J. E. Morris, *The Welsh Wars of Edward I* (Oxford, 1901), is most important; M. C. Prestwich *War, Politics and Finance under Edward I* (London, 1972) looks at the wars of the reign from a different angle. For Wales, see also *The Welsh Assize Roll 1277–84* ed. J. C. Davies (Cardiff, 1940), and *The Merioneth Lay Subsidy Roll, 1292–3* ed. K. Williams-Jones (Cardiff, 1976), both with long introductions, and far more important than their titles suggest. *The History of the King's Works* vol. i, ed. R. A. Brown, H. M. Colvin, A. J. Taylor (London, 1963), deals fully with Edward I's castle-building. H. M. Cam *The Hundred and the Hundred Rolls* (London, 1930) is important for the early part of the reign. For the later political crises, see in particular H. Rothwell 'The Confirmation of the Charters, 1297', *EHR* lx (1945); *Documents Illustrating the Crisis of 1297–8 in England* ed. M. C. Prestwich (London, Camden Society, 1980).

Chapter Two

Of particular note among the chronicles dealing with the Scottish wars are the *Chronicon de Lanercost* ed. J. Stevenson (Edinburgh, Bannatyne Club, 1839); and the *Scalacronia of Thomas Gray of Heton*, ed. J. Stevenson (Edinburgh, Maitland Club, 1836): both these works were translated by H. Maxwell (Glasgow, 1913, 1907). J. Barbour *The Bruce* ed. W. M. Mackenzie (London, 1909) is the fullest account from the Scottish side. For eye-witness accounts of campaigns, see *The Roll of Carlaverock* ed. T. Wright (London, 1864) and the *Chronique de Jean le Bel* ed. J. Viard and E. Déprez (Paris, 1904). For record sources, there are *Documents and Records Illustrating the History of Scotland* ed. F. Palgrave (London, 1837); *Documents Illustrative of the History of Scotland* ed. J. Stevenson, 2 vols (Edinburgh, 1870); *Calendar of Documents Relating to Scotland* ed. J. Bain, 4 vols (Edinburgh, 1881–8); *Rotuli Scotiae* ed. D. Macpherson et al., vol. i (London, 1814); *Anglo-Scottish Relations, 1174–1328: Some Selected Documents* ed. E. L. G. Stones (London, 1965). E. L. G. Stones and G. G. Simpson *Edward I and the Throne of Scotland, 1290–96* 2 vols (Oxford, 1979) is an extremely important edition of the texts of the Great Cause.

The most important modern accounts of the Scottish wars of independence are G. W. S. Barrow, *Robert Bruce* (London, 1965);

R. Nicholson *Edward III and the Scots* (Oxford, 1965), and his more general *Scotland: the Later Middle Ages* (Edinburgh, 1974). A. A. M. Duncan's review of Barrow's book in the *Scottish Historical Review* xlv (1966) is important. For the later period, E. W. M. Balfour-Melville *Edward III and David II* (Historical Association, 1954) and J. Campbell 'England, Scotland and the Hundred Years War in the Fourteenth Century' in *Europe in the Late Middle Ages* ed. J. R. Hale, J. R. L. Highfield and B. Smalley (London, 1965) are both useful. On military organization, see J. E. Morris 'Mounted Infantry in Medieval Warfare' *TRHS* 3rd ser., vol. viii (1914); N. B. Lewis, 'The Recruitment and Organization of a Contract Army, May to November 1337' *BIHR* xxxvii (1964). The impact of war in the north of England is covered by J. V. Scammell, 'Robert I and the North of England', *EHR* lxxviii (1958); E. Miller, *War in the North* (Hull, 1960); J. A. Tuck 'Northumbrian Society in the Fourteenth Century' *Northern History* vi (1971).

Chapter Three

The *Vita Edwardi Secundi* ed. N. Denholm-Young (London, 1957), is one of the best chronicles of the whole period, and this edition provides a translation. Other chronicles are to be found in *Chronicles of the Reigns of Edward I and Edward II* ed. Stubbs, and many of those cited below for chapters six and eight go back to Edward II's reign. The only published wardrobe account for the reign is *The Household Book of Queen Isabella of England* ed. F. D. Blackley and G. Hermansen (Edmonton, Alberta, 1971). References to the main unpublished royal wardrobe accounts are conveniently found in the bibliographies to the works by J. R. S. Phillips and J. R. Maddicott cited below.

There is no adequate biography of Edward II, but his early years have been comprehensively discussed in H. Johnstone *Edward of Caernarvon* (Manchester, 1946). The interpretations of the reign in T. F. Tout *The Place of Edward II in English History* 2nd ed. (Manchester, 1936) and J. C. Davies *The Baronial Opposition to Edward II* (Cambridge, 1918) held sway for many years, but fresh ideas have been put forward by J. R. Maddicott *Thomas of Lancaster* (Oxford, 1970); J. R. S. Phillips *Aymer de Valence, Earl of Pembroke* (Oxford, 1972); R. M. Haines *The Church and Politics in Fourteenth Century England: the Career of Adam Orleton, c. 1275–1345* (Cambridge, 1978). Unfortunately the important study by Natalie Fryde *The Tyranny and Fall of Edward II, 1321–1326* (Cambridge, 1979) appeared too late to be taken into account in this chapter. Her evidence of Edward II's personal interest in financial matters, and her discovery that he possessed a treasure of some £60,000 at the end of the reign are particularly relevant. K. Edwards, 'The Political Importance of the English Bishops during the Reign of Edward II' *EHR* lix (1944) is very useful. S. L. Waugh 'The Profits of Violence: the Minor Gentry in the Rebellion of 1321–1322 in Gloucestershire and Herefordshire' *Speculum* liii (1978), provides a useful corrective to views of politics from the centre. The death of Edward II has been most recently discussed in G. P. Cuttino and T. W. Lyman 'Where is Edward II?' *Speculum* liii (1978). The rule of Isabella and Mortimer still awaits its historian; it is briefly discussed in Natalie Fryde's book, cited above.

Chapter Four

The main records of parliament, the rolls, are printed in *Rotuli Parliamentorum* vols i and ii (London, 1783–1832); that for 1305 is in *Memoranda de Parliamento, 1305* ed. F. W. Maitland (RS, 1893). The writs of summons for the reigns of Edward I and Edward II are in *Parliamentary Writs* ed. F. Palgrave (London, 1827–34).

The best brief account of the medieval parliament is G. O. Sayles, *The King's Parliament of England* (London, 1975). It has a full bibliography, with references to the many important articles Sayles wrote with H. G. Richardson. *Historical Studies of the English Parliament* vol. i, ed. E. B. Fryde and E. Miller (Cambridge, 1970) contains many useful reprints of articles. P. Spufford *Origins of the English Parliament* (London, 1967) gives shorter extracts from a wide range of works. The complex and thought-provoking work of Gaines Post has been brought together in his *Studies in Medieval Legal Thought* (Princeton, 1964), and that of G. T. Lapsley in his *Crown, Community and Parliament in the Later Middle Ages* ed. H. M. Cam and G. Barraclough (Oxford, 1951). J. E. Powell and K. Wallis *The House of Lords in the Middle Ages* (London, 1968) is valuable, and less controversial than might be expected of the first-named author. J. G. Edwards *The Second Century of the English Parliament* (Oxford, 1979) covers the period from about 1340. H. M. Cam's important articles are to be found in her *Liberties and Communities in Medieval England* (Cambridge, 1944) and *Law Finders and Law Makers* (London, 1962). J. R. Strayer has an important article on the Statute of York in *Medieval Statecraft and the Perspectives of History* (Princeton, 1971), but of the many studies of this text, D. Clementi's in *Album Helen Maud Cam* vol. ii (Louvain, 1962) is the most convincing. For the controversial *Modus Tenendi Parliamentum* see M. V. Clarke *Medieval Representation and Consent*, a much criticized book, and V. H. Galbraith in *Journal of the Warburg and Courtauld Institutes* xvi (1953). J. S. Illsley discussed the election of knights of the shire under Edward I in *BIHR* xlix (1976), while the local communities responsible for elections were considered by J. R. Maddicott in *TRHS* 5th. series, xxviii (1978).

Chapter Five

The archives of the nobility have not survived on the same scale as those of the crown, but not all that have are published. M. Midgeley edited *The Earldom of Cornwall Ministers' Accounts, 1296–1297* (Camden Soc., 1942, 1945). John of Gaunt's *Registers* were edited by S. Armitage Smith, E. C. Lodge and R. Somerville (Camden Soc., 1911, 1937). *The Register of the Black Prince, 1346–1365* 4 vols (London, 1930–33) hardly gives a representative picture of private administration. The household account of Elizabeth de Burgh, used in this chapter to give details of food consumption, is catalogued in the Public Record Office as E 101/505/17; it is wrongly attributed in the *List and Index* vol. xxxv to Earl Warenne in Edward I's reign.

The outstanding work on the nobility is K. B. McFarlane *The Nobility of Later Medieval England* (Oxford, 1973). G. A. Holmes *The Estates of the Higher Nobility in XIV Century England* (Cambridge, 1957); M. Altschul *A Baronial Family in Medieval England: The Clares, 1217–1314* (Baltimore, 1965); and J. Rosenthal *Nobles and the Noble Life, 1295–1500* (London, 1976) are all relevant. *The Lives of the Berkeleys* were written by their steward, John Smyth, in the seventeenth century, and edited by J. MacLean (Gloucester, 1883). *The Complete Peerage* ed. G. E. Cockayne et al. (London, 1910–59) is an invaluable work of reference. M. Jones, 'An Indenture between Robert, Lord Mohaut, and Sir John de Bracebridge for Life Service in Peace and War' *Journal of the Society of Archivists* (1972), is a useful listing of all the early indentures of retainer. J. R. Maddicott *Law and Lordship: Royal Justices as Retainers in Thirteenth and Fourteenth-Century England* (Past and Present Supplement 4, 1978) discusses another side of retaining. J. W. M. Bean *The Decline of English Feudalism* (Manchester, 1968) is useful. N. Denholm-Young's volumes *History and Heraldry, 1254–1310* (Oxford, 1965) and *The Country Gentry in the Fourteenth Century* (Oxford, 1969) contain a mixture of wisdom and eccentricity. For Burghersh's remains, see C. Green and A. B. Whittingham

'Excavations at Walsingham Priory, Norfolk, 1961' *Archaeological Journal* cxxv (1969). R. M. Wilson *The Lost Literature of Medieval England* (London, 1952) is useful. The most recent discussion of food is B. A. Henisch *Fast and Feast* (Pennsylvania, 1976), while the early chapters of M. Girouard *Life in the English Country House* (New Haven, 1978) set architecture into a social context. For biographies of Thomas of Lancaster, Aymer de Valence and Henry of Grosmont, see other sections of this bibliography.

Chapter Six

The main English chronicles dealing with the war are *Chronicon Galfridi le Baker* ed. E. M. Thompson (Oxford, 1889); *Adae Murimuth, Continuatio Chronicarum. Robertus de Avesbury, De Gestis Mirabilibus Regis Edwardi Tertii* ed. E. M. Thompson (RS, 1889); *Chronicon Henrici Knighton* ed. J. R. Lumby (RS, 1895); *Anonimalle Chronicle, 1331 to 1388* ed. V. H. Galbraith (Manchester, 1927). *The Life of the Black Prince by the Herald of Sir John Chandos* ed. M. K. Pope and E. C. Lodge (Oxford, 1910), is not as informative as might be hoped on military details. From the continental side, the *Chronique de Jean le Bel*, ed. J. Viard and E. Déprez, and Froissart's *Chronicles* are outstanding. For the latter, I have used the edition by Kervyn de Lettenhove, *Oeuvres de Froissart* (Brussels, 1867–1876), but that by S. Luce, G. Raynaud and L. and A. Mirot (Paris, 1869–1966) is perhaps the most definitive. Various translations are easily available.

For the prelude to the Hundred Years War, E. Déprez *Les préliminaires de la guerre de cent ans* (Paris, 1902); H. S. Lucas *The Low Countries and the Hundred Years War; F.* Trautz, *Die Könige von England und das Reich* (Heidelberg, 1961). On the Gascon question, there is an important series of articles by P. Chaplais, in *BIHR* xxi (1948); *Le Moyen Age* lvii (1951), lxi (1955), lxix (1963). G. P. Cuttino *English Diplomatic Administration, 1259–1339* 2nd ed. (Oxford, 1971), and 'Historical Revision: the Causes of the Hundred Years War' *Speculum*, xxxi (1956) are useful. The best general account of the war is still E. Perroy *The Hundred Years War* (London, 1965). A wide synthesis is given by K. Fowler *The Age of Plantagenet and Valois* (London, 1967), while his *The King's Lieutenant* (London, 1969) examines the career and campaigns of Henry of Grosmont. B. Tuchman *A Distant Mirror* (London, 1978), gives a wide-screen technicolor account. The best account of a campaign is H. J. Hewitt's *The Black Prince's Expedition, 1355–57* (Manchester, 1958). For Brittany, M. Jones *Ducal Brittany, 1364–1399;*

and on Spain, P. E. Russell *The English Intervention in Spain and Portugal in the time of Edward III and Richard II* (Oxford, 1955). J. Le Patourel has written important articles, notably 'Edward III and the Kingdom of France' *History* xliii (1958), and 'The Treaty of Brétigny, 1360' *TRHS* 5th series, x (1960). From the French point of view, much has been written. See in particular R. Cazelles *La société politique et la crise de la royauté sous Philippe de Valois* (Paris, 1958); R. Delachenal *Histoire de Charles V* (Paris, 1909–31). J. Viard wrote two important articles on the campaign of 1346–7 in *Le Moyen Age* 2nd series, xxvii (1926). Such a list as this is inevitably highly selective; that for chapter 7 provides further works on the Hundred Years War.

Chapter Seven

The Public Record Office contains a mass of unpublished documents relevant to the organization of English armies. See in particular the wardrobe accounts, such as E 36/203 and 204, and E 101/393/11. A useful collection of material is provided by G. Wrottesley 'Crécy and Calais' *Historical Collections, Staffordshire, William Salt Society* xviii (1897). P. C. Timbal *La guerre de cent ans vue à travers les registres du parlement (1337–1369)* (Paris, 1961) uses the records of the French *parlement*. Much of the literary evidence is to be found in *Political Poems and Songs* vol. i, ed. T. Wright (RS, 1859).

Many of the topics discussed in this chapter are covered in *The Hundred Years War* ed. K. Fowler (London, 1971). A. E. Prince did much work on the organization of English armies; see his articles in *EHR* lvi (1931); *Speculum* xix (1944); *Historical Essays in Honour of James Tait* ed. J. G. Edwards, V. H. Galbraith, E. F. Jacob (Manchester, 1933). N. B. Lewis has made important contributions in *BIHR* xxxvii (1964), and *TRHS* xxviii (1945); J. W. Sherborne has concentrated on the later years of the reign in *EHR* lxix (1964); *Past and Present* xxxvii (1967); *BIHR* xlii (1969); *BIHR* l (1977). H. J. Hewitt *The Organisation of War under Edward III* (Manchester, 1966) was a highly important pioneering study, as was M. H. Keen *The Laws of War in the late Middle Ages* (London, 1965). The literary evidence is well treated by J. Barnie, *War in Medieval Society* (London, 1974). For the navy, see T. J. Runyan in *Journal of British Studies* xvi (1977). The French army has been fully studied by P. Contamine *Guerre, état et société à la fin du moyen âge* (Paris, 1972).

Chapter Eight and Chapter Ten

In addition to the chronicles cited for chapter six, see the related *Chronica Johannis de Reading et Anonymi Cantuariensis, 1346–1367* ed. J. Tait (Manchester, 1914) and *The Brut* ed. F. W. D. Brie (Early English Text Soc., 1906, 1908). *Chroniques de London* ed. G. J. Aungier (Camden Soc., 1844), and *Chronicon Anglie* ed. E. M. Thompson (RS, 1874) are also important.

There is no adequate modern biography of Edward III, but P. Johnson *Edward III* (London, 1973), provides a brief well-illustrated survey. B. C. Hardy *Philippa of Hainault and her Times* (London, 1910) is badly dated. H. Cole *The Black Prince* (Abingdon, 1976); B. Emerson *The Black Prince* (London, 1976); R. Barber *Edward, Prince of Wales and Aquitaine* (London, 1978), all largely concentrate on the Black Prince's military career, and there remains a need for a modern scholarly study. S. Armitage Smith *John of Gaunt* (London, 1904) suffices until a new biography is written. For the early years of Edward III's reign, and the crisis of 1340–1, D. Hughes *Social and Constitutional Tendencies in the Early Years of Edward III* (London, 1915). N. M. Fryde 'Edward III's Removal of his Ministers and Judges, 1340–1' *BIHR* xlviii (1975), is the latest in a long series of articles by many historians on the crisis; it provides references to the earlier work. For the crisis of 1376, G. A. Holmes *The Good Parliament* (Oxford, 1975), and on the process of impeachment, G. Lambrick 'The Impeachment of the Abbot of Abingdon in 1368' *EHR* lxxxii (1962) and A. Harding 'Plaint and Bills in the History of English Law' in *Legal History Studies* 1972 ed. D. Jenkins (Cardiff, 1975) are the latest contributions to a long debate. G. Unwin *Finance and Trade under Edward III* (Manchester, 1918) is still valuable, but see also the article by E. B. Fryde, 'Financial Resources of Edward III in the Netherlands, 1337–40' *Revue Belge*, xlv (1967), and his work in *History* n.s. xxxviii (1952) and *TRHS* 5th series ix (1959). On the currency, A. B. Feavearyear, *The Pound Sterling* 2nd ed. (Oxford, 1963) is still valuable, but see the recent work by N. J. Mayhew, 'Numismatic Evidence and Falling Prices in the Fourteenth Century' *EcHR* 2nd series xxvii (1974), the articles in *Edwardian Monetary Affairs* ed. N. J. Mayhew British Archaeological Reports xxxvi (1977), and *The Dawn of Modern Banking* Center for Medieval and Renaissance Studies, Los Angeles (New Haven, 1979). The best general survey of the Church is W. A. Pantin *The English Church in the Fourteenth Century* (Cambridge, 1955). Edward III's anti-papal legislation is discussed by C. Davies in *History* xxxviii (1953); E. B.

Graves, in *Haskins Anniversary Essays* ed. C. H. Taylor (Boston and New York, 1929); and by F. Cheyette in *Traditio* xix (1963). On law and order, see J. G. Bellamy *Crime and Public Order in England in the Later Middle Ages* (London, 1973), and the same author's *The Law of Treason in England in the Later Middle Ages* (Cambridge, 1970). There are many articles dealing with this topic; see in particular B. Putnam *TRHS* 4th series xii (1929); A. Harding *TRHS* 5th series x (1960); E. L. G. Stones *TRHS* 5th series vii (1957); J. G. Bellamy *EHR* lxxix (1964). The latest of many articles dealing with Robin Hood and related problems is by J. R. Maddicott in *EHR* xciii (1978).

Chapter Nine

For the economic problems of Edward II's reign, I. Kershaw 'The Great Famine and Agrarian Crisis in England, 1315–1322' *Past and Present* lix (1973) is excellent. J. Z. Titow *English Rural Society, 1200–1350* (London, 1969) and B. F. Harvey in *TRHS* 5th series xvi (1965) present very different views of the pre-plague economy. It is invidious to select a few out of the many excellent detailed studies of individual estates, but reference should be made to P. D. A. Harvey *A Medieval Oxfordshire Village: Cuxham, 1240–1400* (Oxford, 1965); I. Kershaw, *Bolton Priory: The Economy of a Northern Monastery 1296–1325* (Oxford, 1973); E. Searle, *Lordship and Community: Battle Abbey and its Banlieu, 1066–1538* (Toronto, 1974), among many others. Many statistics on prices and wages were collected by J. E. Thorold Rogers in *A History of Agriculture and Prices in England* 7 vols (Oxford, 1866–1902); for a modern approach to manorial statistics, J. Z. Titow *Winchester Yields* (Cambridge, 1972), and D. L. Farmer in *EcHR* 2nd series xxx (1977).

There is a massive literature on plague. On the medical aspects, J. N. Biraben *Les hommes et la peste en France et dans les pays européens et méditerranéens* vol. i (Paris, 1975); *The Plague Reconsidered* (Local Population Studies Supplement (Matlock, 1977)), which includes the excellent critical review by C. Morris of J. F. D. Shrewsbury, *A History of Bubonic Plague in the British Isles* (Cambridge, 1970). A useful discussion of the carriers of plague is in W. S. Patton and A. M. Evans *Insects, Ticks, Mites and Venomous Animals* (Croydon, 1929). P. Ziegler *The Black Death* (London, 1969) is an excellent general account of the plague, while the most recent discussion of its consequences is J. Hatcher *Plague, Population and the English Economy, 1348–1530* (London, 1977). This has an excellent bibliography. More recent still is E. B. Fryde's article in *Medieval Legal Records* ed. R. F. Hunnisett and J. B. Post (London, 1978). A. R. Bridbury, 'The Black Death' *EcHR* 2nd series xxvi (1973) is important and challenging. M. Mate, 'The Role of Gold Coinage in the English Economy, 1338–1400', *The Numismatic Chronicle*, cxxxviii (1978) makes some very significant suggestions.

Controversy over the costs of war was begun by K. B. McFarlane in *Past and Present* xxii (1962), and taken up by M. M. Postan *Past and Present* xxvii (1964). More recent discussions include J. R. Maddicott *The English Peasantry and the Demands of the Crown* Past and Present Supplement no. 1 (1975); E. Miller's article in *War and Economic Development* ed. J. M. Winter (Cambridge, 1975); articles by A. R. Bridbury in *Trade, Government and Economy in Pre-Industrial England: Essays presented to F. J. Fisher* ed. D. C. Coleman and A. H. John (London, 1976), and *EcHR* 2nd series xxx (1977).

Index

INDEX

Kilsby, William, 218, 220
king's evil, 82, 170, 188
Kirkby, John, 16–17
Knighton, Henry, 229, 245, 257, 260
Knollys, Robert, 184–5, 191, 201–2, 266

Lacy, Alice de, Countess of Lancaster, 94, 108, 155–7
Lacy, Henry de, Earl of Lincoln, 38, 51, 66, 83–5, 106, 151, 157, 297
Lancaster, dukes and earls of, see Edmund; Henry; John of Gaunt; Thomas: palatinate of, 298
Langland, William, 259, 286
Langton, Walter, bishop of Coventry and Lichfield, 25–6, 36–7, 147, 293, 297; corruption, 33–4, 38–9; dismissed by Edward II, 82; recalled, 84, 105
La Roche-Derrien, 175
La Rochelle, naval battle off, 184, 197, 272
Latimer, William (d. 1381), 203, 286–91, 293
lawyers, 22, 46, 131, 133, 145, 285
Leake, treaty of, 87–8
Leicester, Earl of, see Montfort, Simon de
Lestrange, Eblo, 156–7
Lewer, Robert, 102–3
Life of Edward II, 80, 100, 105–6
Limoges, 184, 209, 280
Lincoln, 24, 86–7, 116–7, 131, 231; Earl of, see Lacy; earldom of, 155
Lionel of Antwerp, Duke of Clarence, 141, 233, 239, 280–1
Livre des Seyntz Medicines, 159, 161
Llywelyn ap Gruffudd, Prince of Wales, 7, 12–15, 18–19, 41
London, and Londoners, 9, 73, 94, 112, 128, 181, 234, 248, 251, 261, 286, 292, 296: bishop of, 257, 292; and Edward II, 79, 97–8; mayor of, 219, 292; merchants, 287, 289; parliamentary representatives, 124, 132–3; plague in, 255, 259; St Paul's, 27, 209–10; and Stone of Destiny, 58; tournament in, 205; Tower of, 22, 24, 96–7, 99, 103, 107, 112, 192, 219
Loudoun Hill, battle of, 53
Louis IX (St), King of France, 7, 170, 186
Low Countries, 23, 44, 97, 168, 226, 236, 242, 259, 270: Edward I and, 2, 166; Edward III and, 2, 168, 170, 172–3, 175, 194, 201, 211–2, 217–18, 222–3, 235; see also Brabant; Flanders; Guelders

lushbournes, 237
Lyons, Richard, 287–9, 291

Maes Moydog, battle of, 18, 67
Magna Carta, 19, 31, 110, 219–21, 290
Malestroit, truce of, 174–5
March, Earl of, see Mortimer, Patrick
March, William, 27, 34, 39
Marcher lords, 6, 102; and Welsh wars, 102; and Edward I, 30; and Despensers, 89–90, 107–8, 114; and Black Prince, 152, 277–8
Marches, see Scotland; Wales
Mare, Peter de la, 288, 290–2
Margaret, daughter of Edward I, 36, 131
Margaret, Queen of Scots (Maid of Norway), 43, 52
Margaret, Queen of Scots, sister of Edward I, 43
Marshal, office of, 190; see also Beauchamp, Thomas; Bigod; Brotherton; Montague, William; Mortimer; Percy
Martlesham, Edmund de, 159
Mary, daughter of Edward I, 156
Mary, daughter of Edward III, 283
Mauny, Walter, 174, 190, 202–4, 206, 239, 243, 257, 277, 299
Mauron, battle of, 179, 198, 209
Melton, William, Archbishop of York, 55, 59, 86
Menstreworth, John, 185
merchants, 71, 196, 210, 290; grant of customs by, 27, 33, 122; and Edward III, 216, 223–6, 235–7, 274, 287; Flemish, 20; German, 117; Italian, 27, 39, 83, 224, 299; see also Bardi; Frescobaldi; Pessagno; Pole; Ricciardi
Methven, battle of, 53, 66
Middleton, Gilbert de, 56, 74, 103
Minot, Laurence, 210–12
minstrels, 38, 159, 239–40
Mirror of Justices, 125
Modus Tenendi Parliamentum, 92, 115, 121, 128–9, 130, 135
Moleyns, John, 152, 215, 221, 242
Montague, William, Earl of Salisbury (d. 1344), 87–8, 113, 149, 152, 158, 173, 190, 204, 206
Montague, William, Earl of Salisbury (d. 1397), 185, 278
Montfort, John de, III, Duke of Brittany, 174
Montfort, John de, IV, Duke of Brittany, 184–5, 287
Montfort, Simon de, Earl of Leicester, 6, 12, 35, 92–3
Montgomery, 30; treaty of, 12

333